LEADERSHIP SKILLS UNLEASHED

18 TRANSFORMATIVE STRATEGIES FOR MANAGERS AT ANY LEVEL – DEVELOP A GROWTH MINDSET, OVERCOME IMPOSTER SYNDROME, AND CREATE A CULTURE OF BELONGING.

2-BOOKS-IN 1

MARGUERITE ALLOLDING

SL
SHE LEADS

1st Editon

Author: Marguerite Allolding

Publisher: She Leads Strategies, LLC

TABLE OF CONTENTS

FEARLESS FEMALE LEADERSHIP
9 Essential Strategies to Overcome
Gender Biases, Build Confidence, and
Empower Your Career

IMPACTFUL INCLUSIVE
LEADERSHIP
9 Powerful Strategies That Encourage
Diversity, Foster Equity, and Cultivate
Inclusivity to Transform Your Workplace

FEARLESS FEMALE LEADERSHIP

---

9 ESSENTIAL STRATEGIES TO OVERCOME GENDER BIASES, BUILD CONFIDENCE, AND EMPOWER YOUR CAREER

INTRODUCTION

∼

Did you know that as of 2020, women held a global average of 19.7% of board seats in several organizations? Although this is a significant figure compared to the 2.8% since 2018, it still underscores the underrepresentation of women in top decision-making roles (Tina, 2023).

Imagine you're in a meeting where you've got these brilliant ideas to share, and of course, you do. However, they get flipped over, only to be praised moments later when a male colleague presents the same concept. Or picture the frustration of constantly needing to prove yourself, working twice as hard to gain the same recognition and respect as your male counterparts who might have done only 30% of the amount of work you got done. These all-too-familiar scenarios highlight the challenges women face in the world of female leadership.

But here's another eye-opener: the leadership training market is projected to reach a staggering $26.7 billion by 2024 (Technavio, 2020). Undoubtedly, the demand for effective leadership is soaring, and the 2023 Leadership Statistics from TeamStage show that 76% of people between 55–60 believe men and women can lead equally (Tina, 2023). Although women continue to face significant barriers on their path to the top, the data proves otherwise because there can and should be an inclusive and equitable future for women in leadership.

Let me take you back to a chilly winter morning when I sat at a conference table surrounded by the Executive Leadership Team (ELT). As one among three women and about six men in the room, I couldn't help but feel excitement and trepidation at this critical meeting. It was a forum to determine the fate of one of the most influential brands in our company, and I was ready to contribute my expertise and ideas as always.

As the discussion unfolded, I noticed a subtle shift in the room's dynamic. My male colleagues seemed to dismiss my suggestions. It was as if my voice was fading into the background, drowned out by the echoes of gender biases and outdated stereotypes.

Frustration began growing within me because I knew I had the skills, knowledge, and passion to make a significant impact, and my contributions needed to be more valued and noticed, but that wasn't the case.

These scenarios have ruffled many women's confidence through the years because, with such attitude in the workplace, they grapple with self-doubt and imposter syndrome, the byproducts of generations of gender biases in executive positions. The constant fear of failure and the belief that everyone is scrutinizing their every move cripples faith in their potential, stifling innovation and erasing the desire to push forth new ideas that propel companies forward. When you yearn for career advancement but struggle to find your purpose and navigate the path to success, it can leave you in doubt. Or when you crave support, collaboration, and a strong network to inspire and be inspired by others, knowing deep down that you have the qualities necessary to lead if only you're given a chance, but no one notices, it isn't very encouraging.

Globally, more women encounter a lack of training and exclusion from meaningful decision-making processes, leaving them feeling the weight of gender inequality in their professional lives. In fact, some colleagues and leaders aged 35 to 54 still cling to archaic gender biases, resulting in men passing women over for promotions, being demoted, or receiving unequal pay compared to their male counterparts (Greenwood, 2023).

Furthermore, women seeking leadership positions battle insecurities that prevent them from speaking up and sharing their brilliant ideas. The fear of being unheard or dismissed prevents you from contributing innovative perspectives and creative wisdom. You may not fully develop your emotional intelligence to face the challenges ahead, so instead of trying, you remain silent while others move along in their careers. On top of it, another struggle of balancing work and personal life becomes ongoing when you try to nurture relationships and maintain a sense of self amidst the demands of your career. The weight of these competing priorities can take its toll, leaving you searching for a better way to achieve the elusive work-life balance.

The good news is, despite the myriad of strains, and worrisome statistics provided earlier, there is hope.

This book is a beacon of light for women seeking to transcend the obstacles and limitations imposed upon them by societal stereotypes. Within these pages, you will discover the tools, strategies, and insights to overcome self-doubt, shatter those brick walls of low self-esteem, and become a fearless female leader. You need to rewrite the narrative and redefine what it means to lead, starting with understanding who you are and where your success story begins. Rise above the limitations, embrace your full potential, and create a future where you and more women who aim for quality leadership are no longer the exceptions but the new narrative.

To achieve all of this, there are nine strategies you need to hinge on in this book because, with it, you will:

1. Learn to lead with authenticity and build trust with those around you.
2. Discover all the necessary soft skills, like empathy, adaptability, emotional intelligence, and optimism, to effectively lead teams and traverse different life hassles.
3. Master the art of communication and interpersonal relationships, which involves becoming a great listener, a persuasive speaker, and a non-verbal communicator.
4. Become a risk-taker, well-prepared to make calculated decisions that push you and your team toward success.

5. Collaborate more and work assiduously with any team to leverage the strengths of each team member and achieve shared goals.
6. Develop a leadership style that aligns with your personality and values while effectively achieving results.
7. Adopt a growth mindset to embrace challenges as opportunities for learning and expanding ideas.
8. Find your why—the driving force behind your leadership journey—to stay motivated and focused on your goals.
9. Arrive at the core of your journey by being the fearless female leader, leaving a lasting legacy for future generations of women hungry to make a difference.

That's the desired end this book is sure to provide. I know this because I am the first recipient of these benefits. It took me over 20 years to grasp and implement my leadership qualities for maximum success, and believe it or not, these strategies were my guide.

Once you follow these steps committedly, it will create a new difference to evolve a new you.

- You will embrace a life free from the fear of failure, turning it into boundless opportunities.
- Sudden steadfast confidence will emerge. One that will prepare you to take steps you dreaded in the past.
- You will become assertive and foster innovative teamwork that inspires others to excel.
- Life won't be about surviving but living, as you will achieve a harmonious balance between work and life.
- You will get a revamp in your growth mindset.
- The career path you seek will be propelled to unimaginable heights.

This transformative journey will continue as you internalize the principles in this book and make it the key to an evolving career.

Before I acquired the knowledge and insights I am sharing in this book, my journey toward becoming a fearless female leader was riddled with many challenges. As a 43-year-old married woman with two kids in the bustling New York metropolitan area, I faced the demanding pressures of balancing family responsibilities and pursuing a successful career.

For two decades, I navigated various leadership roles in boutique agencies, small businesses, and large organizations. While I experienced many victories and accomplishments, I also encountered setbacks and made mistakes. Through these trials and triumphs, I gained invaluable wisdom and discovered what it truly takes to be a fearless leader.

I struggled with self-doubt and uncertainty without the guidance and insights I possess today. I questioned my abilities and feared the consequences of failure. The lack of a roadmap to success left me overwhelmed and unsure, but I overcame these obstacles and emerged as a confident and empowered leader.

Armed with the lessons learned from my experiences, I am passionate about sharing this "new" information with you. I want to save you from the pitfalls and challenges I faced and provide you with the tools, strategies, and mindset needed to encounter the complexities of leadership fearlessness with grace.

I am excited to reveal the insights that will take you closer to your goals and enable you to create a lasting impact as a fearless female leader. Will the journey be difficult? Of course, however, the knowledge and guidance within these pages will equip you to overcome any obstacle and emerge as a winner—the confident, influential leader you were always born to be.

You picked up this book, so you're ready to embrace your authority, unshackle your true potential, and rewrite the rules of female leadership. It's time for women to step into their power and create a future where gender equality is not just a dream but a reality. Let's make a lasting impact and shape a world where women's voices are heard, respected, and celebrated.

1

THE POWER OF AUTHENTICITY

We must have the courage to embrace our true selves, even if it feels daunting or unfamiliar.
—May Sarton (*Authenticity Quotes (1309 Quotes)*, n.d.)

~

I t may sound unbelievable, but for most women, striving over the years to create relevance for themselves and their work hasn't been an easy journey. While most break their backs to be heard and seen, the BBC's 2022 Equality Matters issue confirms that 40% of women worldwide are in the workforce, 23% are CEOs, and 29% are fortunate to hold senior management roles (Bishop, 2022). This may look good considering the numbers; however, it's troubling all thanks to the boggling fact that most women who possess enormous potential and seek the perfect space to showcase their abilities to work, lead, and deliver are plagued with the reality of gender discrimination.

Gender discrimination is no longer a topic of concern for the United Nations or gender-based organizations to discuss and continuously evaluate; it's become a horrid reality that's shutting down women's opportunities to be their authentic selves, especially in the workplace.

What Is Authenticity?

Authenticity for any female leader is about being honest, embracing her genuine self, and never apologizing for what she represents. Genuineness brings fearlessness because your focus starts getting better at what you're good at until you're labeled the game-changer in the leadership.

The New York Times publication and a host of research could confirm that women make the most profitable decisions at the most stressful times in the workplace. It pinpoints that the success rate of women heading business affairs and driving organizations is far more outstanding irrespective of the demands of climbing the ladder.

The authenticity of female leaders is necessary to empower them to break bounds, defy societal odds, and stay true to themselves and their cause. It begins from within and transcends into their respective roles in their personal lives and professional environment.

Authenticity in the Workplace

Authenticity for women is their ticket to building trust in the industry they represent. Once you decide to be different, unique, and exceptional, you create for yourself the golden opportunity to unlock the business' success and other benefits.

So, a good workplace must meet specific criteria for authenticity to come into plain sight so that women can be felt, heard, and seen like their male colleagues:

1. **Trustworthiness:** It should set women apart as genuine and trustworthy individuals that work hard and are credible enough to deliver and sustain profitable relationships with colleagues, clients, and stakeholders. Their authenticity is about trust, sincerity, and commitment to work and deliver, which will breed support and stronger connections.

2. **Diversity, equity, and inclusion (DEI):** With authenticity comes workplace diversity, equity, and inclusion (DEI). Anyone who can embrace their true identity sets the stage for an environment that appreciates values and respects diverse perspectives, experiences, and identities. Feeling safe to be

yourself cultivates a working culture of acceptance and belonging, where individuals can contribute their unique talents and ideas. Women need this to thrive in their career path as it will give them bold, opinionated, and brave confidence in role execution.

3. **Integrity:** Authenticity aligns actions with core values. Stay true to your beliefs, principles, and all you stand for pushes you to make congruent decisions with who you are. A female leader with this quality will feel fulfilled and inspire others around you. Leaders who lead with integrity pay close attention to how they present themselves to others, and in doing so, they inspire trust, loyalty, and respect, and it positively impacts team members in organizations.

4. **Innovation and creativity:** Authenticity also promotes innovation and creativity. Bringing your genuine self to work helps you tap into your unique perspectives and talents, and, at this point, your innovative thinking is revealed and encouraged. Nothing is more attractive than a female leader who knows her opinions and can share fresh ideas irrespective of the outcome. Even when they think you don't have it, show them that you're bursting with creativity, and you won't stop until they see what's there, ingenuity.

5. **Supportive work environment:** Authenticity in the workplace should spawn a high level of well-being and job satisfaction. When you know you can be yourself at work, the chances are you'll work passionately because not only are your feelings considered, but your career growth is just as significant to you as it is to your team and supervisors, which is refreshing. It allows you to find meaning and purpose in your work, leading to higher engagement and productivity. That way, there is no room for burnout which over 60% of women experience before they hit 40 (Weller et al., 2021). The stakes are high in their journey to discover themselves as mothers, career women, and female leaders, so they try to do too much to stand out. But, with attention to authenticity, they own the stage by creating a work environment that supports women's well-being and meets their job satisfaction.

How to Be Authentic?

For a female leader to be fierce in her leadership role and show authenticity in the execution of it, the following points are to be kept in mind:

- **Identifying your skills:** What are your strengths and weaknesses, and how can you release a mind-blowing conversion rate? Once you understand your qualities, your role will be easy to maneuver because your confidence and communication ability will cascade.
- **Networking:** In the workplace and as an entrepreneur, recognizing your brand and establishing a strong network that empowers you to showcase your expertise is paramount. In my years of working, the power of networking was the one thing I never took for granted as I began to understand myself in the workplace. It gave me the professional identity I needed to stand out because I let engagement and excellent interpersonal relations guide my journey. The cornerstone of my success was based on my adeptness in networking and cultivating meaningful connections, serving as catalysts for expediting work completion. That credibility and strong relationships you make will always single you out as authentic and lead you into the hands of people who are transparent in their actions and accountable for their transactions.
- **Continuous learning and growth:** Suppose you're shying away from grand opportunities to shine and showcase your capabilities. In that case, it's time you change everything because continuous learning and growth are about investing in yourself by converting mistakes into prospects and achievements.

A fearless leader must always be eager to sell herself through her work, values, and achievements. How will they know you matter in the workplace if you don't show your skills to them?

Make them see your true self and appreciate your exceptionalism because it always comes back rewarding in the long term.

Once you start in that manner, you can be like Mindy. Initially, she struggled with confidence in the workplace, doubting her abilities and fearing judgment. But a spark ignited within her one day, and she encountered stories of fearless women who overcame similar challenges. Determined to find her authentic voice, Mindy sought supportive mentors, attended workshops, and connected with empowering women. Slowly, her confidence grew, and she realized she had unique strengths to offer. With newfound passion and authenticity, Mindy became committed to sharing her ideas and earning respect from colleagues. She became a beacon of inspiration, empowering others to embrace their power. Mindy's journey showcased the transformative power of authenticity, passion, empathy, and optimism, proving that confidence can be cultivated and dreams can be achieved.

But, to get to where she did, there are strategies that every female leader must apply and imbibe:

1. **Personal development and internal growth:** Start investing in yourself and focusing more on personal growth. Don't be stuck in the mud and expect to create relevance; connect more through workshops, courses, or self-reflection on delivering your ideas better. Once you build a supportive network, you keep evolving until you get to that place where you become the best version of yourself. A personality people will enjoy working with and learning from.

2. **Establish psychological safety for yourself and others:** To stay real, vulnerable, and honest, there must be a safe space to encourage open communication, active listening, and support for each other's ideas and challenges. This shouldn't be missed, as it is the warehouse for successful leadership and performance output. Valuable, diverse perspectives promote open communications and collaborations that motivate colleagues and team members to contribute and get the best work done.

3. **Be vulnerable; it's your superpower:** There is nothing wrong with showing weakness sometimes. Embrace your unique quirks and imperfections because you are showing you are

yourself; believe it or not, magic always comes with it. You get to reveal yourself without realizing openness was all it took. When Brene Brown, the American Professor, gave a TED Talk on Vulnerability, she affirmed that it was the gateway to building trust and stronger connections. Share your passions, values, and journey with your work community. They get to see the real you and connect on a deeper level.

4. **Power up using feedback:** It's your secret weapon to getting honest, constructive criticism that will help you improve and revamp. A leader must never fear how people judge them or their work. There can be no growth there because if people have nothing good or bad to say about you or your work, then there is blandness in your existence. Feedback helps the woman understand her strengths, recognize her blind spots, and refine her leadership style.

5. **Sustain authentic connections:** Build genuine relationships within and outside the workplace. Connect with people who inspire you, share your values, and lift you. It starts by listening keenly without any sense of judgment or conclusions but just being present and showing that respect for opinions and others' perspectives. Authentic connections are pure gold!

6. **Hold firm to strengths and weaknesses:** There is a lot to gain from identifying your strong and weak sides. Learn from them, use them, and when you're surrounding yourself with a team that compliments you, pay attention to how these characters in you can come to play. According to recent studies from Gallup, if a person can get emotionally and psychologically prepared for anything, they will become productive and thrive in their leadership role because they comprehend the science of feelings.

7. **Learn to be a value-driven leader:** Lead with your heart, define your core values, and let them guide your decisions and actions. Be true to yourself, and the journey will be even more fulfilling.

8. **Accept mistakes as stepping stones:** We all mess up sometimes, and that's okay! Embrace your mistakes, be transparent about them, and learn from them. It's all part of being human and authentic.

9. **Practice self-love and self-care:** You're a fearless leader, and as a woman, you need self-care. Prioritize yourself, always. As crucial as your career goals might be, take time for self-care, recharge your energy, and give yourself some affection.

Encourage Authenticity

Many people don't admit it, but caring for yourself makes you confident enough to speak freely about anything. Nothing scares you as much because you've grown, and now, you're ready to help other individuals find themselves on their path to authentic leadership. You can encourage authenticity in the following ways:

1. Lead by example: Remember, you're being watched; everything you do can inspire or dispel others in their decisions. So, lead by example; you could guide and inspire thousands. Your every action, inaction, or interaction is a significant determinant of how people respond to issues and their decision to be genuinely transparent in making authenticity their watchword. Your exemplary life is their execution model.
2. Inclusive leadership: Inclusive leadership is another vital aspect of encouraging authenticity. Create a safe and welcoming space where everyone's voices are heard and valued. Embrace diverse perspectives and encourage open dialogue where conversations and inhibitions are pronounced without fear or reservations. When people feel included and accepted, they are more likely to feel comfortable expressing their true selves.
3. Promote authenticity: Authenticity should extend beyond your behavior and into your products and services. Promoting authenticity by aligning your offerings with your core values is crucial for an entrepreneur. Don't sell something you wouldn't personally buy to prove you have the power to do so. Let your products and services reflect your respect for authenticity, and customers will appreciate your integrity.
4. Share your story: Additionally, sharing your own story and successes can be incredibly empowering. Regardless of how small or big your achievements may seem, they demonstrate

that authenticity leads to positive outcomes. Being vulnerable and open about your journey inspires others to embrace their unique paths and take pride in their accomplishments. Kamala Harris is one woman who, through her autobiography, "The Truths We Hold: An American Journey," spoke openly about her political career and the hurdles she crossed to reach her destination. Today, her story empowers women to know they can break barriers and reach their leadership expectations once they are determined and focused.

5. Build authentic connections: Remember to mix business and pleasure when necessary. Building authentic relationships means showing genuine interest in others as individuals, not just as colleagues or clients. Find common ground, share personal anecdotes, and foster a sense of team spiritedness that makes integrating work-life balance swift and exciting. Trust and authenticity naturally follow when people feel a personal connection, along with job satisfaction that will make people appreciate the leadership and not assume they must abandon themselves for service.

6. Transparency: In your marketing efforts, focus on responsible messaging and transparency—market responsibly by delivering unbiased and accurate information to your audience. Don't make promises you can't keep or misrepresent your products or services. Authenticity in marketing builds trust and loyalty among customers.

7. Consistency: Consistency is vital to promoting authenticity. Be consistent in your words, actions, and values. Inconsistency breeds confusion and erodes trust. When you consistently align your behavior with your beliefs, people will see you as dependable and trustworthy.

8. Accountability: Being responsive and accountable is essential for fostering authenticity. Give people the attention and support they deserve; respond promptly to inquiries, feedback, and concerns; take ownership of your mistakes and learn from them. Accountability demonstrates integrity and a commitment to doing what's right no matter the eventuality.

Segue

Besides these tips, most importantly, recognize that the key takeaway for every female leader is to understand that authenticity begins and ends with being true to self and empowering others. Once you pursue your goals both ways, the potential for success is limitless.

EMOTIONAL INTELLIGENCE

Emotional intelligence is the innate power within us, a force that transcends the
tangible. It empowers us to skillfully navigate the depths of human behavior,
effortlessly embrace social complexities, and consciously make authentic choices
that manifest remarkable outcomes.
—*Travis Bradbury (Lonczak, 2023)*

~

I n climbing the ladder of becoming a successful leader, you can leave nothing to chance. Once there, many things are expected of you, but most importantly, your ability to overcome hurdles and manage situations will assure your team about the future. Hence, the approach begins with how you respond to the different emotional displays that arise from encounters, confrontations, and networking. There must be a proper way to balance it all and stay ahead as a unique leader. That's where emotional intelligence comes up.

Let's understand the above said with an instance from my professional journey: In a challenging scenario between myself and my team members, we faced a crucial deadline for a Board of Directors meeting, where we were to present in front of top executives from our parent company in Japan and the esteemed ELT team. The pressure was mounting, causing stress levels to skyrocket and emotions to run high. With limited time to prepare our presentation, it was essential to impress them with the remarkable progress we had made since our last encounter. Recognizing the significance of this moment, I chose to lead with a more authentic and supportive approach, fostering a connection rather than resorting to a bossy or authoritative demeanor. I firmly believed that by embracing our collective strengths and nurturing a positive atmosphere, we could conquer any challenge and emerge victorious. We embarked on this crucial meeting with determination and optimism, ready to showcase our accomplishments and win hearts.

First, I listened to my team members to understand all their worries, and then in acknowledging their feelings, I validated their experiences. I didn't do it to get into their good books; I wanted to test how empathy would make them feel safe enough, to be honest in their opinions during the open dialogues. Although it all seemed chaotic, with so many views flying through the room, I still had to maintain calm and manage my emotions. This enabled me to facilitate constructive conversations, encouraging team members to collaborate, share perspectives, and find common ground.

My approach toward the situation inspired my team members; it gave them insight into the importance of emotional intelligence and how it had become a vital tool for any leader who wants their team to be productive. Statistics show that in research done by 80 scientists over 40 years, it was apparent that emotional intelligence is a more in-demand skill than technical as it provides satisfaction and ensures productivity.

What Is Emotional Intelligence?

It isn't a scientific element but a skill that enables individuals to understand and manage their own emotions and the emotions of others. As a female leader, your ability to perceive and regulate emotions effectively and interpersonal interactions plays a crucial role in the workplace. With it, you can

- build strong relationships—by understanding and empathizing with the emotions of their team members, female leaders can foster positive relationships based on trust, respect, and collaboration. They can connect with others on an emotional level, which enhances communication and teamwork.
- make informed decisions—emotional intelligence enables female leaders to consider how their choices affect other individuals and teams. They can weigh different perspectives, manage conflicts constructively, and take steps to balance the organization's needs with their employees' well-being.
- inspire and motivate—female leaders with high emotional intelligence understand what drives and motivates individuals. How? Because they have spent much time watching people, listening to them, and connecting with them, they now recognize the struggles and desires people seek. It makes it easy for them to effectively communicate goals and expectations to resonate with their team's emotions and aspirations. Moreover, employees feel they can lean on their leaders for support and guidance as they aim to rise in the industry, making them the perfect role models.
- navigate challenges—with the resilience and adaptability to navigate challenges and setbacks, female leaders can have well-groomed emotional intelligence. While encountering difficult situations, they can hold their strength and support their team members enough to cope with stress and overcome obstacles. The ability to handle challenges comes with strategic confidence and stamina attained through a series of transitions and transformations.
- promote inclusive and positive work culture—this is the era of diversity and inclusion, and having a leader create a positive work environment; with this approach, only they can possess the emotional intelligence to ensure no one is left out in building a long-term fulfilling work culture. They are attuned to the emotional needs of their team members and promote a culture of empathy, psychological safety, and mutual support. This contributes to higher employee engagement, satisfaction, and overall well-being of the leader and the employees.

In the study by the renowned author Daniel Goleman, he presented pillars of emotional intelligence as signature characteristics of personality that are nurtured over time with self-study, discipline, and intentionality. He shared self-awareness, self-regulation, motivation, empathy, and social skills. They are the foundation of effective interpersonal relationships, communication, and organizational leadership, and further research shows that leaders with high emotional intelligence are more likely to inspire and positively influence their teams, leading to improved performance. A female leader who exudes finesse in the execution of responsibility and relationality with the masses proves the relevance and absorbability of emotional intelligence.

Let's discuss in deeper detail what these components represent:

1. **Self-awareness:** Recognizing one's emotions, strengths, weaknesses, values, and motivations. Self-awareness enables individuals to understand how their feelings influence their thoughts, behavior, and those around them. It is either an internal or external effect you experience from one of these behaviors; however, the inevitable fact is that being self-aware gives you the edge in the emotional intelligence approach as a leader.

2. **Self-regulation:** This component is about effective management. Any female leader who knows how to control their emotions, impulses, and reactions strategically, adapts to change and remains calm in challenging situations can rest assured that their authenticity will shine through their regulated sense of focus.

3. **Empathy:** It's about how you share in the emotions of others. As a boss, you have a peculiar case of a staff whose agreed shift affects their mental health and ability to work productively; how would you address it? Would you replace them in a snap because their sloppiness might cost you a multi-million-dollar contract, or would you share in their predicament by finding ways to mitigate the situation or at least reach a reasonable agreement? This is where the question of empathic leadership comes into play. It involves actively listening, observing nonverbal cues, and being able to put oneself in another person's

shoes. Despite your role as a leader, empathy allows you to connect with others on an emotional level and respond compassionately.

4. **Social skills:** This encompasses a range of abilities related to effective communication, relationship building, and teamwork. This component involves communicating clearly, resolving conflicts, collaborating, and influencing others positively. Strong social skills facilitate healthy and productive relationships. Also, most studies reveal that social skills can assist your intuitive abilities. Your sense of prediction and foresight in reading people and situations strengthens and becomes more distinct because of your connections with people. Somehow, it's like you've seen a scenario play out several times and can tell how it might turn out, which gets you prepared, aware, and emotionally in control.

5. **Motivation:** It is the longing for a drive and enthusiasm to achieve personal and professional goals. It involves setting challenging goals, having a sense of purpose, and maintaining optimism even in the face of obstacles. Motivated individuals are resilient and proactive in pursuing their aspirations.

According to research conducted by Future Talent Learning, emotional intelligence matters in leadership due to its ability to positively influence strategy and decision-making. Leaders with vital emotional intelligence can effectively navigate complex situations, adapt to change, and make informed choices considering organizational and employee well-being. This promotes a supportive and inclusive work environment, fostering engagement and satisfaction.

How to Manifest Emotional Intelligence?

So, how does emotional intelligence manifest? It involves communicating assertively, resolving conflicts constructively, and handling stressful situations with composure. Once these are in place, an organizational system will work effectively. Any leader who aims to attain all these characteristics and more for the latter to thrive can do it, but it comes with a learning process. Once you can identify the tips for becoming emotionally intelligent enough to create a functional and personal empire, the next step is to use them at every chance.

The nine golden tips to becoming emotionally intelligent are:

1. **Communicate:** Being authentic is clearly communicating your emotions to your employees. Let them comprehend what you don't say and what you do at any given opportunity. It makes the environment move coordinately because your team can make decisions based on their understanding of your emotional dispositions. They have worked with you over time and can tell the best-suited approach to any situation, irrespective of your absence or presence.

2. **Self-reflection:** In nurturing emotional intelligence, knowing, understanding, and reading self is critical; that way, people connect with you easily. It exudes authenticity if you take the time to self-reflect and be aware of who you are and what you represent regarding emotions, strengths, weaknesses, and focus. The impact on others is profound as they absorb your character; they can see you achieving synchronization in working output.

3. **Be attentive:** When you genuinely desire to test your emotional reading capacity, set up meetings, workshops, and gatherings and assess the passion level of individuals. Yes, it's a working environment, but that doesn't mean it's not open to having an emotional atmosphere of disagreements, sentiments, and indifference. As long as you deal with humans, it's bound to come up, and an emotionally intelligent leader can listen attentively, observe the tempo of the discussions, and make decisions that would meet everyone halfway. As a result, they would feel heard, appreciated, and valued.

4. **Be imaginative:** Many people would advise you to put yourself in their shoes; that's hard, considering no one knows how tight or loose the other's shoes are. I always say to keep your imagination broad to help you see things from a realistic perspective. If you, a male CEO, get an employee report on your desk every other week about a sickly pregnant lady due to her falling behind on her projects, you won't be able to put yourself

in her shoes (we know why); however, if you imagine having a wife, working her heart out to be valued despite her condition, then you'll learn how to show empathy to the plight of a pregnant employee whose trying her best to work hard. Emotional intelligence makes you a person of compassion and support to your employees, which automatically means work success.

5. **Encourage collaboration:** Create an environment where you don't have this massive gap between you as the leader and your employees. As often as possible, teamwork must be so everyone feels valued and needed. With collaboration comes diverse perspectives where individuals are empowered to contribute their unique strengths and be open about their weaknesses, so everyone compliments each other to maximize profit.

6. **Show passion and optimism:** Enthusiasm, dedication, and positivity for your work can inspire your team to share your passion and strive for excellence. Passionate leadership motivates and energizes those around you, sending a vibe whenever you are present. Even if employees are going to do overtime, they'll do it happily, knowing they have a leader who will ensure they are well compensated and stay supportive and optimistic through the entire tedious journey.

7. **Promote work-life balance:** Recognize the importance of well-being and support your team members in achieving a healthy work-life balance. Give them time off and flexible schedules and provide resources for managing stress like a small game room, a short nap corner, or even a monthly happy hour where employees can get together to unwind and share stories; it bonds colleagues with their bosses and creates a whole new network of interpersonal relationships, a vital tenet of emotional intelligence.

8. **Lead by example:** Model the behaviors and values you expect from your team. They will know the expected standards once you show integrity, fairness, and ethical conduct while establishing trust and respect. Nothing more, nothing less. As a woman who hungered to get on the best side of my colleagues and one day be my own boss, I always aimed to lead by example,

and for me, it was about taking responsibility for my mistakes and admitting when I was wrong. I wanted people around me to tell me my weak points, and the moment I showed that vulnerability, it fostered an environment of accountability, growth, and freedom.

9. **Make informed decisions:** A lot weighs on the shoulders of most leaders. In the case of a female leader who tries to make her employees respect her role and appreciate her contribution, it can be even more demanding. However, the rule doesn't change but upgrades. Her decisions in any case presented must come from a place of emotional comprehension where she understands all sides and remains as firm as she can until the best outcome emerges. This tip is most important because it shows authenticity to lead in fairness and justice and not be prejudiced by any perspective.

How to Use Emotions Wisely

An essential characteristic of a successful leader is harnessing the opportunity to use emotions wisely to think profoundly and address issues smartly and strategically, so much so that most employees and individuals don't know what to expect. It's a skill born from being coherent, diplomatic, and output-driven.

Strategic Thinking and Problem-Solving

Strategic thinking is a skill that enables leaders to envision the future and develop an effective plan of action to achieve organizational goals. It involves considering long-term objectives by assessing any project's anticipated mission and vision, reviewing the possible pitfalls that could come up irrespective of how good the blueprint might look, and identifying growth opportunities. To do this successfully requires lots of data and resources from past and present for analysis to avoid being subjective in conclusions and critical in findings. Women leaders who are in touch with their emotions and understand the power of critical thinking often exhibit strong strategic abilities, as they have a clear vision and can navigate complex business landscapes.

To enhance strategic thinking skills, several approaches should be considered.

- Firstly, a deep understanding of the organization's purpose and values is essential. What are the company's mission, vision, goals, and traction plan? This clarity helps align decision-making with every other aspect of the company's desired goal.
- Secondly, effective strategic thinkers actively gather information, analyze trends, and seek diverse perspectives to make informed decisions. They can anticipate potential obstacles and develop innovative solutions by considering multiple viewpoints. There must be a bi-vocal insight into everything to see the big picture.
- Thirdly, they are future-oriented and embrace a growth mindset. They allow change and are willing to take calculated risks. This mindset will enable them to seize opportunities and adapt their approaches accordingly. A Forbes publication asserted that although women show more growth and output mindset than men in the workplace, they are underrepresented in the role of CEO, and their strategic thinking capacity comes through later in life. This could be because their confidence level is affected, or the overwhelming drive to prove themselves sometimes takes away the focus to yield deep thinking. It's why cultivating strong communication and collaboration skills is essential for the effective strategic thinking of female leaders. Open dialogue and collaboration close unhealthy gaps and help leaders build consensus where their new ideas and valuable insights from others are combined and laid on the table to create what works for now and the future.

After years of rising in her previous role before becoming her own boss, a leading female CEO of a Consumer-Packaged Goods (CPG) company had this to say about the relevance of being strategic as a leader:

Strategic thinking stems from a deep knowledge of your business and the factors shaping your market, consumers, and suppliers. It goes beyond surface-level understanding and requires a detailed grasp of the processes driving your company. By delving into the specifics, you gain invaluable insights and prevent intermediaries from clouding your judgment. Understanding at a granular level empowers you to navigate political dynamics, avoid hidden agendas, and make informed decisions. Embracing this approach is essential for staying well-informed and effectively fulfilling your role.

Problem Solving

With strategic thinking, several tenets of leadership are met, from being organized, detail-oriented, and focused to becoming the best of all, a problem-solver.

People long to have leaders who can solve their problems, pay attention, and offer the best approach for everyone to leave the battlefield with a smile. Problem-solving is more than a talent but a critical leadership skill that empowers individuals to tackle challenges, make informed decisions, and drive positive organizational change. Successful women leaders demonstrate problem-solving skills when they combine analytical thinking with creativity and resourcefulness and approach problems with confidence, persistence, and an empathetic mindset. Care to know why? Well, a scientific angle is least explored where problem-solving is concerned between a man and a woman. In research conducted by Harvard in 2001, evidence showed that the frontal lobe and limbic cortex of the female brain, which was responsible for problem-solving responses and emotional conduct, were more prominent than in a male. This confirmed why women always show a higher sensitivity rate in handling issues. They tend to assess all persons and aim the best way possible not to hurt anyone. It's a compassionate reflection that can be fruitful but sometimes limiting when trying to satisfy everyone.

To effectively solve problems as a leader, a structured approach can be helpful. Once a problem presents itself, a leader mustn't try to prove their autonomy to make decisions, as this can turn out badly. There are steps to make the conclusion meaningful and authentic.

1. **Define:** Firstly, define the problem by looking at both sides to ensure a thorough understanding of the situation.
2. **Gather information:** Secondly, gather relevant information. Every circumstance happens with scenarios, facts, and figures that will be comprehensively analyzed. Suppose an employee comes with a complaint about a colleague or client. In that case, substantial evidence, data, feedback, and stakeholder perspectives must be used to measure and assess the gravity of truth or insinuation.

3. **Brainstorm:** Then comes the tricky part, brainstorming the right solutions. A study from an anonymous women's activist affirmed that because a woman possesses an empathic nature of paying attention to everyone's emotional behavior in any given situation, she tries to lay various solutions on the table. Considering all variables, she identifies a more encompassing approach, evaluating its feasibility, potential outcomes, and alignment with organizational goals. The minute all are checked, next comes effective implementation.

4. **Implement:** Implementing shows that communication and collaboration with stakeholders have been executed, and there is active support and engagement.

5. **Reflect:** Finally, reflect on the problem-solving process, identifying lessons learned and opportunities for growth. This reflective practice enhances future problem-solving abilities, so nothing is left to chance.

Confidence and Integrity

Confidence is a crucial characteristic of a fearless female leader. When you are confident, you trust your ability to make sound judgments and be bold in your decision-making which is an enormous inspiration to others. Confident leaders radiate self-assurance, instill trust, and motivate their teams to achieve greatness. Above all, when a woman exudes that stand-firm shoulder-high aura, it's one force to battle workplace discriminations which many women suffer.

How much belief do you have in yourself? Most leaders today came through successfully in their position either because they were surrounded by people who saw their potential and pushed them to take it a step further or were determined to beat the odds by shutting down the naysayers and focusing on bringing their dreams a step higher. It's never easy once you take the first step, but it's a lifetime of being brave and sure once you take a swing at it.

To cultivate confidence, there are various strategies to consider, and it can start with your outer body posture.

Stand Strong!

How do you stand when you're before people? Do you show your mental fear on the outside by looking downwards, scared, and a little withdrawn in your body language? That says a lot. To beat this, the first step is never to take every situation so seriously. Like Gabourey Sidibe, the American actress who would turn heads with her plus-size figure, would say, "One day I decided that I was beautiful, and so I carried out my life as if I was a beautiful girl." For her, as it should be for most people, once you care less about how people see and treat you and give your all to what's in front of you, the nerves slowly fade away, creating room for confidence to shine. Next, a growth mindset is essential, where challenges are seen as opportunities for learning and establishing. Successful women leaders understand that setbacks and failures are part of the journey and use them as stepping stones to future success.

Upgrade Yourself Always!

There always needs to be more knowledge to make you a perfect leader who has reached the peak of their career. No matter the amount of success amassed, a leader always aims to gain new ideas and be a step ahead of every new challenge. This comes with reading more innovative materials and listening to people and their opinions. You'll find it easy to come up with authentic ideas and share some of your own because you are well-informed and intellectually prepared to contribute to any discussion confidently.

Seek Feedback!

Seeking feedback and learning from others is another way to boost confidence. Actively seek mentorship or guidance from trusted individuals who can provide insights and support your growth. By embracing continuous learning and improvement, you develop new skills and expand your knowledge base, enhancing your confidence in your capabilities.

Attitude is Everything!

Maintaining a positive attitude and celebrating successes, no matter how small, shows you don't see things myopically. When you give yourself some credit by recognizing achievements and progress, you'll visualize success and set realistic goals confidently.

Focus on your objectives; it will take you to another comprehensive behavior and integrity character.

Be Transparent!

Here, a leader's moral principles are put into question. For a fearless female leader, it's about transparency, acting ethically in all circumstances, and upholding core values. These all seem tough; however, leaders who demonstrate integrity inspire trust, credibility, and loyalty from their teams and stakeholders. They are all about doing what's right regardless of what people say or the temptations that would try to spring them on a different path.

To lead with integrity, you must communicate honestly and transparently. Let employees see that openness in you when information is passed so they have no reason to suspect foul play or hidden agendas. Recent research proves that about 60% of female CEOs foster trust and transparency within their team as they don't hold back in the show of emotions (Tina, 2023). Although some may see this as a weakness, sensitivity is an asset to building integrity and winning your favor.

Be Accountable!

Another asset is being accountable for your actions, good or bad, and owning up to the outcome. When mistakes happen, be prepared to face the consequences rather than give excuses and play the victim. Demonstrate a willingness to learn, grow from the ordeal, move past it, and be ready to do better. One prominent rule customer service representatives hold firmly is, "Take the next available flight to get to the right destination." It just means that when you're trying to meet an angry customer's need, and they seem obstinate about their choices, take the subsequent wise decision of escalating the issue to your supervisor. It shows your commitment to job success and eagerness to improve when another situation arises. This authenticity and vulnerability foster a culture of integrity and continuous improvement.

Communication is the Gist!

Finally, promote open and respectful communication across boundaries where you have those moments when all your heart is in the right place, and you need to be hardcore in your decisions. It's normal and necessary that people feel fulfilled with leaders encouraging diverse perspectives, respecting all opinions, talking, and walking the walk.

Persistence, Determination, and Resilience

These are essential qualities of successful leaders, particularly for women navigating their careers and seeking to make a lasting impact in their respective fields.

To persist fuels the drive to keep going, even when faced with challenges. Staying steady on a course with an unwavering belief that with perseverance, anything is achievable, no matter the obstacles. Setbacks are the fuel that propels successful women leaders to soar even higher on their path to greatness. If you ever met a woman who rose without that personality that's persistent to the core, it's most unlikely. Persistence isn't a natural character; it's a learning mindset. Through continuous effort and a refusal to give up, anyone can pave the way for growth and accomplishment.

To enhance persistence, there are practical strategies to consider.

Clear Your Vision!

You need a clear vision of your goals and regularly remind yourself of your purpose. Suppose it has to become a mantra for you, perfect! The goal is to embrace a growth mindset, viewing challenges as opportunities that can take you to the groundbreaking level of your life. A review of great women like J.K Rowling, Martha Stewart, and Madam Walker will tell you that persistence always pays when you pay attention to the end product of your desire.

Seek Support!

Another thing, surround yourself with a supportive network of mentors and peers who inspire and uplift you to respond better to awkward circumstances. You can harness persistence and achieve remarkable results by staying focused, seeking support, and pushing through adver-

Emotional Intelligence 33

sity which will build another noteworthy character of interest; determination.

Be Determined!

Determination is another crucial quality that propels fearless female leaders forward once they stamp their fit on the right course of action. It involves a tireless commitment, resilience, and the drive to persevere despite obstacles. Determined leaders have a clear sense of purpose and an unyielding belief in their abilities. They take decisive action, relentlessly pursue their goals, and inspire others with unwavering dedication.

To cultivate determination in your career, consider practical tips such as setting clear and specific goals, breaking them down into actionable steps, and tracking your progress. Surround yourself with positive influences and seek out role models who embody determination and inspire you. Embrace challenges as personal and professional growth opportunities, and celebrate even the smallest victories. By nurturing determination, you will forge your path with unwavering resolve and make a lasting impact.

Be Resilient!

Have you ever encountered a female leader who's so dogged about their beliefs and principles, whether it's appreciated or not? That's called Resilience. The ability to adapt, recover, and bounce back from adversity. Resilient leaders possess inner strength and the capacity to navigate change, setbacks, and stress gracefully. They maintain their composure, inspire their teams, and find innovative solutions to overcome challenges.

To become more resilient, focus on developing four core areas: physical, mental, emotional, and spiritual resilience. This involves caring for your physical well-being, fostering a positive mindset, building emotional intelligence, and connecting with a purpose. Practice self-care, seek support from your network, and embrace a growth mindset that views setbacks as opportunities for learning and growth. By nurturing resilience in all aspects of your life, you will become better equipped to handle the demands of leadership. You will see the roadmap of your goals before they come to life if you apply another powerful character trait—vision.

Visionary Thinking and Innovation

Visionary thinking and innovation are crucial for aspiring female leaders who want to impact their careers and industries significantly. By embracing the vision and fostering innovation, women leaders can drive positive change, create opportunities, and inspire those around them.

Having a clear vision provides a guiding light for leaders. It involves seeing beyond the present and envisioning a better future. Visionary leaders can articulate their goals, inspire others with their vision, and create a roadmap to achieve them. By communicating their vision effectively, they rally their teams and stakeholders, fostering a sense of purpose and direction.

To enhance your leadership vision, consider practical steps such as reflecting on your passions and values, researching industry trends, and seeking input from diverse perspectives. Continuously refine your vision based on feedback and new insights, and communicate it enthusiastically and clearly. By honing your vision, you can inspire others to join you on the journey toward success.

Innovation

Innovation is another vital skill that enables women leaders to think creatively, challenge the status quo, and drive meaningful change. It involves generating new ideas, taking calculated risks, and adapting to evolving circumstances. Innovative leaders embrace experimentation, encourage a learning culture, and foster an environment that values and nurtures creativity.

To foster innovation in your career, consider practical tips such as seeking diverse perspectives, cultivating a growth mindset, and embracing failure as a learning opportunity. Encourage open communication and collaboration within your team, and create space for brainstorming and idea-sharing. Embrace emerging technologies and stay informed about industry trends to identify opportunities for innovation. You can drive positive change and stand out as a leader by nurturing your innovative mindset.

Collaboration and Inspiration

In leadership, collaboration and inspiration are two essential pillars that empower female leaders to achieve remarkable success. By embracing collaboration, these leaders harness the power of teamwork, fostering an environment where diverse perspectives are valued, and collective achievements are celebrated. Additionally, female leaders uplift individuals and teams through their ability to inspire and motivate others, propelling them to surpass their potential. Let us explore these concepts further and discover how they contribute to the growth and empowerment of female leaders.

Collaboration is the cornerstone of effective leadership for successful women. They understand they can foster collaboration and tap into their teams' collective wisdom and diverse strengths. Embracing collaboration allows female leaders to create an inclusive environment where everyone's ideas are heard, respected, and valued. This enhances creativity and innovation and strengthens the bonds among team members. Collaboration enables women leaders to build strong relationships, encourage open communication, and create a sense of belonging within their teams.

Successful female leaders actively seek input from team members to excel in collaboration, recognizing that diverse perspectives lead to better decision-making. They establish clear goals and foster a culture of trust and respect, where individuals feel comfortable sharing their ideas and challenging the status quo. Effective verbal and nonverbal communication are crucial in collaboration, ensuring that messages are conveyed clearly, expectations are understood, and conflicts are resolved constructively.

By prioritizing collaboration, female leaders create an environment that cultivates teamwork, boosts productivity, and maximizes the potential of every individual.

In addition to collaboration, we have inspiration, a power tool for female leaders to employ to motivate and empower those around them and themselves. I often dissect inspire to mean "in" and "spite" where I chose to create the affirmation that:

- In spite of setbacks, I chose to move ahead.
- In spite of what my head might be telling me, my heart is in the right place.
- In spite of what people may conclude, it's not about them; it's the effort that counts.
- In spite of limitations, my eyes remain on the prize.

These affirmations may look casual, but they are for leaders to understand that inspiring others begins with firing up their authentic selves; then, they can ignite passion, drive, and a shared team vision. Through words, actions, and unwavering belief in their team members' abilities, they create a culture of positive energy, resilience, and continuous growth.

To inspire those around them, successful female leaders adopt various approaches. They lead by example, demonstrating integrity, authenticity, and a strong work ethic. By sharing their stories of challenges and triumphs, they create relatability and foster a supportive environment where everyone feels encouraged to pursue their dreams and aspirations. They provide guidance and mentorship, nurturing the talents and skills of their team members and helping them unlock their full potential. Celebrating achievements, no matter how small, inspires a sense of accomplishment and encourages individuals to set and reach ambitious goals.

Through collaboration and inspiration, female leaders have the power to transform workplaces, industries, and communities. They build bridges, break down barriers, and create a space where everyone's voices are heard and valued. In this collaborative and inspiring environment, individuals are empowered to unleash their creativity, take risks, and contribute their unique perspectives, leading to innovative solutions and extraordinary achievements.

As we embrace collaboration and inspiration, let us celebrate the achievements of successful female leaders who exemplify these qualities. The commitment to collaboration and their ability to inspire and motivate others serve as a guiding light, empowering women to break barriers, shatter glass ceilings, and lead purposefully. By embracing collaboration and inspiring others, female leaders pave the way for a future where everyone's potential can be realized, and gender equality and inclusivity thrive.

To Adapt and Sustain Inclusion

Adaptability is a key skill for aspiring female leaders who navigate the ever-changing landscape of today's professional world. Adaptability means embracing change, staying agile, and continuously learning and growing. It's about resilience in the face of challenges and seizing growth opportunities.

To cultivate adaptability as a leader, consider practical tips such as practicing mindfulness to stay present and focused, seeking diverse perspectives to leverage different ideas, and embracing new technologies and methodologies. Embrace a growth mindset that embraces change as an opportunity for personal and professional development. You can confidently navigate uncertainty and inspire others to embrace change by staying adaptable.

Inclusion is another vital skill for female leaders who seek to create diverse and inclusive environments where everyone feels valued and empowered. Inclusive leaders foster a sense of belonging and embrace diversity in all its forms. By actively seeking diverse perspectives, encouraging open dialogue, and creating an inclusive culture, they unlock the full potential of their teams and organizations.

To improve your inclusive skills, consider practical steps such as educating yourself about different cultures and experiences, actively seeking diverse perspectives, and addressing biases and microaggressions. Foster an environment where everyone's voices are heard and create opportunities for individuals to contribute and excel. By embracing inclusion, you can harness the collective power of diverse perspectives and develop a culture of belonging.

Communicate Your Emotions Smartly

Are you trustworthy enough to communicate your emotions smartly?

Communication and trustworthiness are essential qualities for successful female leaders. Effective communication involves conveying information clearly, listening actively, asking insightful questions, and adapting your communication style to different audiences. It's about fostering open and transparent communication channels that promote collaboration and understanding.

Trustworthiness is the foundation of strong leadership. Trust is built through consistent actions, transparency, and integrity. Trustworthy leaders demonstrate reliability, keep promises, and act honestly and authentically. By building trust with colleagues, teammates, and employees, leaders create a supportive and productive work environment where people feel safe to take risks and contribute their best.

Segue

In developing essential soft skills, you must remember that character and emotional intelligence are the beginning of your journey as a leader. With tips for enhancing each skill, you're well on your way to delving deeper into the fundamental capabilities required for success. In the upcoming chapters, we will explore the power of effective communication—a necessary skill qualifying you to connect, inspire, and influence others with profound impact. Get ready to unlock the true potential of your leadership prowess in this transformative next step.

3

THE ART OF COMMUNICATION

Communication - the human connection - is the key to personal and career
success.
—Paul J. Meyer. (Indeed Editorial Team, 2022)

∼

L ike many other people, you've probably been in a position where your palms are sweating like crazy, and you can barely keep your legs together because all eyes are on you as you are making a speech. Well, it's not a new experience. In fact, amidst the organizational upheaval of the beverage company 'Jane' worked for, she found herself in a position where her team was demoralized, communication was strained, and there seemed to be a lack of direction. Recognizing the urgency to turn things around, 'Jane' persevered with determination despite the tension and uneasiness.

She gathered her team for a meeting, maintaining a calm demeanor; 'Jane' began by acknowledging their challenges and frustrations from the lack of effective communication. She then shared her vision for the team's success, articulating it clearly and inspiringly.

'Jane' observed her team members' non-verbal cues and reactions as she spoke, noticing their guarded expressions and hesitance to open up. Realizing that active listening was critical, she paused, inviting each person to share their thoughts and concerns.

'Jane' empathetically acknowledged the team's frustrations and validated their experiences. She listened to their feedback, addressing each concern with empathy and respect.

Every one of the tools she employed signifies the relevance of effective leadership communication. It's how you convey information, ideas, and goals'; or call it the clarity and compelling nature of creating influence using the right words and an appropriate emotional expression. It's the skillful use of verbal and non-verbal communication to inspire and motivate others towards a shared vision and see their work because your words have stuck to them. Once you can ensure clarity and conciseness without too much fluff, with empathy, understanding, and attentiveness, you'll have everyone seated to listen to your every word. When Oprah Winfrey shared her methods for effective communication, she put it down to one of many things; "have a conversation!" For her, there is no need to get all formal and serious to convey a message. Share stories and have a great laugh while you're at it.

Types of Communication

For successful execution, the different communication types and components representing them must be understood.

1. **Proactive communication:** It is an innovative method of communicating a compelling vision for the future. Influential leaders inspire and motivate their teams by clearly articulating a shared vision and the path to achieving it. They use vivid and persuasive language to engage their audience emotionally and intellectually. Leaders inspire team members to align their efforts and work towards a common goal by painting a compelling picture of the desired future state.

2. **Strategic communication:** It conveys strategies, goals, and plans to achieve organizational objectives. Leaders must

communicate the organization's strategic direction, priorities, and milestones effectively to ensure everyone is aligned and working towards the same goals. This type of communication involves clarity, specificity, and the ability to break down complex strategies into actionable steps. Effective leaders provide context, explain the rationale behind decisions, and guide their teams in understanding how their work contributes to the broader system.

3. **Inspirational communication:** It aims to motivate and energize individuals or teams. Successful leaders use storytelling, powerful anecdotes, and personal experiences to connect with their audience on an emotional level. They inspire others by sharing examples of success, perseverance, and the positive impact of their work. Inspirational communication creates a sense of purpose, builds morale, and fosters a belief in what is possible.

4. **Adaptive communication:** It is the ability to tailor one's communication style to different individuals, teams, or situations. Effective leaders understand that other people have unique preferences, communication styles, and information needs. They adapt their communication approach to ensure messages are understood and resonate with their audience. This includes using different modes of communication (verbal, written, and visual), adjusting the level of detail, and considering cultural or contextual factors.

Components of Communication Style

Oral Communication

It refers to the spoken words and vocal delivery used by leaders to convey their messages. It includes face-to-face conversations, team meetings, presentations, and public speaking. Key aspects of effective oral communication for leaders include:

- **Clarity:** Leaders should articulate their thoughts clearly and concisely, using language that is easily understood by their audience.

- **Tone and delivery:** Leaders should pay attention to their tone of voice, emphasizing key points and using appropriate pauses and inflections to engage and captivate their listeners.
- **Active listening:** Leaders should actively listen to others, encouraging open dialogue and creating an environment where everyone feels heard and valued.

Written Communication

It is about using words to convey messages, instructions, reports, and other forms of written communication. Effective written communication for leaders includes:

- **Clarity and conciseness:** Leaders should express their ideas clearly and concisely in written documents to ensure the intended message is easily understood.
- **Structure and organization:** Leaders should organize their written communication logically and coherently, using headings, bullet points, and paragraphs to enhance readability.
- **Tone and style:** Leaders should adopt an appropriate tone and style that aligns with the purpose and audience of the written communication. They should maintain professionalism, clarity, and positivity.

Non-Verbal Communication

It involves body language, facial expressions, gestures, and other non-verbal cues. Effective non-verbal communication for leaders includes:

- **Eye contact:** Leaders should maintain appropriate eye contact to convey attentiveness and engagement.
- **Body language:** Leaders should know their body posture, gestures, and facial expressions, ensuring they project confidence, openness, and approachability.
- **Proximity and physical presence:** Leaders should be mindful of their physical presence and use appropriate proximity to convey accessibility and attentiveness.

Listening

It is a critical component of effective leadership communication. Leaders who actively listen demonstrate empathy, understanding, and respect for their team members. Effective listening for leaders includes:

- **Active engagement:** Leaders should be fully present and engaged when listening to others, giving their undivided attention, and focusing on the speaker's message.
- **Empathy:** Leaders should strive to understand the emotions and perspectives of the speaker, putting themselves in their shoes and responding with compassion.
- **Clarification and feedback:** Leaders should ask questions for clarification, paraphrase and summarize what they have heard to ensure understanding, and provide constructive feedback when appropriate.

A leader who commits to these components represents the authentic voice of the people. One famous American female leader who exemplifies effective leadership communication is Eleanor Roosevelt. As the longest-serving First Lady of the United States, she utilized her position to communicate effectively and advocate for social justice and human rights. She was meticulous in using words throughout her newspaper column, "My Day"; in her public speeches, she garnered support for her cause; on trips to communities, conversations were always crucial to her, and above all, she took advantage of the media to reach a broader audience to share in her fight for human right. She was an all-rounder and reflected on what future female leaders should promote.

Assessing her character and journey, it's safe to say that effective leadership has numerous benefits to the leader who desires to lead alongside their team.

Benefits of Effective Communication

1. **Empowered and focused teams:** Effective communication provides clarity and direction, ensuring everyone, including you as a female leader, is on the same page. This empowers your

team members, enabling them to work towards common goals with confidence and focus.

2. **Trust and collaboration at the forefront:** As a female leader, you understand the importance of building trust and fostering collaboration. By actively listening to your team members, respecting their ideas, and encouraging open dialogue, you create an environment where everyone feels valued and included. This promotes stronger bonds and enables effective teamwork.

3. **Resolving conflicts with grace:** Conflict resolution is a crucial skill for any leader, and as a female leader, your ability to communicate effectively can bridge gaps and reach resolutions. By staying calm and respectful and considering different perspectives, you can facilitate constructive conversations that lead to ideal solutions, fostering harmony within your team and beyond.

4. **Nurturing customer relationships:** Strong communication skills are vital to building successful relationships with your team and customers. As a female leader, your attentive listening and clear explanations create customer rapport and trust. Understanding their needs allows you to provide tailored solutions and exceptional service, ensuring long-lasting customer loyalty.

5. **Aligning goals for success:** Aligning goals within your organization can be complex, but effective communication simplifies the process. By clearly conveying the organization's aspirations and objectives, you enable your employees, including other female leaders, to understand their roles and contributions. Regular communication builds trust, rapport, and a shared purpose, driving everyone toward common objectives.

6. **Minimized conflicts for a harmonious workplace:** Effective communication tactics help reduce conflicts or tensions within your team. Ensuring everyone receives the same information and clarifying expectations creates a fair and respectful environment where misunderstandings are minimized. This

fosters a harmonious workplace where all team members, regardless of gender, feel heard and valued.

7. **Engaged and motivated employees:** Your communication skills connect and engage employees, leading to higher satisfaction and healthier company culture. By actively listening, recognizing employees' skills, and fostering relationships, you empower your team members, including other women, to contribute fully and enjoy their work. This boosts morale and motivates them to perform at their best.

8. **Increased productivity and efficiency:** Effective communication gives employees, including fellow female leaders, a clear understanding of their roles and expectations. This clarity enables them to perform efficiently, leveraging their skills and resources effectively. By promoting open communication channels, you enhance productivity throughout the organization.

9. **Encouraging innovation and diverse perspectives:** Your commitment to open communication empowers employees to express their ideas and opinions, fostering innovation within the organization. You create an environment that encourages creative thinking and problem-solving by valuing diverse perspectives, including those of other female leaders. This approach drives continuous improvement and fuels the organization's success.

10. **Building strong and cohesive teams:** Effective communication strengthens team bonds and promotes trust among team members. You create a synchronized and supportive work environment by providing clear direction, setting guidelines, and ensuring everyone is on the same page. This cohesive teamwork, including collaboration with other female leaders, elevates the organization and leaves a positive impression on the public.

Active Listening—An Important Communication Rule

When someone asks, "What are the leadership communication rules to help evolve a fearless female leader?" I say—active listening.

Why? The following are the benefits of active listening in leadership:

1. Active listening empowers female leaders to enhance business communication within the organization. Female leaders foster clear and effective communication by genuinely engaging with team members, colleagues, and stakeholders, driving better decision-making and overall outcomes.

2. Female leaders who can absorb information become role models for their teams, nurturing effective communication skills. By valuing diverse perspectives and encouraging open dialogue, female leaders inspire a culture of trust where everyone feels valued and empowered to share their ideas and concerns.

3. Attentiveness by female leaders creates a supportive environment, boosting employee morale and engagement. When employees feel heard and understood, job satisfaction increases, improving productivity and loyalty.

4. Female leaders build strong connections with their team members by having a keen hearing, reducing turnover rates. By valuing their opinions and contributions, female leaders foster loyalty and commitment, creating an environment where employees feel supported and motivated to stay.

5. Noting important information equips female leaders with conflict-resolution skills. By attentively listening and facilitating constructive dialogue, female leaders promote empathy and understanding, leading to more effective conflict resolution and a harmonious work environment.

6. It can empower employees, especially women, to express their unique perspectives. Female leaders create an inclusive space where diverse voices are valued, fostering collaboration, respect, and innovation.

7. Female leaders who pay close attention, encourage exploring new ideas and possibilities. By seeking diverse opinions and being open to different perspectives, female leaders foster better decision-making, innovative solutions, and a culture of continuous learning.

Challenges to Active Listening Skills

- **Distractions:** Noise, interruptions, or multitasking can make concentrating and actively listening to others challenging. Female leaders may face these distractions in various work settings, but being mindful of the importance of focused listening can help overcome this challenge.
- **Preconceived assumptions:** Bias or having a predisposition can hinder effective listening. Female leaders should be aware of their preferences and strive to approach conversations openly, suspending judgment and actively seeking to understand different perspectives.
- **Time constraints:** Busy schedules and tight deadlines often create time constraints for female leaders. Limited time may lead to rushed conversations, where listening takes a backseat. Overcoming this challenge requires prioritizing active listening and allocating dedicated time for meaningful conversations.
- **Emotional barriers:** Strong emotions, such as stress, frustration, or personal biases, can impede effective listening. Leaders should be aware of their feelings and strive to manage them during conversations, allowing for a more empathetic and objective listening experience.
- **Lack of empathy:** There can hardly be any meaningful conversation without traces of empathy. Female leaders may face challenges in empathizing with diverse perspectives or experiences. Therefore, it is essential to cultivate compassion actively, practice active listening to understand, and connect with others on a deeper level.
- **Information overload:** In today's fast-paced world, female leaders occasionally encounter information booms from several sources, making it difficult to process and retain as much data as possible while listening. Employing techniques such as summarizing key points, taking notes, or seeking clarification can help manage this challenge and ensure adequate comprehension.
- **Communication styles and cultural differences:** How you relate with people based on your cultural mannerism and roots

can play a big part in how you receive information. As a leader, you should be sensitive to these differences and adapt your listening approach to actively bridge any gaps in understanding.

Why Does it Matter?

Effective listening is crucial because it allows us to understand others, build relationships, collaborate effectively, resolve conflicts, foster personal and professional growth, and enhance consumer satisfaction. When you listen attentively with a desire to comprehend

- you can grasp perspectives with interest.
- show the needed concern where helpful.
- integrate diverse ideas and find common ground.
- learn from others.
- meet consumer needs adequately.

It is a fundamental skill that promotes meaningful communication, connection, and positive outcomes in various aspects of life.

Strategic Steps to Effective Listening and Leadership Communication

1. **Be present:** Create a focused and conducive environment for communication, free from distractions. Give your full attention to the speaker, demonstrating active engagement.
2. **Practice empathy:** Seek to understand others' perspectives and emotions. Show genuine interest and concern, fostering a supportive and inclusive atmosphere.
3. **Suspend judgment:** Avoid making premature assumptions or forming opinions. Keep an open mind and listen without bias, valuing different viewpoints.
4. **Ask clarifying questions:** Seek clarity and a deeper understanding by asking relevant and thoughtful questions. This approach demonstrates your engagement and encourages the speaker to elaborate.

5. **Reflect and summarize:** Summarize the main points and reflect on the speaker to ensure accurate comprehension. This strategy reinforces understanding and validates their contribution.

6. **Provide feedback:** Offer constructive feedback and affirmations to the speaker, acknowledging their ideas and input. This tactic encourages continued participation and fosters a positive communication dynamic.

7. **Adapt communication style:** Tailor your communication approach to meet different individuals' and situations' needs and preferences. Flexibility in your communication style promotes effective understanding and rapport.

8. **Encourage participation:** Create an inclusive environment where individuals feel safe to express their opinions and perspectives. Actively encourage and value contributions from all team members.

9. **Practice active listening:** Demonstrate active listening through nonverbal cues, such as maintaining eye contact, nodding, and using appropriate body language. Show that you are fully present and engaged in the conversation.

10. **Continuously improve:** Cultivate a continuous learning mindset and improve your communication and listening skills. Seek feedback, reflect on your performance, and actively work towards enhancing your leadership communication abilities.

Segue

Communication is the cornerstone of fearless leadership, elevating your impact from valuable to invaluable. Embrace the continuous improvement of your communication skills with every individual in your working environment, forging connections that empower and inspire. Through active listening, empathy, and open dialogue, create a safe space where diverse perspectives are celebrated and valued. As you cultivate this environment, you will overcome challenges and unlock the art of risk-taking. In the next chapter, we will explore the strategies to embrace calculated risks confidently, enabling you to lead with unwavering courage and embrace the transformative journey of fearless leadership.

YOUR FEEDBACK IS APPRECIATED!!

Fellow Leaders, you're halfway through "FEARLESS FEMALE LEADERSHIP," and I'd love to hear your thoughts. Your feedback not only helps me but also fellow leaders seeking valuable insights.

It's simple to leave a review on Amazon: Visit the book's Amazon 'Write a customer review' page by clicking the link or scanning the code below with your phone.

By sharing your experience, you're contributing to a community of leaders helping each other thrive. Your words of wisdom can inspire and guide them, making their journey smoother and more fulfilling.

Your insights matter – thank you for being part of my journey!

4

THE ROLE OF RISK-TAKING

If you take no risks, you will suffer no defeats. If you take no risks, you will win no victories.
—Richard M. Nixon (Risks Quotes, n.d.)

∼

Recent research states that one reason most people avoid taking risks is not because they can't but because of the fear of failing (LinkedIn, n.d.). Remember the word "fear"? An annoying little voice in your head constantly whispering, "*Watch out! Something bad might happen!*" But let me tell you, giving in to fear won't get you anywhere. It'll keep you stuck in your comfort zone, missing out on incredible opportunities and driving yourself crazy with "what ifs."

Now, let's talk about risks. They're like those thrilling roller coasters you're too scared to hop on. Sure, there's a chance you might scream your head off or feel a little queasy, but hey, that's part of the adventure! Taking risks propels us forward, pushing us to grow and discover our true potential. The legendary Helen Keller once said, "Life is either a daring adventure or nothing at all." (*A Quote From the Open Door*, n.d.)

Sure, it's totally normal to feel some fear when faced with risks. But here's the thing: fear shouldn't be calling the shots. You gotta look fear in the face and say, "*Not today, fear, not today!*" Trust me; you'll gain strength, confidence, and a kick-ass attitude by taking on those challenges head-on. As our buddy Mark Zuckerberg wisely said, "The biggest risk is not taking any risk. In a world that's changing fast, the only strategy guaranteed to fail is not taking risks." (*Mark Zuckerberg Quotes*, n.d.)

As a leader desiring to make a difference, the important motto for you, after integrity, should be risk-taking. The world keeps changing daily, and every attentive and present leader must work with the times and find best practices to navigate any circumstance, no matter the complexity.

The need to take risks is an unending demand to help every leader connect with innovations and project growth that will skyrocket their companies and businesses to the next level. How will you gain access to big clients and projects if you're all about the comfort zone? Do you think your employees will think outside the box if they notice you always aim to play safe? Once you think through all this, you'll appreciate the essence of calculated risks as the path to success, getting ahead of competitors, learning adaptability in any scenario the economy presents, and motivating and inspiring your team and clients to keep trusting your ability to deliver and best of all, seizing grand opportunities to break bounds and give the company a competitive edge.

Remember, "calculated risks" means under no condition should you feel the need to be impulsive in taking risks without thinking things through. That's not being smart but showy on your ability to dive head-on without swimming. Calculated risks are thoughtful evaluations of the potential benefits and drawbacks before deciding. They mean never misusing your emotions to cloud your sense of judgment. No great leader ever got far that way; in fact, to take risks that count:

- Be aware and clear on the potential risks and rewards.
- Aim to be authentic and transparent in your dealings.
- Assess all options presented to you.
- Seek advice on the value to be gained from the risks.
- Above all, show an openness to learn, fail, and rise again.

In leadership, these modes can do wonders for you and your team in the future, achieving productivity.

One of the most significant characteristics of a great leader is their desire to take risks that count: no running and hiding. According to a Yale School of Management study, leaders who take risks are often rewarded, particularly in competitive environments. These rewards can come from increased recognition, career advancement, and financial gains (Georgeac, 2021).

When Steve Jobs, co-founder of Apple Inc., took a significant risk by introducing the iPod in 2001, he didn't know it would be the product revolutionizing the music industry. At that time, the market was dominated by CDs and portable cassette players, and people were content with that, not knowing there were even better ways to enjoy music. The iPod's success was uncertain. However, Jobs believed in the potential of digital music and took the calculated risk of introducing a new and innovative product. It paid off. The iPod became a game-changer and set the stage for Apple's future success.

As a leader, when you can see what no one else sees after doing the due diligence of weighing all the pros and cons, rest assured that you'll get the following:

- The confidence of those who depend on you.
- The commitment of those who work with you.
- The attention of those who might want to ignore you.
- The open doors of more significant projects will elevate you.

Now you see that taking calculated risks places you on a new level. But, it begins first and foremost by overcoming your fears. You must train your brain to act when necessary and leave room for doubt and negativity. Notice that to take calculated risks is to drive success and re-channel the attitude of fear. Try doing that in three steps:

1. Rather than dwelling on the fear of failure, let your mindset take a different direction and view it all as a learning opportunity. See failure as a natural part of growth and

development where lessons are learned to prop yourself
forward.

2. Never allow fear to paralyze you; channel it into motivation and
   determination. Use it as a catalyst for action, pushing yourself to
   step outside your comfort zone and take calculated risks.

3. Take baby steps and manageable risks that gradually build your
   confidence. Break down bigger goals into smaller milestones,
   allowing you to experience success. Celebrate these
   achievements, no matter how small, as they reinforce your
   ability to overcome fear, take action, and take even bigger risks
   in the future.

The Alternatives

In addition, some alternatives can be considered on your journey to
fighting the fear of failure. I recommend this most to women seeking to
make a difference as fearless female leaders:

1. Identify and challenge any negative or self-limiting beliefs
   contributing to fear. Recognize that self-doubt is expected but
   not always rational. So, use the weapon that works for you to
   mold your mind. Practice positive affirmations, focus on your
   strengths, and celebrate your achievements. Remind yourself of
   your capabilities and the value you bring as a leader; that way,
   fear won't have its grip on you.

2. Cultivate a growth mindset that hinges on continuous learning
   and sees setbacks as opportunities for growth. There is no such
   thing as an insurmountable obstacle; that's what you need to tell
   yourself constantly when in doubt. Reframing failure as a
   chance to learn and improve, you can approach risks with a
   more optimistic and open mindset.

3. Foster an environment that values and celebrates diversity and
   inclusion. Encourage diverse perspectives, create opportunities
   for underrepresented voices to be heard, and support the
   development of women leaders. When leaders feel empowered
   and valued, it can help mitigate the fear that may arise from
   societal pressures and biases.

A study published in the Journal of Personality and Social Psychology found that individuals who overcome the fear of failure and take risks have higher self-esteem and life satisfaction. Knowing they didn't bail out at the last minute isn't only a comfort but a sign that, with a little effort, they can reduce the fear of failing and taking risks. Also, a better way can come in more strategic steps:

1. **See failure as a learning tool:** An opportunity for growth where you are, allows you to refine your strategies and approach for future success.

2. **View failure as a stepping stone to greatness:** Once you recall how many successful leaders have experienced failures, use their stories as catalysts for achieving extraordinary outcomes.

3. **Practice self-compassion:** Be kind to yourself when faced with setbacks; understand that taking risks is a courageous act that requires resilience and self-encouragement.

4. **Pencil down the benefits of past failures:** How have previous failures provided valuable lessons, insights, and experiences that have shaped your leadership skills and decision-making?

5. **Surround yourself with a supportive network:** Seek out mentors, colleagues, or a peer group that can provide guidance, encouragement, and a safe space to discuss challenges and bounce back from failures.

6. **Set realistic expectations:** Understand that taking risks involves uncertainties, setbacks, and the potential for significant rewards and growth. Align your expectations with the process of learning and improvement.

7. **Focus on small steps:** Break down significant risks into minor, manageable actions that can help build confidence and momentum. Celebrate each step forward, regardless of the outcome.

8. **Nurture a growth mindset:** Cultivate a philosophy that supports challenges and sees setbacks as opportunities for growth rather than fixed limitations or indicators of failure.

9. **Seek feedback and continuous improvement:** Actively seek feedback from trusted sources to gain insights into areas for improvement and refine your approach to future risks.

10. **A big cheer to your successes:** Acknowledge and celebrate your achievements and successful risk-taking endeavors, recognizing the courage it took to step out of your comfort zone and make a positive impact.

It's a challenging but laudable choice. For instance, you leave the comfort of a job that pays well and ensures your financial security to pursue your passion in the hope of growth. That takes a lot of guts and planning. Informed decisions and taking calculated risks are imperative if your career and leadership passion is to see the light of day.

Risks That Count

As a female leader desiring to be fearless and driven, **how do you take risks that count?**

- **Weigh your risk-taking capability:** Reflect and evaluate your past experiences with risk-taking, considering how your unique experiences as a female leader have shaped your risk appetite so far. You have the statistics, so only you can give the correct answer.
- **Give room for failure:** Never deny potential obstacles and setbacks their fair share of existence; they must come, like it or not. But developing contingency plans to mitigate risks and recognizing the power of resilience and adaptability as critical attributes of successful female leaders will help prepare you for everything.
- **Define clear goals:** What are your desired outcomes? What are your objectives for the risks you are considering? Ensuring they align with your vision as a leader and contribute to your long-term career growth and empowerment—this is what counts the most.
- **Identify strengths and weaknesses ahead:** Assess your skills, knowledge, and resources, considering the unique strengths and capabilities you bring to the table and leveraging them to make informed decisions about the risks you are willing to take.

- **What do you and others stand to benefit from:** Evaluate the potential positive impacts of the risk-taking on your career, team, and organization, recognize the potential for advancing gender equality, break barriers, and inspire other aspiring female leaders. With this gain, the risk will be worth taking.
- **Seek guidance from experts:** Consult mentors, advisors, or successful female leaders who can provide valuable insights and perspectives specific to the challenges and opportunities women face in leadership roles, empowering you to make informed risk-taking decisions.
- **Get comfortable taking tiny risks at first:** Start with smaller, manageable risks to build confidence and gradually increase your risk tolerance, recognizing that taking calculated risks is an integral part of the journey towards achieving gender equality in leadership.
- **Be ready to adapt:** When you think about risk, think agility and flexibility because risk-taking often involves navigating through gender biases and stereotypes and being able to adjust your strategies and approaches to create positive change.
- **Be around like-minded people:** A supportive network of diverse female leaders and allies who share your passion for breaking barriers is an excellent way to support one another in taking risks. Most of all, it's a collective method to advance women's leadership.
- **Remember self-awareness:** Continuously reflect on your strengths, weaknesses, and the unique challenges female leaders face, using self-awareness as a tool for personal growth, resilience, and inspiring others through your journey.
- **Be diverse:** Diverse perspectives, ideas, and approaches should always be a welcome development. Be aware of the importance of inclusivity in decision-making and its positive impact on innovation, problem-solving, and driving positive change.
- **Be accountable:** Hold yourself responsible for your risk-taking endeavors and openly communicate your goals and aspirations as a female leader, inspiring others and creating a culture that encourages women's leadership and risk-taking.
- **Follow the 3 A's of risk-taking:**

1. Act decisively.
2. Assess the outcomes.
3. Adapt your strategies and approaches based on the lessons learned.

You should embody the resilience and determination needed to succeed as a female leader.

- **Fail, but get up and proceed:** If you've heard the saying "fail fast but rise faster," you'll know that failure shouldn't be an excuse to sit back and dwell on the "had I known." Failure should be your stepping stone for growth and improvement, as you have been provided valuable lessons, paving your way toward success as a resilient leader.
- **Be ready to innovate:** Cultivate a mindset of curiosity, creativity, and a willingness to challenge the status quo, seizing opportunities for innovation from taking calculated risks and driving positive change in your leadership journey.

Segue

Unleash your potential by overcoming fear and embracing change, innovation, and learning opportunities. Don't let fear rob you of victories; instead, seize potential opportunities and grow from the valuable lessons they offer. Did you know overcoming fear is crucial in developing practical collaboration skills? When you let go of fear, you become more open to working with others, sharing ideas, and embracing diverse perspectives. Now, let's shift our focus to enhancing your collaboration skills in the next chapter.

5

FIGHT IMPOSTOR SYNDROME

Alone, we can do so little; together, we can do so much.
—Hellen Keller (Conley, 2022)

❧

E very good structure didn't just take building materials and the knowledge to bring it to life; it took the commitment and dedication of people who worked tirelessly until they saw a finished edifice. There are countless buildings like the Empire State Building in the United States, the Eiffel Tower in France, and the ancient Pyramids of Egypt. These monuments have survived centuries of historical changes. They are still a wonder in the world because of teamwork, the collaboration of efforts and ideas, and respect for each other's perspectives and contributions.

Today, these skills are among the most in-demand requirements for the world's transition to higher interconnectivity and effective leadership. To position yourself as one with authority not nurtured in isolated brilliance but with the encompassing effort of collaboration and teamwork, you must believe in and support the strength of being team-spirited on your journey.

Collaboration isn't just about people combining their ideas because it would look good together, like date matchmaking; it pays attention to views from different sources. Somehow, everyone on a team is heard, their contributions and opinions are checked side-by-side with the desired outcome, and a decision is made. This approach in recent studies has become paramount, especially as about 75% of U.S. workers acknowledge that collaboration is vital for effective leadership and the work environment to thrive. They feel strongly about it because a report from KPMG affirms that, once again, 75% of female executives across over 150 leading global organizations have suffered imposter syndrome at some point (Boskamp, 2023). It shows that the connection between these figures is profound, and collaborative skills can significantly influence the leadership outcome in several industries.

What Is Impostor Syndrome?

Where the phrase impostor syndrome is used, it's synonymous with doubt, second-guessing, laid-back and low esteem. Not only do you have the skills, but you're also excellent at what you do. Regardless, there is still a fear of letting your work shine, and more times than not, you feel like some scam who doesn't have what it takes to win those big clients or execute those high-powered jobs.

When you're starting up your own sole proprietary business, that tends to happen because it's you against thousands of other competitors in similar companies. So, your work doesn't only have to speak for you; it needs to stand out. And, although you achieve that status of being significant and relevant, you still feel undeserving of the recognition for some reason.

But, like most phenomena, imposter syndrome slowly manifests itself through the character of the victim in several ways:

- Being successful is never enough. Most leaders with impostor syndrome disorder are often labeled high-achievers because they don't believe success is enough to quantify good leadership. They are fixated on their goals and go all out to make it happen, even if it breaks them.

- Overworking is a part of life. There is no room for playtime in their world because somebody must do everything perfectly. Mistakes are often viewed as significant blunders, potentially indicative of incompetence. Leaders with this trait are difficult to relate to as their employees walk on eggshells around them.
- The most common problem is self-doubt. More often than ever, the belief is that one's work is too unworthy to find its place among exceptional work. Even when trusted sources credit it as unique and authentic, it never changes the mindset of self-torture and belittling of efforts.
- Praises are more like savage statements than acknowledgment. Sensitivity to what's being said and how it's said can be a contention. Already, discontentment with their work makes any praise or recognition sound like a savage way of ridiculing their skills. For a leader with a big ego, their pride can be wounded easily without much effort since the sensitive behavioral response is profound.

In essence, imposter syndrome begins inborn and grows to create a character that's overly sensitive and judgmental of themselves and those around them. Richard Patterson, an American author, is among the famous personalities with their fair share of imposter syndrome disorder. His statement on the phenomena was striking as he described it as a character within most confident professionals where they get anxious and over-zealous to succeed before they're perceived as deceptive and their skills fraudulent. For him, these weird feelings make the victim work extra hard to clear their name and protect their records. (Patterson, 2023)

Archetypes of Imposter Syndrome

Honestly, this reason justifies the essence of impostor syndrome. But, like a white lie, there is no right way to celebrate a character trait that makes you second-guess your capabilities. To understand it better and approach it strategically, psychologists have taken the time to undergo studies that will clarify the different archetypes of Impostor Syndrome.

1. **Perfectionist:** This personality is all about high standards for themselves. They get so anxious about how things will turn out and if their work will be labeled as crap, regardless of their accomplishments. Good is never enough, except it's great.

2. **Soloist:** When you love to do things on your own and be the star of your show, that's the soloist. They find leadership hard because they don't know how to delegate or accept help. They fear that asking for assistance will expose their incompetence and make them look like they can't handle the weight. In fact, no one has the right to take the shine off them because doing it alone proves exceptionality.

3. **Natural Genius:** They're the know-it-all, so new knowledge for them is hard work. What happened to all their skills and talent? These folks will be least attentive when in a workshop or seminar because their competence, if anything, should come effortlessly and instantaneously. They struggle on the first try, and their self-perception is that they're naturally talented individuals.

4. **Expert:** You believe your knowledge or experience is only a drop in an ocean of water. Year after year, you bag certificates and increase qualifications and still find yourself in the zone where you doubt your legitimacy. It's a case of being an expert by name but not by belief.

5. **The Comparer:** According to Mike Robbins, this individual is caught in a comparison trap with the tendency to be a jealous character who spends more time comparing themselves to others, believing that everyone around them is more competent and accomplished. They feel inadequate and fear being exposed as less capable, so without knowing it, this envy surfaces once they notice someone else doing what they should be doing.

Instead of wishing to be like them, try appreciating what you have.

How to Overcome Imposter Syndrome?

The one thing a victim of impostor syndrome has is talent. They have the skills but need more trust to celebrate their potential. So, how can you overcome your negative thoughts about yourself?

1. **Acknowledge:** Like any other disorder, acknowledgment is the first step to recovery. Accept that you are a victim of impostor syndrome based on all the signs discussed, and then begin the journey of healing by telling yourself it's not unusual and can be corrected. When you admit your wrongdoing, you weaken the chances of repeating the same act twice since you've become aware, present, and hungry for change.

2. **Play down on criticism:** It's good to criticize your work so the best can come out of it. However, in the case of an imposter syndrome mindset, it's safer to go minimal on pinpointing and downgrading your efforts. You might think it's a humbling way to win attention, but you're slowly instilling low self-confidence in yourself. Even if there are hiccups here and there, appraise how well you've performed and prepare more strategically for more significant projects.

3. **Call your impostor syndrome's bluff:** This might sound like pushing yourself to the edge to prove a point. And yes, it is but with a foresight to see yourself disengaging the thought that you don't have what it takes to stand out. Prove everyone—especially yourself—wrong by trusting and taking it all the way.

4. **Listen and learn:** Many people in your circle, probably those you've read about, have been there before. Take a moment to listen to their story and learn from their experiences. No one can help you better than someone who's been there. They know the signs; they'll tell you when to fight hard or pipe low.

5. **Ask for help:** Once you notice it's getting out of hand and your work and position are in jeopardy because of innate negativity, it's time to seek professional support. Let the therapists do their job and help you navigate this challenging phase.

6. **Be mindful:** Choose your words and thoughts carefully as they shape a significant part of your impostor syndrome recovery. As

a leader, being positive is a non-negotiable attitude to becoming an achiever and a profiting executor. No matter how bad it all looks, focus on why you want to make the best out of the worst situation.

7. **Take self-care seriously:** Sometimes, the weight on your shoulder strengthens the doubt. You tell yourself, "I'm tired, so why should I try so hard when it all comes down to nothing?" Instead of all that, aim to take a break in whatever way works for you. Swimming, meditating, taking long walks, getting a sauna treatment, you name it. Always step aside to reboot so your thought level reevaluates things rationally.

8. **Practice collaboration and teamwork:** Once you admit that, yes, you are good, but you don't have all the answers, it will push you to find out who does. And then, you'll appreciate the importance of employees and building a synergized work setting where everyone aims for the success of the other's project. No room for envy, comparison, or judgment, just support, hard work, respect, and team effort.

The strongest weapon impostor syndrome uses to hamper the success of its victim is to kill their self-confidence. You never feel right about anything, and it's the worst place to be when you're a leader. People depend on your optimism and confidence to have a reason to hope, and if that's dashed, then what? Does it mean you'll no longer get the respect and submission of your employees?

If it only takes confidence and determination to make a good leader, then most recognized names today wouldn't make it past the first few months in their positions.

Note that when a leader lacks confidence and has traces of self-doubt, they may sound the same; however, there are some acute differences.

Building confidence involves recognizing and leveraging strengths, setting and achieving goals, seeking feedback, and continuously learning and developing skills. These actions are positive approaches to help individuals develop a sense of competence and self-assurance in their professional abilities.

On the other hand, combating self-doubt focuses on addressing and challenging negative thoughts, beliefs, and insecurities that may undermine confidence. It is about restraining negative self-talk, embracing mistakes and failures as learning opportunities, seeking support from others, and practicing self-care to nurture a positive mindset.

How to Crush Self-Doubt?

The strategies to combat self-doubt and deal with negative thoughts are the same. Try these six tricks:

1. **Challenge negative thoughts:** Your thoughts must constantly be reevaluated whenever you're around people. Once you notice you're about to get into the zone where you practically nurse negative ideas, replace them with positive and realistic ones.

2. **Focus on strengths and accomplishments:** You have records of great success stories; remind yourself of them and all the strengths that have contributed to them. Use these thoughts to boost your confidence and reflect on your capabilities.

3. **View failure as a learning opportunity:** View failure and when you're in doubt as a chance to learn, grow and try again. In one of her lyrics, the late American Singer Aaliyah said, "What if you don't succeed; dust yourself up and try again." Adopt a growth mindset to see setbacks as stepping stones to future success.

4. **Attempt self-compassion:** What recharges you? Is it exercise, relaxation, yoga techniques, or spending time with loved ones? Prioritize it and treat yourself with kindness and understanding during challenging times and moments when you fall below expectations.

5. **Celebrate achievements:** Imagine yourself succeeding and overcoming a back-breaking obstacle; how would you celebrate? Would you take on a bigger challenge to validate your accomplishments, no matter how small? Would you rework your mindset to have better self-belief and motivation? Question your mode of recognizing efforts and be open to good cheer.

6. **Seek feedback and support:** Surround yourself with trusted mentors, colleagues, friends, and professionals to help where necessary. You need people who can provide constructive, open conversations to gain perspective and reassurance that you're in this place of doubt for now, but it's a step toward something amazing.

These tricks, once applied, raise a personality that's slowly beginning to see yourself differently.

Boost Your Confidence

In leadership, it is important to exude positivity even when the situation looks pretty bad. Gaining that level of respect from subordinates starts with boosting your confidence and making bold decisions. There are several ways to do it, and one thing you must remember is that confidence is about something other than standing tall, speaking professionally, taking a slow and steady stride, and convincing people easily. It's about doing everything possible as a leader to escape and stay safe from that fear of being wrong. It's a horrible place to be enslaved by imposter syndrome. So, start now to boost your confidence by:

1. **Reforming yourself:** Ensure your disposition, attire, and discussions exude high confidence. This is the first trick most people disregard but have proven to be over 70% helpful to job seekers and leaders (Cohn, 2021). When they take a good look at you, there needs to be an aura that will make them assured of your capabilities. It starts from the outside.
2. **Surrounding yourself with positive, beneficial activities:** Everything about your life and desire to grow should be linked to positive actions. Take professional training, join workshops and seminars to empower your skills, and attend conferences where you rub shoulders with positive-minded peer groups and top leadership individuals. These all seem casual, but they significantly affect how you think, act, and react where confidence comes into play.
3. **Challenging your safety net:** You've played it safe for far too long. Aren't you tired of being the nice girl who's too diplomatic sometimes? Go over and beyond to see what comes of it. For instance, maybe you have always dreaded giving presentations to the entire sales and marketing team. You could step outside your comfort zone by volunteering to deliver the next presentation or co-host with a teammate. Usually, you would look for any opportunity to escape that responsibility. It's time to

leave the safety net behind, go into the ocean, and see what's out there. You'll either sink or swim, but you'll learn.

4. **Rewriting history:** If you have a background of being the rejected stone who's been ignored, overlooked, underrepresented, and taken for granted, rewrite that story. Don't work into your new position, thinking history will repeat itself. Take a new approach to being positive and forward-thinking. This goes especially for female leaders with doors slammed in their faces. Channel those past experiences into present strengths to stir your course to success.

One of the many ways to encourage confidence in female leaders, especially in the workplace, is to leverage the diversity of thought within a working environment, which we will discuss in detail in the next section.

Stereotypes and gender bias must be addressed to ensure there is only room made for mutual respect and team building. Always recognize that everyone thinks differently, and their differences can help unlock innovation and creativity to match and surpass industry standards.

How to Leverage Diversity in the Workplace?

How can female leadership be fostered to nurture respect, teamwork, and innovation in the workplace without compromising their intentions? I say, by leveraging the diversity of thoughts, you can achieve that in the following ways:

- **Have open dialogues:** The work environment has a serious undertone and a formal setting. So, to keep the mood light and the employees responsive, encourage a safe space where team members feel comfortable expressing their unique perspectives and ideas. Encourage more dialogues where they can speak freely and participate in active listening to ensure that diverse viewpoints are heard and respected.
- **Make inclusion a culture:** The value of inclusion must be emphasized. And so, for female leaders to feel safe and create a more embracing space, diverse perspectives and inclusive culture should be an essential part of work ethics. Recognize and celebrate the contributions of individuals from different

backgrounds, experiences, and identities. Encourage collaboration and teamwork, embracing the power of diversity, and you will see how far the creativity and productivity level will bloom.

- **Perform a mixed-duty delegation:** Form teams with a mix of individuals from various backgrounds, expertise, and ways of thinking to come together and perform different responsibilities. This diversity can lead to richer output, increased creativity, and innovative problem-solving. Consider rotating team members across projects to ensure the cross-pollination of ideas with a mixture of people's strengths and weaknesses to complement each other for personal improvement.

- **Constructive debates and health conflicts:** These should never be seen as a hole in the wall or a source of tension; they should be welcomed as new possibilities and opportunities for growth and improvement. When managed effectively, diverse perspectives can lead to better decision-making and outcomes.

- **Invest in diversity training and education:** Provide training and educational opportunities to raise awareness about unconscious bias, stereotypes, and the benefits of diversity of thought. Equip team members with the knowledge and skills to navigate diverse perspectives, promote inclusivity, and challenge any biases hindering collaboration.

Segue

As a leader, setting the record straight so everyone works freely and happily is always a great place to start. Remember, you're also on a path to combat impostor syndrome to stay positive-minded and create the right vibes among the people around you. Let them feel motivated and inspired working around you. Every team is a massive part of the success of a leader and their company, so posterity will speak for you once you employ a leadership style to win and sustain your employees' confidence. You can explore Chapter 6 to understand how great leaders stood the test of time and maintained wealth and recognition.

6

THE POWERFUL DYNAMICS OF THE FEMALE LEADERSHIP STYLE

A leader takes people where they want to go. A great leader takes people where they don't necessarily want to go but ought to be.
—Rosalyn Carter (Fallon, 2023)

～

What makes female leadership different? You might say women show empathy because they have high emotions. But there is more; their emotional intelligence makes them able to apply authenticity to their intentions and attentiveness to the details of human activities. Their leadership is about bringing diverse perspectives to the table, encouraging a collaborative team-building work environment, championing an inclusive playing ground, and working resiliently to see organizational success.

Looking back at the former Prime Minister of New Zealand, Jacinda Ardern, her leadership stood out among the most exceptional with global recognition because of her empathetic approach towards crisis situations and her leadership style, which was diplomatic, inclusive, and full of integrity.

Leadership over the years has witnessed a series of changes. The years of having older generation leadership are slowly fizzling away, giving room to many younger characters; inclusion and diversity are becoming integral to fostering good leadership. People have become specific about the leadership styles and values they seek that will inspire them. Having a style is your way of leaving an indelible mark on how you run things so there can be progressive leadership. To achieve a style that works and is accepted by the majority, there are factors to consider, the first being consistency and predictability.

1. Consistency is about you doing everything that makes your leadership transparent, predictable, and reliable. The perfect way to build a solid foundation where team members are assured that they can trust your integrity and decision-making process because you are all about communication, interpersonal relationships, and problem-solving mechanisms.
2. Nothing beats trust; in today's leadership style, it's a massive requirement if you want your team to stand by you. Can you keep your promises and follow through on commitments? Are the people who depend on you assured of fairness and equity where loyalty is concerned? If it's all yes, rest assured that your team won't only have the psychological safety of knowing they are appreciated and respected, but it would give room for an increased workforce.
3. What's most beneficial is the reputable record you create for yourself. Indira Nooyi, the former CEO of PepsiCo, had a style of leadership that labeled her a visionary because of her ability to see consumer trends way ahead of time. When she launched the "Performance with Purpose,' it was about sustaining growth while looking into social and environmental impacts. She adhered to values, principles, and ethical standards, establishing herself as reliable and trustworthy. There is nothing more profiting than showing credibility and opening doors of opportunities to attract top talent.
4. Consistency leads to improved cooperation and communication, eliminating favoritism and ensuring the team's fairness. Team members understand the leader's expectations,

which enhances teamwork, productivity, and mutual understanding.

From inception, it's plain to see that being a consistent leader is about building a character that provides insurance to your leadership. So, every style has its ups and downs and results therein. Take a look at these 12 different leadership styles and understand their complexities.

1. **The Autocrats:** All that concerns them is that they lead, you follow, and you don't have to like it. Your opinion doesn't count because you're a pawn in a chess board moving at the leader's wimp. Such leaders can think fast on their feet, make quick decision-making, and be efficient in crises. But they'll have more employees walking out the door because they kill creativity and innovation with their autocracy. The work atmosphere will always be low and unexciting.

2. **The Democrats:** Without the voice and commitment of the team, they feel useless and baseless, as what they stand for is collaboration. This is a great and sure way to boost employee engagement with the mission to promote diversity and inclusion. On the lower end, waiting for people to be the deciding panel for your next step can slow down your leadership process, make you appear incompetent enough to make decisions, and sometimes leave you with nothing tangible to work with.

3. **The Laissez-Faires:** They have that "I don't care" attitude where they provide minimal guidance and allow employees to make decisions and work autonomously. Employees enjoy the privilege of freedom and autonomy; however, it lays a poor structure for the environment. Where the system is structureless, there can be a lot of chaos and disorganization.

4. **The Transformers:** Inspiration and motivation is their middle name, as they always aim for exceptional performance and personal growth. They undoubtedly promote personal development and push themselves too hard to see it through. This could lead to burnout, and the dreaded impostor syndrome might worsen if it prolongs.

5. **The Transactionists:** Leadership is like a business deal emphasizing demands, rewards, performance rate, and clear expectations. This can benefit economic development but what about team building and collaborative approaches? These are ignored and sidelined with minimal importance rendering a non-empathetic working environment.

6. **The Servants:** The focus is to serve, protect and support others, putting their needs first. It promotes teamwork, collaboration, and a positive work culture. The sad part is that these leaders often get exploited for their good nature to serve. They get pinned down as weak and sometimes indecisive in a bid to be diplomatic.

7. **The Charismatics:** These are the leaders with a lot of character. They have charm, enthusiasm, and an aura of empowering people. Because of their personality, it's easy to feel motivated and inspired around them. But then, when you take away the personality, it just means there is no substance. Such leaders lose traction pretty quickly, except there is something more about them other than charisma.

8. **The Situationists:** A leadership style that adapts to the individual and situational needs of the team. This can be good but will require lots of assessment, check and recheck for decisions to be made. The process is cumbersome, and long-term development is often overlooked.

9. **The Coaches:** They are focused on guiding and developing individuals to reach their full potential. To ensure the success of any worthy cause you're pursuing, investing time and seeking guidance from a skilled and dedicated coaching leader is essential. With their expertise and professional approach, the purpose and objectives of the cause may be protected. The aim of replicating their skillset is defeated.

10. **The Bureaucrats:** This style emphasizes following rules and procedures strictly. They want a system that works with compliance and consistency as their watchwords. An excellent structure, but it could be more flexible and stiff with room for opinions and innovations.

11. **The Adaptives:** They are open to adjust to any situation and flow with the tide. That's the style of leadership that shows flexibility and openness to change.

12. **The Authentics:** The leaders with this leadership style are genuine, transparent, and true to themselves and their values. They hold strongly to ethical behavior and credibility, mostly making them seem too rigid and inflexible. This resonates as the most outstanding style of leadership to be embraced by all, especially females who seek to lead fearlessly.

Authentic Leadership

Though many leadership styles exist, for optimal success, authentic leadership stands out for how it makes individuals establish their true selves and capabilities. In today's society, authenticity sets you apart as someone who doesn't joke with integrity and truth. Gaining people's trust is paramount, and if it takes you losing a few friends and trusted allies along the way, so be it. With such character, authentic leaders can inspire people because they are present, aware, and committed to success. They create an environment where team members feel safe to take risks, share ideas, and collaborate effectively.

Honestly, authentic leadership is essential because of its reputation for building trust and addressing people's aversion to deception and inconsistencies. People naturally have an incline to distrust and suspect others, especially when there are little traces of contradictions here and there. These inconsistencies can distract talented employees from their work, resulting in a negative streak that reduces productivity. However, authentic leadership, characterized by trust, transparency, and support, tackles this issue. By being credible, authentic leaders inspire their team members to excel, collaborate effectively, and achieve shared objectives.

Historical records of authentic leaders like Mary Barra (CEO, General Motors), Malala Yousafzai (Activist), and Michelle Obama (Former First Lady), among others, unveil how you can identify the characteristics of an authentic leader in five traits:

- **Self-awareness:** Authentic leaders understand their values, emotions, strengths, and weaknesses. They've spent years through their personal experiences knowing about themselves and their impact on others. This self-discovery has them actively seek to align their behavior with their core principles so people can appreciate what they stand for.
- **Transparency:** They are open, honest, and transparent in their communication. As much as possible, they ensure information is updated, and transactions are accounted for to avoid hidden agendas and foster an environment of trust within their teams.
- **Truthfulness:** For them, outstanding leadership is about honesty and integrity. Every action must be done with a humble mindset to maintain the right standing by admitting mistakes and sustaining integrity in decision-making.
- **Willing:** A leader who is willing to learn, unlearn, recognize limitations, and acknowledge the contributions of others. That's authentic and humble. When you learn from others, long to hear their feedback, and use it to your advantage, you promote your integrity and empower team members.
- **Empathy and integrity:** They always strive to demonstrate empathy by understanding and valuing the perspectives and emotions of others. They show genuine care and consideration for their team members' well-being while still trying to align with their values and ethical standards. It's a character that's noble and humane at the same time.

The list is endless. It's because authentic leadership is unique and highly embraced by team members. In the hands of an authentic leader, team members feel motivated because these leaders know how to create an environment where individuals feel valued, supported, and inspired.

When 'Ramona,' a 37-year-old media communications graduate, sat down for an interview at a prestigious advertising agency, she felt like a fish out of water. Despite her credentials, her personal struggles, including obesity and low self-esteem, greatly overshadow her potential. She wondered if she could succeed among the elite graduates that filled the company's ranks. Yet, halfway through the interview, a remarkable thing happened. The CEO saw past 'Ramona's' insecurities and recognized a hidden gem. Ignoring societal bias and conventions, she saw a woman who, despite battling impostor syndrome, held the untapped potential to propel the company forward.

The CEO seized the moment, engaging 'Ramona' in a heartfelt discussion about her worth and value to the company. This wasn't favoritism— it was empathic leadership in action, a potent tool for igniting dormant potential. Authentic leaders excel at this. They empower their team members, foster collaboration, provide constructive feedback, and celebrate accomplishments, steering their teams towards shared objectives. They see beyond perceived limitations and help their people uncover their best selves.

It's why authentic leaders can motivate teams and introduce a method that can swiftly combine with the leadership style of some of the previously mentioned styles for optimal success.

Best Leadership Style Combinations

1. Transformational leaders inspire and motivate their team members by setting high expectations, fostering creativity, and promoting individual growth. So once you combine it with authentic leadership, a powerful blend inspires others to reach their full potential while building trust and authenticity within the organization.
2. Servant leaders prioritize the well-being and development of their team members. They work well with authentic leaders to build a supportive environment where leaders genuinely care about their employees and have a shared sense of purpose.
3. Democratic leaders involve their team members in decision-making, valuing their input and perspectives and seeing ways to rope their ideas into the scheme of things. Connecting this with authentic leadership promotes transparency, open communication, and inclusivity. Here employees feel empowered to contribute ideas and foster a sense of ownership and engagement.
4. Coaches are all about developing the skills and abilities of their team members through mentorship and guidance. Like

authentic leaders, their goal is to provide a support structure
and growth-oriented culture for their team members.

All these connections show that authentic leadership is a perfect partner
for almost any individual who wants their mode of leadership to
resonate differently.

How to Maintain Authenticity?

Any female leader who wants to develop and maintain authenticity for
the long term should never forget these eight short quick steps:

1. Reflect on your core values and beliefs.
2. Practice self-awareness and self-reflection.
3. Seek feedback from others.
4. Develop emotional intelligence.
5. Build genuine relationships.
6. Embrace vulnerability and authenticity.
7. Align your actions with your values.
8. Continuously learn and grow as a leader.

Following these steps, you'll leverage a leadership style aiming for
success, especially in the workplace, because you've come so far in establishing trust and credibility through consistent transparency. People feel
inspired and motivated when you lead passionately with unwavering
commitment. Best of all, your open communication and collaborative
approach have unlocked your teams' full potential, driving more innovation and increased productivity.

All these have created an authentic female leader whose leadership style
demonstrates empathy, support for growth and development, and a positive workplace culture that attracts top talent, enhances employee
engagement, and paves the way for long-term success in the organization.

Segue

Your leadership style has a significant impact on those around you. It
sets the tone, inspires others, and commands respect, regardless of

biases. Always leverage your leadership style to its fullest potential and maintain consistency once you have identified your most effective approach. Doing so will cultivate a growth mindset that aligns with your leadership style, enabling continuous improvement and success. Do you have a growth or fixed mindset? Chapter 7 will educate you better.

7

THE FEARLESS GROWTH MINDSET

The best thing you can do for the whole world is make the most of yourself.
—*Wallace Wattles (Hannah, 2020)*

⁓

P erhaps you didn't know this, but achieving success in life has never been done through a fixed destination. It's fluid and evolves with our changing mindset because our goals never stop expanding even though we have accomplished our initial desires. Maintaining this leadership perspective requires adopting a growth mindset where our intelligence is nurtured and developed based on the boundless capacity to acquire new skills.

Only you have the power to unleash the extraordinary growth mindset within you. But what is this mindset all about?

A growth mindset is an understanding that your abilities and intelligence can be developed and improved through effort, consistent learning, and persevering through tough challenges. To keep yourself upbeat, always recognize that your talents and skills are not fixed traits but can be enhanced with new knowledge and positive influence. According to the Harvard Business Review, a growth mindset challenges the misconceptions that we either have what it takes to grow or we don't, leading to success. Notice that the right attitude, strategies, and support can lead you to grow continually and achieve greater performance and fulfillment in various areas of your life. An American Leadership Coach, Linda Scott, says, "Being an adult and having a growth mindset, you must possess the hunger to learn, fail, make findings, expand, and evolve." (*LinkedIn*, n.d.)

Common Myths

It means a growth mindset is a process that can be sequential sometimes, which explains why there is a common myth about either having it or not having it. You're either born with the innate desire to grow or appreciate the comfort zone and are too scared to make changes. Although this might sound like a trait of many people, research has shown that everyone can develop a growth mindset with intentional effort and practice. For instance, 'Jenny' worked as a jeweler for a company for over 15 years, and it paid her bills and gave her enough time for her family, which is great. Then one day, it dawns on her that she is made for more and can become her own boss. All it takes is doing research, assessing all the risks and successes involved, and taking the bold step of trying to start as a fearless leader with a potentially growing mindset. This is called emancipating from being okay with the normal to trying something new and promising, which is what a growth mindset is all about.

Another myth is the belief that effort alone can lead to success. While effort is essential, it must be coupled with practical strategies, feedback, and continuous learning to maximize growth. It's why 'Jenny' could pull off and envision her potential as a standalone owner. You need to create room for a mental assessment of what you want and what it will take to get there. That's the start.

There is also the myth that people mistakenly think that a growth mindset dismisses the importance of natural talent or that it guarantees instant success. In reality, a growth mindset values and requires effort and innate abilities because the combination emphasizes the importance of embracing challenges, persisting through setbacks, and seeking opportunities for growth and improvement.

To develop and maintain a growth mindset, it is crucial to acknowledge that growth and learning are lifelong processes. The Harvard Business Review believes you must prioritize confronting and addressing limitations and shortcomings as valuable learning opportunities rather than personal deficiencies. Spending time cultivating self-awareness and seeking feedback from others can help identify areas for growth and improvement. Don't feel too proud or shy to have your ideas and works criticized and evaluated because there is no improvement for hidden work. Constantly challenge yourself and your ideas by stepping out of your comfort zones and taking proactive steps to move forward on continuous development. Once you're at this point, it's the beginning of breaking free from all fixed mindset ideology.

Growth vs. Fixed Mindsets

Observing all the components of a growth mindset presents an apparent contrast to a fixed mindset. While a fixed mindset assumes that our abilities and intelligence are static traits that cannot significantly change, a growth mindset believes in the potential for growth and development. With a growth mindset, individuals understand that their current skills and talents are starting points and that they can expand their abilities through dedication, learning, and effort. If Ben Carson had listened to the voices that criticized his poor learning skills, he wouldn't have become the renowned American neurosurgeon, author, and politician who is celebrated today. That's what a growth mindset can do—it fosters a belief in the power of progress and the capacity for personal transformation.

Critical Devices

But it all begins with some critical devices:

- Don't be ambiguous and scared to experience challenges, setbacks, and self-doubt. It is a shared human experience that needs to happen so you understand there is room for improvement and resilience.

- Aim to use effective strategies, seek support, and believe in your potential for growth.
- Replace limiting beliefs and negative self-talk with positive and affirming statements. Say proudly, "I can learn" and "I can improve."
- Cultivate optimism, curiosity, and a willingness to embrace new opportunities for learning and development.

Above all, let your thinking patterns and beliefs switch into a more daring and adventurous mode where your vision and mission are value-based, and expansions personified.

Developing a Growth Mindset

No matter how far you go in life, keep developing a growth mindset by:

- **Cultivating a sense of purpose:** Find meaning and direction in your growth journey, keeping your goals and aspirations in mind.
- **Celebrate others, especially your team:** Foster a collaborative and supportive environment by recognizing and celebrating the achievements and growth of your team members.
- **Value growth over speed:** Prioritize continuous improvement rather than focusing solely on immediate results. Embrace the process of development and progress.
- **Take action:** Put your growth mindset into action by consistently taking steps towards your goals, learning new skills, and applying them practically.
- **Welcome constructive criticism:** Welcome feedback and constructive criticism as opportunities for personal growth and development. See them as valuable insights for improvement.
- **Reframe failure:** Change your perspective on failure, viewing it as a steppingstone to learning and growth. Embrace the lessons and insights gained from failures.

- **Engage in reflection and self-thought:** Regularly reflect on your experiences, challenges, and successes to gain deeper insights and adjust for continuous growth.
- **Learn from team mistakes:** Recognize that mistakes happen and view them as learning opportunities. Learn from the mistakes of others on your team to avoid similar pitfalls and foster collective growth.
- **Embrace the power of "Yet":** Replace limiting beliefs with the understanding that you can develop skills and abilities over time. Shift from "I can't do it" to "I can't do it yet," emphasizing the growth potential.
- **Celebrate growth and progress:** Acknowledge and celebrate your achievements, regardless of their size. Recognize your progress, using it as motivation to continue pushing yourself and striving for excellence.

By striving for excellence, it's not enough to see yourself at the top; you must find the best ways to get up there and maintain a high standard. It comes with its demands, one of which is the act of upskilling.

Upskilling

In today's world, upskilling is becoming the in-demand lookout for most employment agencies. Leaders are beginning to see how important it is to up their game, challenging their employees to be more daring in stepping up their own game. This can only mean that upskilling is the future of development and improved performance. Adding more knowledge to what you have because you want to create relevance is the beginning of upskilling. In a survey conducted by LinkedIn in 2020, 94% of employees confirmed they would stay longer with a company that invested in their career development, and 58% of employees said they would be more likely to recommend their organization as a great place to work if they felt supported in their upskilling efforts (*LinkedIn*, n.d.).

Benefits of Upskilling

With the statistics provided above, we can infer that the benefits of upskilling are numerous and continue to grow with time.

- Upskilling programs generate a strong return on investment (ROI) and are often cheaper than addressing workplace problems. With upskilling, the performance grows at its best, leaving room for little to no slips that can cost the company huge debts.
- Providing free training increases employee retention rates and reduces turnover and hiring costs. With more employees willing to take on upskilling learning, it's easier to swing people around job roles rather than bring in new talent. Plus, employees always look for room to grow, so why not give them the best and see them at their best? With Upskilling, employee engagement improves, and their demands for professional development and training opportunities are well satisfied.
- Employee productivity is optimized by improving their understanding and proficiency in relevant technologies. In the age of technology, employees must be carried along, and what better way to do it than to upskill their knowledge and prepare them for the evolving technological era?
- Employees feel an increasing motivation to try and learn new things.
- Upskilling enhances consumer satisfaction by improving the employee experience and enabling them to solve consumer issues better. Their sense of empathy and enthusiasm to meet needs and build better communication comes with passion and professionality.
- Organizations stay competitive by keeping up with industry trends and acquiring new skills to meet the changes in the market. Nothing passes them because they always aim to be way ahead.

That's the idea behind adding more skills to what you have. There is never a case of too much because everything is relevant.

Upskilling vs. Reskilling

There have been several misconceptions about the connections and similarities between "Upskilling" and the concept of "Reskilling."

Although both aim toward career development and improved job performance, their approaches differ.

In upskilling, you're all about acquiring additional skills and enhancing existing skills to keep up with evolving job requirements and industry trends within a particular field. You want to attain a more profound understanding or proficiency in specific areas, so you work at expanding expertise and staying relevant. While reskilling involves acquiring entirely new skills to transition into a different job or field. It typically occurs when individuals need to shift their career paths due to technological advancements, changes in industry demand, or other factors that make their existing skills obsolete and need an upgrade.

For instance, Sarah, a software developer, recognized the changing demands of the industry. She pursued upskilling to deepen her knowledge of emerging technologies like machine learning. Intrigued by blockchain, she reskilled herself and became a proficient blockchain developer. Sarah's combined efforts in upskilling and reskilling allowed her to navigate the evolving technology landscape and build a rewarding career path. She wasn't scared of the extra demands on her to learn and relearn; instead, she was hungry to try another path to her career. Like Karen Salmansohn, a motivational speaker and author, says, "A successful woman builds a firm foundation with the bricks others have thrown at her." (*Karen Salmansohn Quotes (Author of How to Be Happy, Dammit)*, n.d.)

Upskilling Strategies

As an influential female leader, you should encourage individuals, especially women, to embrace challenges and setbacks as opportunities for growth. By continuously building upon their skills and adapting to new circumstances, they can construct a solid foundation for success, regardless of obstacles.

To achieve this, every leader needs an excellent upskilling strategy to provide a long-lasting skill with 110% ROI traction. These can be:

- Identify skills gaps and target specific areas for improvement. Don't be content with the usual. Always aim to bring something new and fresh to change the status quo.

- Provide ongoing training and development opportunities, such as workshops, webinars, and online courses. As often as possible, every trend in the market should be discussed in roundtables to see how this can be learned and incorporated with best practices maintained.
- Implement mentorship programs and job rotations to offer valuable learning experiences. As a leader, make the job interesting for employees by switching things up occasionally to avoid making the job monotonous.
- Conduct assessments and evaluations to determine skill needs. Checkmating employees' work delivery and standards will help assess how everyone's deficiency can be restructured and strengthened.
- Integrate upskilling into daily routines, such as dedicating time during lunch breaks for self-study and fostering knowledge-sharing sessions with colleagues for mutual upskilling and learning.
- Utilize online learning platforms like Coursera, Udemy, LinkedIn Learning, and more to encourage employees to access free growth opportunities. Along the way, they can leverage resources and workshops provided by professional associations and organizations. Some of the courses can be (*Leadership Courses: Online Training to Inspire and Lead*, n.d.):

1. "Leadership and Influence" by Dale Carnegie.
2. "Leading with Emotional Intelligence" by Daniel Goleman.
3. "Strategic Leadership and Management" by Stanford University.
4. "Leadership Communication" by Harvard University.
5. "Leading Teams: Inspiring Excellence" by the University of Michigan.
6. "Executive Leadership Development Program" by Wharton School of Business.
7. "Leading for Success: Emotional Intelligence in Leadership" by Case Western Reserve University.
8. "Leadership in 21st Century Organizations" by Copenhagen Business School.

9. "Leadership and Management" by University of California, Irvine.

They are moves that shape the mind for growth, opportunities that shouldn't be taken lightly if, as a leader, you want to be remembered for fearlessness and authenticity. Take note, though, that as good as this gets, there are still pitfalls every leader must avoid while journeying into a growth mindset through upskilling.

Pitfalls

Understand that this is a digital era, and the approach to learning has taken a new dimension. You can either key into it or stay old-fashioned, a common mistake most leaders make. You must rely on something other than formal education or training programs about theories and principles with loads of reading. Half the time, you will lose your audience to confusion and indifference. You must consider the practical application and balance theoretical knowledge and hands-on experience.

Another pitfall is providing available skills instead of what is necessary. As a leader who fully understands their company, you must know what is relevant and required to make your employees stand out. Irrelevancies will only keep employees behind the competition when new opportunities arise. So, continuously reassess skills because industries evolve rapidly; you must envision what will be valuable.

It is essential to conduct a comprehensive self-assessment of your workforce to avoid a one-size-fits-all approach. Recognize that while some employees have the potential to learn and improve their skills, others thrive when immersed in hands-on tasks. As a collaborative leader, these evaluations are always at your fingertips to understand that different individuals may have unique learning preferences. It is in your place to provide diverse learning opportunities that can cater to these various styles and needs so you can create a variety of learning and a hunger for upskilling. This, in turn, leads to enhanced job retention and high recommendation to any organization.

Strategies to Avoid Pitfalls

Achieving upskilling requires smart strategies applied at the slightest opportunity while avoiding pitfalls. Learning doesn't have to feel demanding or tiresome because there are ways to make it convenient, engaging, and exciting simultaneously.

- **Break-time sessions with experts:** Organize sessions during lunch breaks where outside specialists share their knowledge on specific subjects. Encourage participation and create a supportive environment for continuous learning.
- **Virtual learning and training:** Utilizing technology with online software is a great way to provide employees with the flexibility to train remotely at their convenience. Allocate necessary resources and promote participation to ensure successful implementation.
- **Mentoring by experienced employees:** Tap into the expertise of internal mentors to provide on-the-job training and guidance. Foster a learning culture and recognize achievements to encourage both mentors and mentees.
- **Microlearning sessions:** Offer short, focused training sessions, such as videos followed by exercises and quizzes, that can be completed in minutes. Provide easily accessible materials and track progress to ensure effective learning outcomes.
- **Develop a comprehensive plan:** Identify skills gaps and create a tailored upskilling plan. Allocate resources, provide guidance, and track progress to achieve desired outcomes.
- **Foster a learning culture and encourage participation:** Promote the benefits of upskilling, actively engage employees in opportunities, and create an environment that values continuous learning.
- **Provide support, guidance, and recognition:** Offer necessary support and advice to employees throughout their upskilling journey. Recognize and reward achievements to motivate and reinforce the importance of ongoing development.

Segue

You see it, too, don't you?

Being hungry for growth can take you to places you never thought possible. That's the power of having the right mindset. So, embrace upskilling, and keep striving for more success. It's an endless journey that fuels your development and makes you the kind of leader every employee yearns to work side by side with. As we move forward, let's explore the next chapter, where you will discover what drives you for success.

8

FIND YOUR "WHY" AND LEAD WITH PURPOSE

Hard work is painful when life is devoid of purpose. But when you live for something greater than yourself and the gratification of your ego, hard work becomes a labor of love.
—Steve Pavlina (Nemeth, 2020)

❀

I f you haven't understood that your being in this life is not by accident but intentional, then you don't know how valuable you are. The first rule to living a fulfilled and purposeful life is knowing you were born to make a difference to yourself and the people around you. Once you're thinking this way, you create room to pursue success and see how worthwhile it is to find yourself and use your superpower to inspire others.

In trying to find purpose, individuals always have questions lined up:

- Why am I different?
- Why is it vital for me to learn this or that?
- Why do I need to do this and that?
- Why does it matter to them or me?

These questions are expected and relevant for anyone seeking to grow, succeed and create visionary ideas to inspire and motivate more people. Women always go through this phase at some point in their lives. So many questions about life pop up in their head, and it feels like an enormous weight is on their shoulders because they need answers and fast. A lot depends on how the answers they receive impact their lives and those who look up to them. The famous writer/author Maya Angelou said, "Each time a woman stands up for herself, without knowing it possibly, or even claiming it, she stands up for all women." (Top 25 Quotes By Maya Angelou *TOP 25 (of 1010) | A-Z Quotes*, n.d.)

In working to create relevance for women's place in leadership, especially in the workplace, you are awakening more women to understand their purpose, find themselves, and align their needs to establish the best version of themselves. This brings us back to the question of "why". How does your "why" matter in helping you succeed and enabling your team to become driven? Among many things, the answer can be found in Maslow's Hierarchy of Needs.

Maslow's Hierarchy of Needs

It's a theory that proposes that every individual has a flow of needs to be met before they can acknowledge that they are living their best life. This flow illuminates the path to passion, motivation, and inspiration that every leader should possess to transfer this self-actualization to their employees for maximum satisfaction equally.

It starts with how you arrive at meeting your needs systematically, so you reach your fullest potential and lead a truly fulfilling life.

Maslow's Pyramid of needs is often called a psychological framework for understanding individual needs and their interplay. Once done, you can gain valuable insights into what drives human behavior and what it takes to achieve self-actualization. In leadership, you can hold the four aces since you'll fully grasp what can make your employees tick and commit to job success.

Simply put, Maslow aligns five stages of fulfilling life needs so everyone gets to understand at what stage they are at to get to the apex point of their life. From the basic physiological needs required for survival, such as food, water, and shelter, to the higher-level needs of love and belonging, self-esteem, and self-actualization, the pyramid displays the human journey toward personal growth.

Suppose you're interested in an existence that involves self-improvement. In that case, this is definitely the model to follow, and it's what many great female leaders have followed to arrive at the pinnacle of their careers.

Recall the story of Malala Yousafzai, a courageous advocate for girls' education, who, despite facing adversity in Pakistan, recognized the importance of fulfilling basic physiological needs, such as safety, education (which was greatly frowned upon for women), and healthcare. She prioritized her safety while continuing to speak out, defying the oppressive Taliban regime and striving for a safer future for girls because she believed there was more for girls than living in relegation. With the loving support of her family and a global network she connected to for her fight, Malala found a sense of belonging, empowering her to persist in her mission and motivating more girls to rise up for their rights. While receiving international recognition and awards, Malala remained humble, using her platform to amplify marginalized voices and fight for equality. Her advocacy has stirred many awakenings in the Middle East, Asia, and Africa. Through her unwavering dedication, Malala achieved self-actualization, establishing the Malala Fund, and advocating for girls' education worldwide. Malala's story unveils a perfect example of how a female leader who accomplishes life needs can drive more leaders and women to overcome obstacles, inspire change, and make a lasting impact.

Maslow's Hierarchy of Needs showcases that specific prerequisites, such as freedom of speech and living in a just society, can greatly help the natural progression of life. Learning and understanding the world around us is essential, serving practical and innate purposes. Although needs are presented in a hierarchy, they are not strictly linear, and individuals often have partially met needs. Furthermore, one behavior can satisfy multiple needs simultaneously. Maslow's insights remind us that our journey through the hierarchy is complex and interconnected, shaping our pursuit of fulfillment and self-actualization.

What Are "Needs"?

With the theory comes a definition of the needs in every individual's desired path for an accomplished life. We can divide our needs into two parts: deficiency and growth needs.

Deficiency Needs

Deficiency needs are the lower level that arises when you feel deprived or lacking in something of a necessity. Call them the essentials of survival and well-being that prompt individuals to seek satisfaction. They include the first four levels of the hierarchy:

- **Physiological needs:** These are the basic biological needs for survival, such as food, water, shelter, sleep, and physical well-being—everything you need to feel comfortable and stress-free, so you don't get overwhelming worries.
- **Safety and security needs:** It's all about having a secure and stable environment free from physical or psychological harm. They include personal safety, financial stability, job security, health, and protection from dangers like harassment, assault, or even disasters.
- **Love and belonging needs:** Everyone needs to network and connect. Your ability to gain acceptance and have meaningful relationships will meet the need to be loved, form friendships, achieve intimacy, belong to a community or group, and have positive interpersonal relationships.
- **Esteem needs:** These needs encompass the desire for self-esteem and recognition from others. They involve feelings of self-worth, confidence, achievement, respect from others, and the need for recognition or status. Deficiency needs might be on the lower level, but they motivate individuals to strive to meet up, knowing that the absence creates a sense of dissatisfaction. However, once met, individuals can progress to higher-level needs, known as growth or being needs.

Growth Needs

These are the higher-level needs in Maslow's Pyramid. Unlike deficiency needs, which arise from deprivation, growth needs to emerge from a desire for personal development and realizing one's potential. If you want to stand out and impact, these needs demand a focus on self-actualization and pursuing meaning and purpose in life. You can pinpoint them as:

- **Cognitive needs:** The desire for knowledge, understanding, and intellectual growth. It's a never-ending quest to acquire all aspects of learning and keeps individuals seeking to expand their intelligence, engage in academic pursuits, and explore new ideas and concepts.
- **Aesthetic needs:** Aesthetic needs involve appreciating beauty, art, and creativity. Your aesthetic pleasure is put to work. What is your love for modern art, music, nature, or other forms of creative expression? These are the desires that are sort-after.
- **Self-actualization:** The highest level of the hierarchy represents the need for personal growth, fulfillment, and realizing one's full potential. Transcendence, as some studies call it, is the high point of your life where you're all about growth and authenticity, and your journey toward self-actualization and personal growth becomes uniquely different from others based on how you want self-actualization to reflect in your story.

Expanded Theory of Maslow's Hierarchy of Needs

The great thing about Maslow's Pyramid is its timelessness. Through generations, it remains the most realistic attempt to comprehend human needs. Although, time has shown that with the evolution of human behavior, man has become hungry for more and dissatisfied with the usual. It's why in the 1970s, researchers embarked on a study to see how they could develop an Expanded Theory of Maslow's Hierarchy of Needs.

It's why the five motivational levels, which have always been known as Maslow's Pyramid, conceptualized in 1943, had three more needs added, as seen above. As many questioned the importance of these additions to what has been known and accepted overtime as to affected individuals and leadership goals, the key takeaway in recognizing these evolving needs was:

- The expanded theory recognizes that particular prerequisites, such as freedom of speech and living in a just society, facilitate needs. Once these external factors are met, it creates an enabling environment for individuals.
- The importance of learning and understanding the world around us is emphasized. The knowledge expands to gain insights about our environment and how you can contribute to meeting specific needs and fulfilling an inherent desire.
- Needs go beyond being hierarchical or linear because individuals often have partially met needs at any given time. Also, their progress through the hierarchy may vary as needs can become more complex and dynamic.
- Needs are more interconnected within the hierarchy than ever before. A behavior or action can address multiple needs simultaneously, bringing about a holistic accomplishment through integrated experiences.

Self-Actualization

In all the dialogues on needs discussed over the years, self-actualization is the most paramount used by individuals and leaders, especially to motivate themselves and inspire others with the truth. They can live their best and most purposeful life if they key into what they define as needful.

For instance, in the workplace, when you refer to self-actualized leaders, it's those who have attained a state where their employees know and recognize that they are authentic, they rose through the ladder by accepting their potential, and they let failures become their stepping stones. And now, these leaders are paying it forward by inspiring more people to go on the same journey causing a positive ripple effect throughout the organization. An effect that's empowering enough to recreate employees that go above and beyond to see projects through confidently.

As an individual threading the job market in search of the perfect place to grow and evolve, how can you identify these leaders? What are the characteristics of a self-actualized individual who can lead you to your golden room? The seven important attributes of these leaders are:

1. **Self-awareness:** They understand their strengths, weaknesses, values, and passions. So no one can deceive them into feeling little or having low self-esteem because they've grown above that level.
2. **Defined purpose:** These individuals are purpose-driven. They have a clear focus on what they want, and it guides their actions and decisions. They aren't random but prepared for every step they want to take as they progress.
3. **Continuous learning:** Any chance for growth is always noticed. New knowledge for them is like buying the latest model of a Ferrari. It's fulfilling, so they go for professional development opportunities, attend seminars, workshops, and conferences, and expand their knowledge and skills.
4. **Authenticity:** One thing you can't take away from them is their genuineness, transparency, and staying true to their values. It gives room for those unique personalities and perspectives to shine through.
5. **Meaningful connections:** They are big on interpersonal relationships and connections by engaging in networking, mentorship, and collaboration opportunities.
6. **Taking risks:** They always desire to step outside their comfort zones and seek new responsibilities. In fact, they want to try as many new things as possible, so there is always the willingness to take calculated risks.
7. **Inspire and empower others:** Success for them alone is only possible if they can support the growth and development of team members and provide mentorship, coaching, and recognition. Only then can they proudly say that it was all worth it.

These are the most unignorable characteristics of anyone who truly believes in self-actualization and wants to be authentic in the workplace. But, understand that character goes beyond this.

Benefits of Self-Actualization

Self-actualization benefits everyone because once you arrive at this point in your life, you feel satisfied and joyful about everything, even if things look difficult. You radiate a positive energy that's infectious for the organization or the community you are part of. You awaken this person inside who is all about the greater good and contributing to societal growth. So, somehow, it's a character that goes beyond you to the person next to you, and before you know it, it covers the whole environment.

When it comes to the purpose of the workplace and leadership, self-actualization comes with many benefits:

- **Enhanced job satisfaction:** When individuals align their work with their personal values, passions, and purpose, they experience a deeper level of job satisfaction because everything is coming together. They find meaning and happiness in their roles, which translates into increased enthusiasm, motivation, and engagement in their work.
- **Increased performance:** Self-actualized individuals are driven, fueling their dedication and commitment to achieving their goals. This heightened motivation and focus lead to improved productivity and performance in the workplace. Their records are outstanding, and more times, they can go above and beyond, taking the initiative and delivering high-quality results.
- **Authentic and inspirational leadership:** It brings about an authenticity that inspires others through actions. By leading purposefully and passionately, they create a positive work culture that encourages and empowers their team members to reach their full potential. They become role models and sources of inspiration, fostering a sense of trust, loyalty, and collaboration within the team.
- **Improved problem-solving:** More employees who self-actualize start to possess a strong sense of self-awareness, which enables them to make more informed decisions and solve problems effectively. They deeply understand their own values, strengths, and limitations, allowing them to approach challenges with

clarity and resilience. This leads to better decision-making and
the ability to navigate complex situations confidently.

- **Positive impact:** When leaders prioritize their self-fulfillment
  and inspire others to do the same, it creates a work environment
  that values personal growth, purpose-driven work, and
  authenticity. It also fosters collaboration, trust, and mutual
  support among team members. This, in turn, enhances
  teamwork, communication, and overall team performance.

It shows how self-actualization unlocks true potential and numerous
benefits in the workplace. The joy of positively contributing to a thriving
organizational culture is established. Somehow every individual, from
leader to employee, starts to live each day to its fullest, knowing they are
all making meaningful impacts in different ways and creating fulfilling
professional experiences.

But, to get to that place where you self-actualize means there is a "why"
in the life goal. Why should this path be important to you as a leader,
and why should you find yourself to achieve that purposeful life?

To answer these questions, you must find your core values. The best way
to find these core values is by asking yourself—what makes you exceptional when you put yourself to the test? Is it self-actualization? You will
see that what's important to you isn't the same for someone else.
However, with these steps, you can acquire self-actualization easily:

1. Engage in introspection and self-reflection.
2. Explore what truly makes you happy and gives you a sense of
   purpose.
3. Understand your values, strengths, and aspirations.
4. Uncover your unique purpose and meaning as a leader.
5. Lead in a purpose-driven way.
6. Ignite a sense of fulfillment in your leadership journey.
7. Inspire others through your purpose and actions.

You will align your leadership journey with what truly matters to you,
fostering a sense of self-actualization and purpose.

Importance of Vision

At this point, when you feel rested and invested in your success, it's normal to question if it's wise to share your purpose or vision. Sharing your purpose as a leader can profoundly impact your team. While it's not necessary to explicitly share every detail, expressing your vision and aligning it with the organization's goals can inspire and motivate others. It can even create new visions to evolve the organization for another level of growth. As more people hear and understand the idea behind the vision, they can contribute to coming up with a fresh perspective. This is as much a plus for you as a leader as it is for your employees. Recognize that leaders who communicate their purpose authentically create a sense of purpose within their teams, fostering a collective commitment towards a common goal.

Once you have identified your purpose and have people channeling their energy in the same lane as yours for optimum purpose, the next step is to implement it. Those practical steps for your daily actions with your vision come with you constantly asking yourself, "What can I do today to live my purpose?" It's simple. Take intentional steps towards your goals by creating a meaningful impact and inspiring others to do the same. It's just what we've been saying, and it doesn't change because that's how you empower yourself and others to lead authentically and passionately.

Now don't think this journey is a walk in the park; in aiming toward self-actualization, it's just as important to address and dispel common myths hindering progress. Debunk misunderstandings about purpose, such as the belief that purpose must be grandiose or solely focused on personal success. Understanding and challenging these myths allows you to embrace your unique purpose and lead in a way that aligns with your authentic self.

Once you've arrived at this stage, congratulations! You are all set to inspire others by becoming the mentor they need to set sail toward their goals.

Mentorship

Mentorship is a powerful tool for personal and professional growth. It offers guidance, support, and the opportunity to learn from someone with experience in your desired field. Research has shown that mentoring works, as it helps individuals develop new skills and reach their goals more effectively. If you're interested in becoming a mentor, it's essential to understand your responsibilities. A great mentor sets goals with their mentees, provides constructive feedback that pushes their mentees to the next level, and challenges them to go ahead of set boundaries. Remember, being a mentor isn't about gatekeeping knowledge; it's about empowering others to succeed in the future using your years of experience.

To get started, try various mentoring activities such as icebreaker exercises (a game of conversation and cool down for people to get acquainted relaxingly), skill-sharing, and inspiring your colleagues and team members.

Advancing women in leadership is crucial for fostering gender equality and creating diverse and inclusive workplaces. Recruiting more women is essential if you want to promote women in leadership roles. Seek out qualified female candidates and ensure the hiring process is fair and unbiased. Additionally, as you provide sufficient training and mentorship opportunities to support their professional development and address any challenges they may face, never forget those with growing skills who need that push away from self-doubt to self-awareness; they are just as important and hungry for growth, and should be carried along. Creating a woman-friendly culture is the future of outstanding leadership because it encourages work-life balance, offers flexible arrangements that won't seem overwhelming, and promotes an inclusive environment that values and respects women's contributions.

Finally, consider advocating for policy changes that promote gender equality, such as implementing supportive policies for maternity leave and childcare, and using digital workplaces to facilitate work-life integration.

Segue

By taking these steps, we can inspire and empower women to thrive in leadership positions. Women need this validation to help them come to terms with their chosen career path, the business dreams they want to pursue, or the promotion they hold dear. Once all these come together, it's clear that they've come to their fearless place of branding their legacy. A chapter of their life that will make all the difference.

9

BE FEARLESS AND BRAND YOUR LEGACY

Legacy is not what I did for myself. It's what I'm doing for the next generation.
—Vitor Belfort (Legacy Quotes, n.d.)

〜

W hen the word "legacy" comes up, many people think it's about wealth, empires, and being a mogul with billboards with your name on them so people acknowledge the generational footprints created through one person's ingenious ideas. It's not a lie, but there is so much more. Ruth Bader Ginsburg, a famous American lawyer, jurist, and Supreme Court associate justice, says it's about "Fight for the things that you care about, but do it in a way that will lead others to join you." (*Ruth Bader Ginsburg Tells Young Women: "Fight for the Things You Care About" | Radcliffe Institute for Advanced Study at Harvard University*, n.d.)

It's that urge to make a difference by making others see things from your perspective, and then they're convinced to join you in standing out for the present and future. You might not know it, but slowly, you're building something profound. It's like a woman who gives birth to a child, believe it or not, a child is a legacy of the name they represent. When you impact meaning and purpose into them, they leave an indelible mark that will uphold their family name for decades. It's the same with a female leader who aims to lead fearlessly.

She doesn't want it so she can prove a point that women need to have equal space to lead and grow like every other male; she needs it to lay a foundation for her growth and the future of young girls and women that will be exceptional for the caliber of leadership the world requires today; one of selflessness and success.

Leave a Legacy!

As a female leader, caring about leaving a legacy is essential for several reasons:

- When you leave a legacy, you inspire other women to follow your lead and drive meaningful change in the professional world. Your accomplishments and your impact serve as a source of inspiration, empowering other women to break barriers and achieve their own success. Call yourself the trailblazer who contributes to shifting the narrative and challenging traditional gender roles. That's who you become and what people see when they look at you.
- Leaving a legacy allows you to change the status quo. It demonstrates your capabilities and achievements and how they have defied stereotypes and paved the way for a more inclusive and equal society. In a study from Pew Society, statistics showed that the gender pay gap in the United States had seen minimal improvement over the past two decades, with women typically earning 82% of every dollar earned by men in 2022, similar to the 80% they earned in 2002. This slow progress contrasts sharply with the significant advancement witnessed in the preceding two decades when women earned only 65% of each dollar earned by men in 1982. It proves that now more than ever, the world needs that female influence and presence to create opportunities for future generations of women. It will help to reduce gender pay gaps and provide a platform for diverse voices to be heard. (*Pew Research Center Finds Gender Pay Gap Has Barely Budged in Past 20 Years, 2023*)

- Moreover, as a female leader, you become a role model and mentor to young girls, show them what is possible, and encourage them to dream big. Your actions and accomplishments convey that women can excel in leadership positions and significantly impact their chosen fields, and that's what the younger generation wants to see. They need to believe that everything is possible with more commitment and drive. You build a more equitable and diverse future by nurturing the next generation of female leaders.
- With a legacy-minded drive, workplaces would be less toxic. Who needs a space filled with back-biting and all sorts of sneaky attitudes? It's demoralizing; it's why your leadership style and values can inspire a positive work culture, fostering collaboration, respect, and inclusivity. There is no drag for superiority based on class, color, or sex but an environment centered on supporting all individuals and contributing to the well-being and success of team members.

Best of all, you become a voice for the voiceless, using your platform to speak out against inequality, discrimination, and social issues, addressing these challenges from the standpoint of someone who's been there and now wants to advocate for change and an inclusive society.

In fact, you'll be pushing towards being the iconic woman they've been waiting for to take them to the next level—someone who has been preparing for a moment like this for years.

Be an Iconic Female Leader!

Now, you must be wondering—how do you become an Iconic Female Leader, Marguerite? I have answers for you:

- By using all the weapons in self-empowering books, especially this one—to transform herself from a girl who accepted the usual to a woman who challenges the unusual so there can be harmonious living.
- By self-assessment and improvement aimed at personal growth, and continuously striving to improve your skills, knowledge,

and leadership abilities. Being a leader means investing in self-development programs, seeking mentorship, and embracing lifelong learning.

- By dreaming big and setting ambitious goals that go beyond societal limitations. No one has the right to tell you that, as a woman, this is as far as you can go or that this is the industry for men; there is little space for women here. Believe in your potential to significantly impact and challenge the status quo. Be fearless in pursuing your aspirations and breaking barriers.

- By developing your skills and expertise so you become indispensable in your field. You already know how it's easy to be put in the background once your ideas no longer seem productive, so continuously enhance your knowledge, acquire new competencies, and stay ahead of emerging trends. Be adaptable, resilient, and willing to embrace change. Position yourself as a valuable asset in your organization or industry, one they can hardly decide without consulting.

- By being bold and confident in what you believe in. Be the advocate for equality, inclusivity, positive change, and the woman who champions the underrepresented. You'll find yourself addressing critical issues that impact women in the workplace.

- By supporting and uplifting others who speak up, creating a culture of inclusivity and empowerment. Foster an environment where everyone feels heard and valued as they raise significant concerns and work collaboratively to drive meaningful change.

- By collaborating and connecting with like-minded individuals and women who share your vision and values. There is so much benefit in forming alliances, joining networks, and participating in professional communities to amplify your impact. You'll find engaging in partnerships and collaborations that promote diversity, innovation, and collective progress easy.

- By cultivating a strong social media presence to amplify your message, connecting with a broader audience, and inspiring others is paramount, especially in this age of technology. Use various platforms to share your experiences, insights, and achievements. Leveraging social media for empowerment, mentorship, and networking is the best way to reach a wider audience of like minds and women who need upliftment.

- By setting high accountability standards for yourself, leading by example, and maintaining integrity. Demonstrate professionalism, ethical behavior, and a strong work ethic where you don't joke with figures and auditing, as it sets a pace for higher expectations and closes all gaps. Strive for excellence and ensure that your actions align with your values. Inspire others through your commitment to personal and professional integrity.
- By cultivating self-awareness to recognize biases and promote fairness and equality. Challenge your assumptions, educate yourself about diversity and inclusion, and actively work to eliminate unconscious biases. Create an environment where everyone feels valued and respected, regardless of gender or background.
- By fostering diversity in the workplace by actively seeking out and hiring talent from diverse backgrounds. Stop paying attention to who comes from where and start promoting equal gender ratios in leadership positions and advocate for inclusive policies and practices. As long as there is productivity and forward-thinking minds, every woman must embrace the power of diverse perspectives, experiences, and ideas to drive innovation and success.

Visualize yourself achieving all the above goals—Now, you're no longer that one voice trying to create relevance; you've built a network for yourself. By being the iconic leader, you used all the tentacles available, from self-improvement to expert support to sharing knowledge. You've gone around, and it's time to let your brand stand through all the networks you've created over time. Building a solid personal brand and making your mark in your industry heavily relies on effective networking. It's about leveraging connections to establish your reputation and amplify your value. Like everything else that needs building, there are strategies you have to adapt to make it achievable and sustainable.

Sustainable Iconic Leadership

1. **Envision your networking goals (The VALUED Model):** What are your networking objectives? You must be clear about this, and then you can visualize the desired outcomes. Understand your value and how networking can enhance it into becoming more than just a brand but a demand.

2. **Be accepting of various leadership networks:** Explore a range of formal and informal leadership networks that go well with your professional aspirations. These networks offer valuable learning opportunities, mentorship, and potential collaborations. There can be many schools of thought in leadership, so when you find what fits with yours, learn how they made it work and use it.

3. **Ignore networking myths:** Make sure to avoid getting swayed by common misconceptions. They won't only discourage you but leave you, always making excuses. Imagine a myth that says networking is only for extroverts! How can that be possible? Recognize that networking is a skill anyone can develop, regardless of personality type. You can go all the way once you know and hold on to this.

4. **Comprehend the networking structure:** Take the time to grasp the networking structure and how relationships are built and nurtured. Cultivate diverse connections, including peers, mentors, and sponsors, across various industries and backgrounds so you can apply a more grounded networking mode. According to the Harvard Review Issue of 2022, achieving a holistic networking approach is about addressing the operational, personal, and strategic angle of leadership structure; otherwise, there will be an imbalance in service delivery. As you pay attention to the organization's affairs (operational), carry yourself along in development (personal), and ensure you're up-to-date on the latest and the most remarkable innovations. (Arscott, 2022)

5. **Network in terms of resources:** Go beyond simply connecting with people and consider networking in terms of valuable resources. Identify what you need to succeed and seek out

individuals who can provide knowledge, expertise, opportunities, or support. This requires your intuitive behavior in singling out quality over quantity. Remember, you're out to be a leader seeking to network productively, so no stone can be left unturned to retrieve the best results.

6. **Share your resources:** It's all about give and take. Be generous in sharing your resources, insights, and experiences by sustaining a collaborative mindset. Contribute to the success of your network by offering assistance and support.

7. **Stay authentic:** It's crucial to adapt your communication style to the situation but remain true to yourself. No need to throw away what you represent because you feel the circumstances outweigh your principles. No need to swing off course; only practice active listening, display genuine interest in others, and foster relationships based on trust and respect. As you give, also be humble to receive when given because it shows ethical behavior.

8. **Utilize power thoughtfully:** If you have influence or power within your network, exercise it thoughtfully and responsibly. Don't get drunk with authority; instead, focus on your impact on others and use your position to empower and uplift those around you rather than solely for personal gain or a show-off.

9. **Communicate effectively:** Enhance your communication skills to convey your ideas clearly, actively listen to others, and tailor your message to resonate with different individuals. Choose your words wisely, so it doesn't pass the wrong intentions, and be mindful of how your communication can impact relationships.

10. **Negotiate with skill:** Whether discussing opportunities, collaborations, or career advancements. Hone your negotiation skills, advocate for yourself, assert your value, and maintain a collaborative and respectful approach so others' ideas are shown to be just as relevant and impactful as yours. Never give room for bickering because your employees see in you the leader who believes in equity.

11. **Build, maintain, leverage, and transition relationships:** Networking is an ongoing investment in building relationships,

nurturing them through regular communication and support, leveraging them to achieve your goals, and being adaptable in transitioning them.

By implementing these strategies, you can develop an authentic and empowering networking approach that will help you cultivate a solid professional network, establish your brand, and unlock new opportunities and collaborations for yourself!

Cultivate a Network!

Below are the top five perfect places for you to cultivate networks:

1. **Professional Associations and Industry Events:** For instance, a female leader in the tech industry could attend conferences like the Grace Hopper Celebration, an event dedicated to women in computing. By participating in industry-specific gatherings, she can connect with fellow professionals, attend informative sessions, and build relationships with individuals who share her interests and goals.
2. **Women's Leadership Organizations:** Joining organizations such as the National Association of Women Business Owners (NAWBO) or Women in Technology International (WITI). They provide access to networking events explicitly tailored to empower women in leadership. These events often feature keynote speakers, panel discussions, and workshops on professional development and networking opportunities.
3. **Online Networking Platforms:** LinkedIn, World Pulse, Hub Dot, and Ellevate Network offer virtual spaces for professional women to connect and engage with each other. For instance, a potential female leader can join industry-specific LinkedIn groups, participate in discussions, and connect with professionals with common career interests. These online platforms enable networking opportunities regardless of geographical constraints.
4. **Business Incubators and Accelerators:** Women entrepreneurs can leverage programs like Women's Startup Lab or Female

Founders Alliance. These organizations provide access to mentorship and resources and facilitate networking events where aspiring female leaders can connect with successful entrepreneurs, investors, and industry experts who can provide guidance and support.

5. **Diversity and Inclusion Initiatives:** Women can participate in events like the Women in Leadership Summit or The Women's Chapter to network with professionals from diverse backgrounds and industries. These initiatives strengthen connections among women leaders, encourage collaboration, and create spaces for sharing experiences and best practices in promoting diversity and inclusion.

By actively engaging in these networking opportunities, potential female leaders can broaden their professional networks, gain exposure to new ideas, find mentors and sponsors, and increase their visibility within their industry. You can embark on a remarkable journey to leave a lasting impact on the workplace and society.

Segue

By actively networking and building meaningful connections in professional associations, you can position yourself to imprint memories and reshape perceptions of women in leadership roles. Your success will become an inspiration, empowering other women to pursue their own paths to greatness. As you gather your skills, embrace continuous learning, and fearlessly put your plans into action, you become a catalyst for change, leaving imprints deep enough to transform history. Now is the time to step forward and create a legacy that will be remembered for generations.

CONCLUSION

～

As we reach the conclusion of this book, it is clear that fearlessness and confidence are driven by tapping into our authentic selves and embracing our strengths and weaknesses. As a female leader, you will learn that pretending to be someone else is futile, as true success and growth come from aligning our actions with our genuine selves. The notion of "faking it until making it" has been debunked, for it hinders our personal and professional development.

Leave all the worries about gender inequality and doubts that may hinder your path to becoming an iconic and fearless female leader. Believe in yourself, for you have the power to achieve greatness. Hold firmly and strongly to the valuable lessons you have learned throughout this journey and embody your leadership with authenticity, inspiration, and lasting impact. Trust in your abilities and forge ahead with unwavering confidence. Yes, you can, and you will make a difference. The doubt must fade away as you step into your true leadership potential.

In this journey, you have discovered **Nine Unforgettable Strategies** to stay ahead in becoming a fearless female leader:

1. The importance of maintaining authenticity while acquiring soft and hard skills to excel as leaders.

2. You've witnessed the power of finding your voice and ears and mastering effective communication to establish mutual respect, understanding, and collaboration with your colleagues.

3. Risk-taking and learning from failure are two things you can identify as instrumental to any fearless leadership journey, debunking the misconception that female executives take fewer risks.

4. There has been inspiration from the teamwork displayed in the construction of the pyramids, recognizing the value of collaboration and mutual respect and inspiring others to work together towards a shared goal.

5. As leaders, we have explored various leadership styles and recognized the importance of knowing your style, remaining consistent, and inspiring others through your fearless leadership.

6. Your mindset plays a crucial role in shaping your perception of success, as it constantly evolves along with your goals.

7. Adopting a growth mindset ensures you stay on track with an ever-expanding vision for your leadership journey.

8. Moreover, you now understand the significance of finding meaning in your work and valuing what you do for yourself and those around you, inspiring them to strive for excellence.

9. Finally, you explored the concept of workplace legacies, understanding that true success lies in achieving your personal goals and leaving a positive and lasting impact on the business world. Engraving a legacy requires humility, grace, and a genuine desire to inspire others, ensuring that your contributions transcend individual achievements.

When you think about successful fearless female leaders, think about Sheryl Sandberg, Facebook's Chief Operating Officer (COO). She has consistently practiced authenticity, empowering others, effective communication, taking risks, and leaving a lasting legacy. Sandberg is known for her influential book *Lean In*, where she encourages women to pursue their ambitions, challenge gender biases, and lean into leadership roles. Through her own journey, she has inspired countless women to embrace their strengths, overcome challenges, and make a lasting impact in their respective fields. Sandberg's unwavering determination, strategic mindset, and commitment to empowering women have positioned her as an iconic figure in the business world and a role model for aspiring female leaders.

You could also say the same for Mary Barra, the CEO of General Motors (GM). Barra made history as the first woman to lead a major global automaker. Under her leadership, GM underwent a significant transformation, focusing on innovation, electric and autonomous vehicles, and sustainability. Barra's inclusive leadership style and commitment to creating a diverse and inclusive workplace have driven positive change within the company. She has strongly advocated empowering women in the automotive industry and has implemented initiatives to promote gender equality and career advancement. Barra's resilience, strategic acumen, and ability to navigate challenges have positioned GM as a leader in the rapidly evolving automotive landscape. Her success story inspires women aspiring to break barriers and excel in traditionally male-dominated industries.

∾

Like these women, I, too, have a story to tell. I spent the last 20 years of my career trying to hone in on my unique leadership style, and while I am still learning and growing, I am proud to say that I have helped dozens of females during my tenure. Many have advanced into leadership positions or even started their own businesses. If I can be a fearless leader, you can too!

Hear this now as you've never heard it before.

As a woman of incredible strength and potential, you harbor the power to shape your destiny and the course of this world. With every turn of the page in this tome of leadership, remember your influence; your reviews on Amazon can inspire countless others to take their leadership aspirations to heart.

Should you believe I have missed anything or have personal insights to share, please feel free to contribute your feedback. I am, like everyone, a constant work in progress, forever learning and evolving. I may not possess all the answers, but together, we can ignite a significant shift in empowering women of this generation.

May your journey be filled with joy, success, and all the rich experiences your resilient heart seeks and merits. With this newfound wisdom, embrace your leadership role, knowing you are paving the way for future women leaders.

$\sim$

REFERENCES

≈

AllBusiness. (2021, August 24). 3 Ways To Be More Authentic (And Successful) In Your Business. *Forbes.* https://www.forbes.com/sites/allbusiness/2021/08/24/3-ways-to-be-more-authentic-and-successful-in-your-business/?sh=24c4db7f5e67

Amplifying Women's Voices for Change. (n.d.). World Pulse. https://www.worldpulse.org/?gclid= CjwKCAjwl6OiBhA2EiwAuUwWZWTGQ3LnED8iecmViuMtixgGJXoL8utmIcBNYOa TGGejGmWoolo2DRoCtgEQAvD_BwE

Arscott, C. H. (2022, November 4). *A Better Approach to Networking.* Harvard Business Review. https://hbr.org/2022/11/a-better-approach-to-networking

A quote from The Open Door. (n.d.). https://www.goodreads.com/quotes/9605-life-is-either-a-daring-adventure-or-nothing-at-all

Authenticity Quotes (1309 quotes). (n.d.). https://www.goodreads.com/quotes/tag/authenticity#:~:text=%E2%80%9CWe%20have%20to%20dare%20to%20be%20our selves%2C%20however%20frightening%20or%20strange%20that%20self%20may%20prove%20to%20be.%E2%80%9D%0A%E2%80%95%20May%20Sarton

Authenticity at Work: Everything You Need to Know. (n.d.). https://www.betterup.com/blog/authenticityatwork#:~:text=How%20to%20be,help%20you%20understand

Authentic Leadership: What It Is & Why It's Important | HBS Online. (2019, December 10). Business Insights Blog. https://online.hbs.edu/blog/post/authentic-leadership

Author. (2022, November 2). *The Maslow's Hierarchy of Needs for Employee Motivation.* Author, T., & Author, T. (2023). 5 Tips to Apply Maslow's Hierarchy of Needs in the Workplace. *Techfunnel.* https://www.techfunnel.com/hr-tech/maslows-hierarchy-workplace/

AttendanceBot Blog. https://www.attendancebot.com/blog/maslows-hierarchy-of-needs/#How_to_Apply_Maslows_Hierarchy_of_Needs_in_the_Workplace

Behind every woman is a Circle of women. Make it official. (n.d.). Lean In. https://leanin.org/circles?gclid=CjwKCAjwl6OiBhA2EiwAuUwWZS2ZWvHHTI7IgvA6jC_QUKKgus LCDhTkOgvlp-Eu87L7FWi4KxsAehoCx-oQAvD_BwE

Bell, J. (2018, August 14). Listening Is An Underrated Leadership Tool. *Forbes.* https://www.-
forbes.com/sites/forbesdallascouncil/2018/08/14/listening-is-an-underrated-leader-
ship-tool/?sh=4cb94b042fe5

Bhoumick, P. (2018). It's Really Matter: Review of the book, Emotional Intelligence: Why it
can matter more than IQ' by Daniel Goleman. *Research Journal of Humanities and Social
Sciences.* https://doi.org/10.5958/2321-5828.2018.00107.9

Biography: Indra Nooyi. (n.d.). National Women's History Museum. https://www.women-
shistory.org/education-resources/biographies/indra-nooyi

Bishop, K. (2022, June 7). Why women have to sprint into leadership positions. *BBC
Worklife.* https://www.bbc.com/worklife/article/20220603-why-women-have-to-sprint-
into-leadership-positions

Blakely-Gray, R. (2021). Authenticity in Business: 7 Strategies to Become the Real McCoy.
Patriot Software for Small Business https://smallbusiness.patriotsoftware.com/authentic-
ity-in-business/#:~:text=On%20a%20scale,you%20get%20it%3F

Brim, B. B. J., EdD. (2023, March 30). How a Focus on People's Strengths Increases Their
Work Engagement. *Gallup.com.* https://www.gallup.com/workplace/242096/focus-
people-strengths-increases-work-engagement.aspx

Boss, J. (2014, June 12). 6 Principles Of A Leadership Legacy. *Forbes.* https://www.forbes.
com/sites/jeffboss/2014/06/12/6-principles-of-a-leadership-legacy/?sh=5f0bc2044a51

Brush, K. (2020). upskilling. *WhatIs.com.* https://www.techtarget.com/whatis/definition/
upskilling?Offer=abt_pubpro_AI-Insider

Boskamp, E. (2023). 35+ Compelling Workplace Collaboration Statistics [2023]: The
Importance Of Teamwork. *Zippia.* https://www.zippia.com/advice/workplace-collabora
tion-statistics/

Change, I. (2020). What Is Growth Mindset and How to Achieve It. *Intelligent Change.*
https://www.intelligentchange.com/blogs/read/what-is-growth-mindset-and-how-to-
achieve-it

Cohn, A. (2021, October 11). *Don't Let Self-Doubt Hold You Back.* Harvard Business Review.
https://hbr.org/2021/02/dont-let-self-doubt-hold-you-back

Conley, M. (2022, March 28). 45 Quotes That Celebrate Teamwork, Hard Work, and
Collaboration.   https://blog.hubspot.com/marketing/teamwork-quotes#:~:text=
Quotes%20About%20Collaboration-,%22Alone%20we%20can%20do%20so%20lit
tle%3B%20together%20we%20can%20do%20so%20much.%22%20%E2%80%93%
20Helen%20Keller,-%22Talent%20wins%20games

Denker, R. (2017, October 31). *5 Ways To Vastly Improve Your Strategic Visioning and Leadership.* https://www.rdpusa.com/5-ways-vastly-improve-strategic-visioning-leadership/

Dweck, C. (2023, April 6). *What Having a "Growth Mindset" Actually Means.* Harvard Business Review. https://hbr.org/2016/01/what-having-a-growth-mindset-actually-means

Elder, A. H. A. S. (2017, July 14). Why You Should Become a Published Writer as a Solopreneur. *Entrepreneur.* https://www.entrepreneur.com/article/295734

Elliott, E. (2021, December 23). 10 Ways to Be an Authentic Entrepreneur and Sell Your Best Self. *Entrepreneur.* https://www.entrepreneur.com/leadership/10-ways-to-be-an-authentic-entrepreneur-and-sell-your-best/403625#:~:text=In%20short%2C%20cus tomers,a%20lot%20earlier.%22

Emotional Intelligence in Leadership: Why It's Important. (2019, April 3). Business Insights Blog. https://online.hbs.edu/blog/post/emotional-intelligence-in-leadership

Fallon, N. (2023). 35 Inspiring Leadership Quotes. *Business News Daily.* https://www.businessnewsdaily.com/7481-leadership-quotes.html

Fateh, A., Mustamil, N., & Shahzad, F. (2021). Role of authentic leadership and personal mastery in predicting employee creative behavior: A self-determination perspective. *Frontiers of Business Research in China, 15*(1), 1-16. https://doi.org/10.1186/s11782-021-00100-1

Find your leadership purpose and write a leadership purpose statement. (n.d.). Truist Leadership Institute. https://www.truistleadershipinstitute.com/publications-research/media-publications/find-your-leadership-purpose-and-write-a-leadership-purpose-statement

FutureLearn. (2023, April 14). *How to improve leadership skills: 7 top tips – FutureLearn.* https://www.futurelearn.com/info/blog/how-to-improve-leadership-skills#1_Identify_your_strengths_and_weaknesses

Future Talent Learning. (n.d.). *What are the top 5 characteristics of emotional intelligence in good leadership?* https://www.futuretalentlearning.com/en/future-talent-learning-blog/what-are-the-top-5-characteristics-of-emotional-intelligence-in-good-leadership

Georgeac, O. a. M. (2021). Are Leaders Rewarded for Taking Risks? *Yale Insights.* https://insights.som.yale.edu/insights/are-leaders-rewarded-for-taking-risks

Goleman, D., Boyatzis, R. E., & McKee, A. (2013). *Primal Leadership: Unleashing the Power of Emotional Intelligence.* Harvard Business Press.

Goleman, D. (2023, April 4). *What Makes a Leader?* Harvard Business Review. https://hbr.org/2004/01/what-makes-a-leader

Goodman, N. (2013, March 14). Train Your Brain to Overcome Fear. *Entrepreneur*. https://www.entrepreneur.com/starting-a-business/train-your-brain-to-overcome-fear/226050

Green, H. (2023, March 29). *Active Listening As A Leadership Skill | Vistage*. Vistage Research Center. https://www.vistage.com/research-center/business-leadership/20180912-active-listening-leadership-skill/

Greenwood, S. (2023, March 1). *The gender wage gap endures in the U.S. | Pew Research Center*. Pew Research Center's Social & Demographic Trends Project. https://www.pewresearch.org/social-trends/2023/03/01/the-enduring-grip-of-the-gender-pay-gap/

Hannah. (2020, February 25). *Top 10 Quotes for Growth Mindset | SATs Companion*. SATs Companion. https://satscompanion.com/top-10-quotes-growth-mindset/

Harper, T. (2021, March 2). Blogging Tips & Events for Content Creators Everywhere | Blogher. *Blogging Tips &Amp; Events for Content Creators Everywhere | Blogher*. https://www.blogher.com/feature/leadership-skills-of-successful-women-687/

Hickey, K. F. (2016, November 23). *5 lessons from Skillshare: on empowering team members to do their best work*. Wavelength by Asana. https://wavelength.asana.com/workstyle-skillshare/

Herrity, J. (2022). Maslow's Hierarchy of Needs: Applying It in the Workplace. *Indeed.com*. https://www.indeed.com/career-advice/career-development/maslows-hierarchy-of-needs

Home - Grace Hopper Celebration. (2023, July 3). Grace Hopper Celebration. https://ghc.anitab.org/

Hopper, E. (2020). Maslow's Hierarchy of Needs Explained. *ThoughtCo*. https://www.thoughtco.com/maslows-hierarchy-of-needs-4582571

Houseofself. (2021). 5 Ways to Reframe Your Fear of Failure. *House of Self*. https://houseofself.co.uk/5-ways-to-reframe-your-fear-of-failure/

Ibarra, H. (2019, August 22). *Women and the Vision Thing*. Harvard Business Review. https://hbr.org/2009/01/women-and-the-vision-thing

Ibarra, H. (2019, February 7). *How Leaders Create and Use Networks*. Harvard Business Review. https://hbr.org/2007/01/how-leaders-create-and-use-networks

Indeed Editorial Team. (2023). How To Find Purpose in Your Work (Benefits, Steps and Tips). *Indeed.com*. https://www.indeed.com/career-advice/career-development/purpose-in-work

Indeed Editorial Team. (2023). How To Leverage Your Strengths in the Workplace. *Indeed.com*. https://www.indeed.com/career-advice/career-development/leveraging-strengths

Indeed Editorial Team. (2023). 10 Benefits of Effective Communication in the Workplace. *Indeed.com*. https://www.indeed.com/career-advice/career-development/communication-benefits

Indeed Editorial Team. (2022). What Is Innovative Leadership? *Indeed.com*. https://www.indeed.com/career-advice/career-development/innovative-leadership

Indeed Editorial Team. (2022). 56 Inspiring Team Communication Quotes To Motivate Your Team. *Indeed.com*. https://www.indeed.com/career-advice/career-development/team-communication-quotes

James, G. (2021, January 5). Science Says: Women in Business Outperform Men. *Inc.com*: https://www.inc.com/geoffrey-james/science-says-woman-in-business-outperform-men.html

Journeytoleadershipblog. (2019). The Importance Of Risk Taking In Leadership. *Journey to Leadership*. https://journeytoleadershipblog.com/2019/04/01/risk-taking-in-leadership/

Karen Salmansohn Quotes (Author of How to Be Happy, Dammit). (n.d.). https://www.goodreads.com/author/quotes/117096.Karen_Salmansohn

Larson, K. (2023, March 8). 31 Big Questions About Business Coaching & Executive Coaching Answered. *Champion PSI*. https://www.championpsi.com/blog/31-big-questions-about-business-coaching-executive-coaching-answered/

Leadership Courses: Online Training to Inspire and Lead. (n.d.). Udemy. https://www.udemy.com/courses/personal-development/leadership/?search-query=leadership&utm_source=adwords&utm_medium=udemyads&utm_campaign=DSA_Catchall_la.EN_cc.ROW&utm_content=deal4584&utm_term=_._ag_88010211481_._ad_535397282064_._kw__._de_c_._dm__._pl__._ti_dsa-391663266418_._li_9053242_._pd__._&matchtype=&gclid=CjwKCAjw9J2iBhBPEiwAErwpecu9x3qyuhLjWK9TvXOS8IleMtouQQbPsCofoqicZKOUA503DJXqNh0C500QAvD_BwE

Legacy Quotes. (n.d.). BrainyQuote. https://www.brainyquote.com/topics/legacy-quotes

Leverage Your Leadership Skills To Improve Your Impact | How To Be A Leader | Leadership And Management | Leadership Skills | Leadership Development | International Institute of Directors and Managers | IIDM - IIDM Global. (n.d.). https://www.iidmglobal.com/ expert_talk/expert-talk-categories/leadership/leadership_skill/id38810.html

Llego, M. A. (2022). The Benefits of Achieving Self-Actualization. *TeacherPH.* https://www. teacherph.com/achieving-self-actualization/

Kitchens, J. (2022, September 6). How to Be an Adaptable Leader and Use Change to Your Advantage. *Entrepreneur.* https://www.entrepreneur.com/leadership/how-to-be-an-adaptable-leader-and-use-change-to-your/428557

LinkedIn. (n.d.). https://www.linkedin.com/pulse/do-you-have-fixed-growth-mindset-linda-scott/

LinkedIn. (n.d.). https://www.linkedin.com/pulse/impact-company-culture-employee-retention-business-umbrella/

LinkedIn. (n.d.). https://www.linkedin.com/pulse/maslows-hierarchy-needs-benefits-self-actualized-employees-scott-king/

LinkedIn. (n.d.). https://www.linkedin.com/pulse/5-reasons-why-people-avoid-taking-risks-munyaradzi-demadema/

LinkedIn. (n.d.). https://www.linkedin.com/pulse/3-proven-ways-more-persistent-leadership-john-eades/

Lonczak, H. S., PhD. (2023). 40 Emotional Intelligence Quotes & Do They Ring True? *PositivePsychology.com.* https://positivepsychology.com/emotional-intelligence-quotes/

Maldonado, Y. (2022, June 6). Over 30% of Americans Suffer From Impostor Syndrome, Study Finds. *NBC10 Philadelphia.* https://www.nbcphiladelphia.com/news/local/over-30-of-americans-suffer-from-impostor-syndrome-study-finds/3259530/

Mark Zuckerberg Quotes. (n.d.). BrainyQuote. https://www.brainyquote.com/quotes/ mark_zuckerberg_453450

McCarthy, D. (2022, December 1). *12 Ways to Become a More Confident Leader – Pragmatic Institute Resources.* Pragmatic Institute Resources. https://www.pragmaticinstitute.com/ resources/articles/product/12-ways-to-develop-leadership-confidence/

Mcleod, S., PhD. (2023). Maslow's Hierarchy of Needs. *Simply Psychology.* https://www. simplypsychology.org/maslow.html

Mentoring activities: 17 examples to try in your next meeting | Together Mentoring Software. (n.d.). https://www.togetherplatform.com/blog/mentoring-activities-to-try

MindTools | Home. (n.d.). https://www.mindtools.com/aal02x7/essential-negotiation-skills

Morgan, J. (2021, December 16). Why Great Leaders Are Risk-Takers - Jacob Morgan - Medium. *Medium.* https://medium.com/jacob-morgan/why-great-leaders-are-risk-takers-22e031313391

Morgan, O. (2021). How to Define Your Purpose as a Leader — Morgan Latif. *Morgan Latif.* https://morganlatif.com/resources/how-to-define-your-purpose-as-a-leader

Morin, A. (2023). Growth Mindset: How to Develop Growth Mindset. *Understood.* https://www.understood.org/en/articles/growth-mindset

MSEd, K. C. (2022). Maslow's Hierarchy of Needs. *Verywell Mind.* https://www.verywellmind.com/what-is-maslows-hierarchy-of-needs-4136760

Nemeth, A. (2020, April 16). 20 Quotes to Inspire You to Find More Purpose in Your Work. *MovingWorlds Blog.* https://blog.movingworlds.org/purpose-at-work-quotes/

Ntsoane, M. (2023, July 15). Helpful tips to discover your PURPOSE as a leader - Esme Witbooi Coaching. *Esme Witbooi Coaching.* https://www.esmelifecoaching.com/helpful-tips-to-discover-your-purpose-as-leader/

Patel, N. (2020). Truth Will Out – Why Authenticity is the Key to Growing Your Business. *Neil Patel.* https://neilpatel.com/blog/truth-will-out/

Patterson, A. R. (2023, July 6). *Richard Patterson.* NetLdn. https://netldn.uk/author/richardpattersonnz/

Pew Research Center Finds Gender Pay Gap Has Barely Budged in Past 20 Years. (2023). *Lexology.* https://www.lexology.com/library/detail.aspx?g=8ad4ecf7-7bff-4ffe-afcf-3cf1f05482d8

Pierce, M. (2022, July 28). *How to Leverage Your Leadership Style for Business Success - Addicted 2 Success.* Addicted 2 Success. https://addicted2success.com/success-advice/how-to-leverage-your-leadership-style-for-business-success/

Risks Quotes. (n.d.). BrainyQuote. https://www.brainyquote.com/topics/risks-quotes

Robbins, M., & Robbins, M. (2022). The Trap of Comparison with Others. *Mike Robbins | Infusing Life and Business With Authenticity and Appreciation.* https://mike-robbins.com/the-trap-of-comparison/

Ruderman, M. (2022). How to Increase Your Resilience as a Leader. *CCL*. https://www.ccl. org/articles/leading-effectively-articles/4-tips-will-increase-resiliency-leader/

Runyon, M. (n.d.). *How active listening can make you a better leader*. The Enterprisers Project. https://enterprisersproject.com/article/2021/11/how-active-listening-can-make-you-better-leader

Ruth Bader Ginsburg Tells Young Women: "Fight For The Things You Care About" | Radcliffe Institute for Advanced Study at Harvard University. (n.d.). Radcliffe Institute for Advanced Study at Harvard University. https://www.radcliffe.harvard.edu/news-and-ideas/ruth-bader-ginsburg-tells-young-women-fight-for-the-things-you-care-about

Schinkel, M. (2023, July 20). 9 Tips for Leading with Integrity - ACHIEVE Centre for Leadership. *ACHIEVE Centre for Leadership*. https://achievecentre.com/blog/9-tips-for-leading-with-integrity/

Scott, L. (n.d.). Do you have a fixed or a growth mindset? *www.linkedin.com*. https://www.linkedin.com/pulse/do-you-have-fixed-growth-mindset-linda-scott/?trk=articles_directory

Sharon. (2023). Great Leaders Take Risks. *SIGMA Assessment Systems*. https://www. sigmaassessmentsystems.com/great-leaders-risk-taking/

Simkins, M. D. (2021, January 5). How Successful Leaders Overcome Self-Doubt. *Inc.com*. https://www.inc.com/melissa-dawn-simkins/4-ways-to-crush-self-doubt-when-your-inner-critic-gets-best-of-you.html

Slack. (n.d.). *Collaborative leadership: an inclusive way to manage virtual teams*. Slack. https://slack.com/blog/collaboration/collaborative-leadership-top-down-team-centric

Staff, L. E. (2023). The Top 6 Rules of Leadership Networking. *CCL*. https://www.ccl.org/articles/leading-effectively-articles/top-6-rules-leadership-networking/

Staff, L. E. (2023). 15 Tips for Effective Communication in Leadership. *CCL*. https://www. ccl.org/articles/leading-effectively-articles/communication-1-idea-3-facts-5-tips/

Staff, L. E. (2022). 8 Steps to More Resilient Leadership. *CCL*. https://www.ccl.org/articles/leading-effectively-articles/8-steps-help-become-resilient/

Strategic thinking skills | Robert Half. (2021, September 6). https://www.roberthalf.co.nz/career-advice/career-development/strategic-thinking-skills

Susancfoster. (2020). 7 Leadership Skills of Successful Women. *LH AGENDA*. https://lhagenda.com/career/7-leadership-skills-of-successful-women/

Tech, F. (2020). null. *Florida Tech Online.* https://www.floridatechonline.com/blog/business/problem-solving-a-critical-leadership-skill/

Technavio. (2020, May 11). Global Corporate Leadership Training Market 2020-2024 | Increased Spending on Corporate Leadership Training to Boost Market Growth | Technavio. *Business Wire.* https://www.businesswire.com/news/home/20200311005401/en/Global-Corporate-Leadership-Training-Market-2020-2024-Increased-Spending-on-Corporate-Leadership-Training-to-Boost-Market-Growth-Technavio

Thakrar, M. (2020, January 16). How To Become An Adaptable Leader. *Forbes.* https://www.forbes.com/sites/forbescoachescouncil/2020/01/16/how-to-become-an-adaptable-leader/?sh=74f3c11c14b6

Tina. (2023). Leadership Statistics: Demographics and Development in 2023. *TeamStage.* https://teamstage.io/leadership-statistics/

Tonya.Johnson. (2023). 12 tips for overcoming imposter syndrome in leadership. *Fast Company.* https://www.fastcompany.com/90862289/12-tips-for-overcoming-imposter-syndrome-in-leadership

Top 10 Skills for Aspiring Female Leaders | The International Educator (TIE Online). (n.d.). https://www.tieonline.com/article/3247/top-10-skills-for-aspiring-female-leaders

Top 25 Quotes by Maya Angelou (of 1010) | A-Z Quotes. (n.d.). A-Z Quotes. https://www.azquotes.com/author/440-Maya_Angelou

Trust in the Workplace: 10 Steps to Build Trust with Employees. (n.d.). https://www.yourthoughtpartner.com/blog/bid/59619/leaders-follow-these-6-steps-to-build-trust-with-employees-improve-how-you-re-perceived

Uță, I. (2023, June 16). 12 Leadership Styles for Successful Leaders (complete list) with Pros & Cons - BRAND MINDS. *BRAND MINDS.* https://brandminds.com/12-leadership-styles-for-successful-leaders-complete-list-with-pros-cons

Valamis. (2023, April 19). Leadership Communication. *Valamis.* https://www.valamis.com/hub/leadership-communication

Valamis. (2023, March 20). Emotional Intelligence in the Workplace. *Valamis.* https://www.valamis.com/hub/emotional-intelligence-in-the-workplace

Wallbridge, A., & Wallbridge, A. (2023). The Importance Of Self-Awareness In Emotional Intelligence. *TSW Training.* https://www.tsw.co.uk/blog/leadership-and-management/self-awareness-in-emotional-intelligence/#:~:text=Self%2Dawareness%20is%20the%20ability,of%20other%20%E2%80%9Csoft%20skills%E2%80%9D

Weller, C., Hickey, W., Kiersz, A., & Su, J. L. (2021, May 29). Most Americans are burned out from the pandemic. These charts reveal the biggest stressors we're facing right now. *Business Insider*. https://www.businessinsider.com/american-burnout-survey-results-age-race-job-region-covid-2021-5#:~:text=There%27s%20a%20stark%20gender%20gap%20in%20self-reported%20burnout.,out%2C%20compared%20to%20only%2055%25%20of%20male%20respondents.

What Authentic Leadership Is and Why Showing Up As Yourself Matters. (n.d.). https://www.betterup.com/blog/authentic-leadership

Why Authenticity in DEI Practices in the Workplace Leads to Good Business. (n.d.). https://partnerstack.com/articles/dei-practices-authenticity-workplace-matters

Why diversity matters. (2015, January 1). McKinsey & Company. https://www.mckinsey.com/capabilities/people-and-organizational-performance/our-insights/why-diversity-matters

Why consistency is important in leadership. (n.d.). https://www.morningcoach.com/blog/why-consistency-is-important-in-leadership

Women in Leadership - How to Promote? (n.d.). Tutorialspoint. https://www.tutorialspoint.com/women_in_leadership/women_in_leadership_how_to_promote.htm

WomensMedia. (2021, February 1). Leadership When You Have Imposter Syndrome. *Forbes*. https://www.forbes.com/sites/womensmedia/2021/02/01/leadership-when-you-have-imposter-syndrome/?sh=5c7076387195

Zenger, J. (2021, March 24). The Extremely Curious Case Of Women's Strategic Thinking. *Forbes*: https://www.forbes.com/sites/jackzenger/2021/03/24/the-extremely-curious-case-of-womens-strategic-thinking/?sh=53dea236c1c6

Ziegler, P. (2022, December 22). How To Become An Inspirational Female Leader In 2023? *Best Diplomats | Diplomatic Conferences | New York*. https://bestdiplomats.org/how-to-become-inspirational-female-leaders/

4 Ways to Conquer Your Fears and Take Smarter Risks | BusinessCollective. (2013, November 14). BusinessCollective. https://businesscollective.com/4-ways-to-conquer-your-fears-and-take-smarter-risks/index.html

5 Benefits of Effective Leadership Communication. (n.d.). SMU Academy. https://academy.smu.edu.sg/insights/5-benefits-effective-leadership-communication-7826

7 steps to leaving a lasting legacy | Tony Robbins. (2023, June 2). tonyrobbins.com. https://www.tonyrobbins.com/business/how-to-leave-a-legacy/

8 Essential Leadership Communication Skills | HBS Online. (2019, November 14). Business Insights Blog. https://online.hbs.edu/blog/post/leadership-communication

8 Leadership Qualities to Motivate Your Team | DeakinCo. (2023, May 3). DeakinCo. | Powering Workplace Performance. https://deakinco.com/resource/8-leadership-qualities-to-motivate-and-inspire-your-team/

IMPACTFUL INCLUSIVE LEADERSHIP

9 POWERFUL STRATEGIES THAT ENCOURAGE DIVERSITY, FOSTER EQUITY, AND CULTIVATE INCLUSIVITY TO TRANSFORM YOUR WORKPLACE

CONTENT WARNING

∾

Chapter 9 includes discussions about workplace discrimination and bias, which may evoke strong emotional responses or memories for some individuals. Please proceed with empathy and self-care. If you feel triggered or overwhelmed, consider taking a break or seeking support.

∾

INTRODUCTION

~

In the heart of bustling workplaces today, the promise of diversity, equity, and inclusion (DEI) echoes, and more placards and persistent voices are speaking about it. However, a tale still needs to be explored as many keep silent on the sensitive part of DEI. Imagine Sarah, a talented Gen Z professional, bursting with innovative ideas and hungrily navigating the corporate labyrinth. Despite her brilliance, she encounters subtle barriers, a stark reminder that generational divides persist. This scenario isn't isolated; it reflects a broader narrative where the vibrant energy of youth is met with systemic challenges.

Racial discrimination also stubbornly lingers, acting as a setback for many in the professional arena. The pursuit of workplace equality proves elusive for individuals with disabilities, while women continue to face the subtle yet pervasive currents of gender bias. Amidst this landscape, people of color confront pronounced prejudices, and those embracing diverse genders and orientations find themselves subjected to unfair treatment. In the collective pursuit of DEI, it becomes evident that despite progress, significant struggles linger in our quest for a truly inclusive working environment. Let's delve into the nuanced realities that shape our professional landscape, exploring the challenges that demand our attention and collective action.

Perhaps you've found yourself in that zone? You're in this workspace, feeling undervalued and overlooked for promotions, facing unfair treatment, and now experiencing discrimination has become your narrative. It's a subtle yet impactful undertone that makes you question your worth, your contributions seemingly eclipsed. So, because you are witnessing stereotypical behaviors and discriminatory practices, it stirs a sense of awakening to the diversity of the world around you and how this workplace keeps you from the bigger picture. You're acutely aware of your potential and eager to contribute more. Yet, the acknowledgment you seek remains elusive, and the promises of change seem slim when familiar faces continue to ascend the corporate ladder. Despite your studies, experience, and hard work, the payoff and hopes to become a senior executive are disproportionate, leaving you grappling with the frustration of unfulfilled assurances of "you're next in line" or "better luck next year." So, who have you become because of this? A breeding ground of discontent fueled by a lack of passion for the job, knowing DEI is nothing more than an abbreviation with no actualization. Hating where you work becomes a rational response when efforts are met with unequal rewards, so you ponder the unsettling question: "Why does the same effort yield disparate outcomes?"

Simple! The answer lies in front of you. It's you!

You are the reason things remain the same: you fail to make your dissatisfaction known so every other workplace can take DEI as a personal concern. The pains you experience can only be the beginning of an idea to turn the system around through an awakening of how inequality and non-inclusion are not condoned and accepted as business as usual. While HR and high-level executives typically wield the power to enact decisions and reforms, the persistent cycle of unfair treatment has left you weary and disheartened. Your sincere desire for a workplace defined by DEI stems from the belief that everyone should reap the rewards of their hard work. Empowered by this conviction, you stand poised to instigate change, whether you witness a deficit of inclusion or personally experience its effects. Hence, the need for this book to come into play for you:

- Reading this book will expose you to diverse viewpoints, so you have an above-the-surface understanding of the intricacies of DEI coming from your perspective and that of other different groups.
- There is no doubt about the level of insight to be gained from this literary work, as it will empower you to make informed decisions to the point where you are equipped with the knowledge to advocate for and implement meaningful changes in your workplace. Once you understand that you are the change you seek, you become driven toward actualizing it.
- A well-versed understanding of DEI principles gained through reading is a powerful catalyst, motivating and enabling you to actively contribute to being the lightbulb fostering a more inclusive and equitable work environment.

These are only but a few of the numerous benefits this book will provide you. It's a whole new journey into taking ownership of your rightful position in the workplace, so no one makes you believe you're there by luck instead of a well-deserved role. Did I mention the ton of results moving forward? Here are just FIVE:

1. **Updated Leadership:** You will gain a comprehensive understanding of how embracing diversity and ensuring equity can elevate your leadership, resulting in workplaces that thrive on the richness of varied perspectives.
2. **Effective Advocacy:** Empowered with insights from the book, you will have the confidence to champion fairness and inclusivity actively. You are the influential voices for positive workplace transformations that transcend biases and discrimination.
3. **Enhanced Team Dynamics:** With team members, you can foster environments where collaboration is more than just a buzzword—it will be a reality that propels teams toward unparalleled success.
4. **Improved Organizational Culture:** As a cultural architect, you will play a pivotal role in shaping workplaces that prioritize

respect so the atmosphere is where everyone feels a sense of belonging and shared purpose.

5. **Professional Growth:** Beyond skill development, understanding and embracing diversity pushes you toward a path of continuous self-improvement, establishing them as change agents capable of driving progress within your professional spheres.

Why am I the best person to tell you this?

I have lived and breathed the corporate world for a number of years. I emerged as a pioneering figure with a rich leadership background spanning more than two decades in the professional field. Settling in New Jersey at the age of 44, I built a life alongside my devoted husband and two delightful children. However, my narrative came to life in a quaint town and unfolded further in the corporate landscape of Chicago before reaching the bustling metropolis of New York. Along this trajectory, I occupied numerous prestigious leadership positions within both expansive corporations and more intimate organizational settings, consistently shattering barriers and redefining expectations.

Honestly, it wasn't easy at the time, but many things became clear to me. I personally witnessed the immense, yet neglected, potential residing in numerous talented women and smaller demographics, often dismissed and undervalued. This ignited a profound passion within me to empower women, amplify their voices, and serve as the inspiration behind my first book, *Fearless Female Leadership*.

I delved into testing methods and strategies suitable for contemporary settings, incorporating data-driven analysis and leveraging DEI principles. Through rigorous research, I uncovered distinctive steps that proved beneficial for a diverse spectrum of individuals, extending beyond the realm of women alone.

It brought me where I am today. A woman who is passionate about making every human being feel relevant within the next place they call home: the workspace. If you have this desire as I do, then you've come to the right place. You can embark on this life-changing journey by embracing the initial move and as you gear up to infuse data-driven DEI principles into your workplace. Get ready to nurture a vibrant, diverse, and wholly inclusive environment.

1

WORKPLACE DEI 101
UNDERSTAND THE ENEMY BEFORE CHANGING IT

Strength lies in differences, not in similarities.
—Covey S. (1989)

◅

#1—Unveiling the DEI Revolution: The Might of Awareness

Were you aware that in today's ever-evolving corporate landscape, an astonishing 75% of organizations accord the highest precedence to DEI (Diversity, Equity, and Inclusion), considering it an indispensable keystone for their future prosperity? These statistics are beyond a trend, but an imperative for advancement and development, which is why, in this chapter, you will be taken on a journey into the core of DEI so that, armed with knowledge and profound insights, you will be endowed with the capability to reshape work environments, cultivate inclusivity, and institute lasting transformation.

#2—DEI: When Did It Become So Relevant?

If this term comes to you as just another abbreviation introduced among the long list of shorter terms for reinventing how humanity can be more encompassing, think again. DEI is more than a term. It's a movement seeking to ensure every workplace environment creates comfortable and embracing room for all kinds of people irrespective of nationality, religion, gender, abilities, or sexual orientation.

DEI is a framework that organizations use consistently because, although they mean different things, they are interconnected in transforming the workplace. Let's see what they encompass:

- **Diversity** is having individuals with various backgrounds, experiences, and characteristics within an organization or community. It doesn't matter what race, gender, ethnicity, age, sexual orientation, physical abilities, religion, or socioeconomic status these people represent. Their diverse identities and perspectives make them exceptional in the environment they embrace.
- **Equity** ensures everyone has the same opportunities, resources, and advantages within an organization or society. It involves recognizing and addressing systemic barriers and biases that may hinder certain groups from achieving their full potential. In essence, equity seeks that leveled playing field so everyone has a fair chance at success. It's what John Legend, the famous musician and activist, stated when asked about his thoughts on DEI.
- **Inclusion**, however, is a practice of fostering a culture of value, respect, and empowerment for people to contribute their unique perspectives and talents. It goes beyond having a diverse workforce; it's about fully participating, collaborating, and thriving so those diverse voices are heard and no one feels excluded or marginalized.

Verna Myers, a prominent advocate for diversity and inclusion, defines it all in more relatable terms this way: "Diversity is 'being invited to the party' (representation), equity is 'being asked to dance' (fair treatment), and inclusion is 'dancing like nobody's watching' (feeling valued and empowered)" (Myers, 2022).

#3—DEI Interconnects Differently

It shows that these three elements are different principles interwoven to provide a holistic approach toward workplace success and productivity. So, what does each element represent?

- Diversity is the "**what**" about various people and perspectives.
- Equity is the "**how**" of the actions and policies that ensure fair hearing and justice, thereby removing barriers.
- Inclusion is the "**how well**" measure of how effectively an organization embraces and values diversity, creating an inclusive culture.

For example, if individuals from diverse backgrounds do not feel welcomed and empowered (inclusion), we need more than diversity initiatives, we need efforts to address systematic biases (equity). However, these equity measures may not lead to meaningful change if the workplace culture does not embrace diversity and actively include underrepresented groups. In the entertainment industry, which has been one of the most active grounds aiming to uphold DEI, the iconic actor Denzel Washington emphasized that for him, DEI from the angle of equity is: "Opening doors for people who have been historically underrepresented and ensuring they have a chance to succeed" (Commencement Speech, University of Pennsylvania, May 2011).

This is not only true but a requirement to lead to Inclusion as that bridge that ties diversity and equity together, ensuring that the benefits of a diverse workforce are fully realized.

#4—The Different Sides to Each Element

One of the strengths of DEI is that it considers various aspects of each element, thereby introducing a range of perspectives that enhance workplace effectiveness. When it comes to "diversity", there can be:

- **Demographic Diversity:** In this setting, you find differences related to observable characteristics such as race, ethnicity, gender, age, sexual orientation, disability, religion, and nationality. Here, creativity and teamwork thrive as each individual brings their idea of problem-solving to the table.
- **Cognitive Diversity:** The thoughts and intellectual approaches to issues are diverse and intuitive, bringing innovative solutions from multiple angles.
- **Experiential Diversity:** Your life experience and background are as important to shaping a workplace as another. Once you bring it to the forefront, it creates room for a better understanding of individual opinions on every issue. No judgments are made; rather, the fact that you have an experience to share makes the environment more relaxing for everyone to work together harmoniously.
- **Generational Diversity:** It's beautiful to see the Baby Boomers, Generation X, Millennials, and Generation Z all in a workplace because of the power of DEI, as each comes in with a unique work style that each generation can learn from.

In "equity", you find:

- **Procedural Equity:** Ensuring that the processes and procedures within an organization or system are fair and unbiased, from hiring practices to decision-making processes. The goal is for all applicants to feel confident in the system, knowing their qualifications matter more than their background and orientation.
- **Outcome Equity:** Focusing on fair outcomes or results, regardless of initial disparities. In a classroom, students of all backgrounds have access to quality education, and the graduation rates rise, bridging the achievement gap so fairness is upheld.
- **Structural Equity:** Addressing systemic and structural inequalities perpetuating discrimination and inequity, like unequal pay due to gender inequality, is the norm. No woman should feel her gender in the workplace will place her on a

lower cadre for promotion or higher pay. Rather, the policies must ensure gender equality to the latter.

- **Economic Equity:** Ensuring that individuals have equal access to economic opportunities and resources. Every community should invest in job training programs to help marginalized groups access opportunities for financial stability and reduce wealth and income disparities where the rich get richer and the poor get poorer. This is the origin of capitalist societies, where class and status are put above creating a comfortable standard of living for all to enjoy.

- **Educational Equity:** All students should have equal access to quality education, regardless of their background. In societies where education seems underfunded, all it takes is a leveled playground to create educational opportunities for all, and the learning must always feel more encompassing. The disparity between public and private schools should not determine the curriculum system and the post-graduation opportunities the students will encounter in the workplace environment. As long as you are good, you deserve to be given a fair chance to exhibit your skills anywhere.

Now, like a tree with diversity and equity as the branches, what stem cells help make "inclusion" the connecting ground for sustainability?

Cultural Inclusion: Inclusion is mostly about value creation, so when you have people from several cultural backgrounds come together, it opens the door to celebrating cultural traditions and fostering cross-cultural understanding. Imagine a workplace where people are encouraged to come for events that showcase cultural displays in food, music, and more. It won't only be a successful way of driving home the essence of inclusion, but it will be the beginning of building long-term ties of cultural appreciation.

- **Professional Inclusion:** For employees to desire to be part of any workplace environment, one of the key attractions is having equal access to career development, advancement opportunities, and mentorship, regardless of their identity. No individual wants to feel bored or redundant in a system that doesn't encourage career growth because, in such places, the chances for promotion and recognition would be slim, and the hope for a pay raise would be a pipe dream. There must always be a consistent working plan for job satisfaction, leading to organizational productivity.

- **Social Inclusion:** A workplace doesn't need to feel uptight just because it's a work environment. The room to socialize and connect should be a welcome way to build positive relationships, networks, and a sense of belonging. If you belong to the working class, you would understand that the next home after the home is the workplace, and it's why having a supportive community of bosses and colleagues makes the workplace feel like a home away from home.

- **Psychological Safety:** If you're in an environment where you have to look around you before you speak up and share your ideas, then there is a problem. Inclusion encourages respect for opinions, so you must always feel comfortable taking risks and stating your case even if it hurts. It's how people learn, grow, unlearn, and relearn for better system structure.

- **Intersectional Inclusion:** It is crucial to recognize that individuals have multiple aspects of their identity and ensure their unique needs and experiences are considered and respected. For instance, medical staff should consider patients' cultural backgrounds and health conditions within a healthcare setting. This dual consideration facilitates the provision of care that is not only more effective but also empathetic.

Intersectionality

Understanding the concept of intersectionality goes beyond looking at one aspect of your identity in isolation. It's not just about your gender or race but the multiple dimensions of identity and social categories and how they intersect and interact with one another to establish the histories surrounding discrimination and privilege. Kimberlé Crenshaw, a legal scholar and civil rights advocate, coined it. For her, intersectionality could be likened to a situation in which a Black woman may face distinct discrimination from that experienced by a White woman or a Black man due to the combined effects of racism and sexism. A situation that is detrimental not only to the workplace or the working class but to an entire world system and the reason why Martin Luther King Jr. would say, *"Injustice anywhere is a threat to Justice everywhere"* (King 1963). With this statement, it is clear that intersectionality aims to encourage a more nuanced and comprehensive understanding of social inequalities and emphasizes the need to address various aspects of identity simultaneously when addressing issues related to diversity, equity, and inclusion.

In this regard, certain policies have been introduced in line with intersectionality to assist in weighing the parameters of organizational success between business goals, job satisfaction, and delivery.

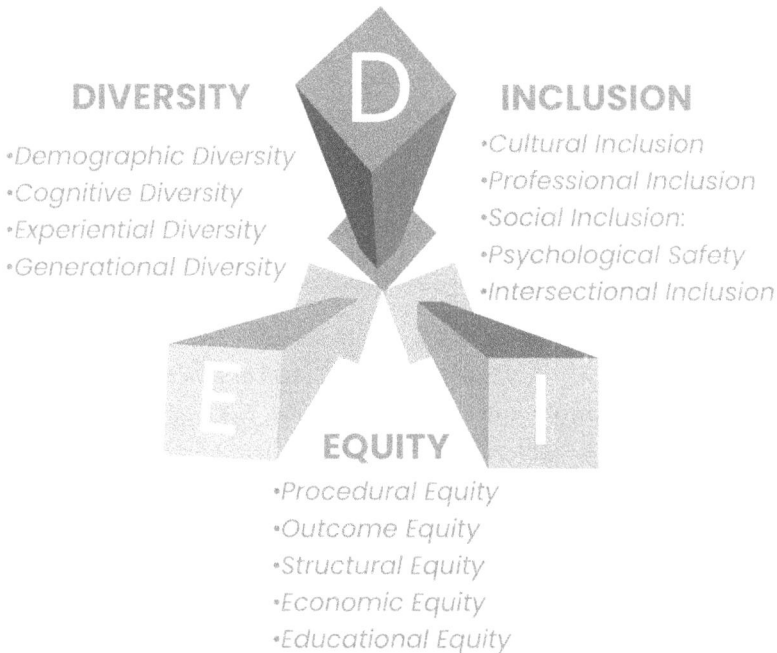

DIVERSITY
•Demographic Diversity
•Cognitive Diversity
•Experiential Diversity
•Generational Diversity

INCLUSION
•Cultural Inclusion
•Professional Inclusion
•Social Inclusion:
•Psychological Safety
•Intersectional Inclusion

EQUITY
•Procedural Equity
•Outcome Equity
•Structural Equity
•Economic Equity
•Educational Equity

ESG (Environmental, Social, and Governance)

Policies that represent a framework companies and investors use to evaluate a company's impact on society and the environment beyond its financial performance. Each component of ESG represents a different aspect:

- **Environmental (E):** What is a company's environmental impact? Here, factors such as carbon emissions, energy efficiency, waste management, and sustainability practices are considered and evaluated.
- **Social (S):** A company's relationships with its employees, customers, suppliers, and communities where labor practices, employee well-being, and community engagement stand as a strong ground for assessing the success of an organization.
- **Governance (G):** It refers to how a company is managed and the structures in place to ensure ethical and responsible decision-making. It includes issues such as board diversity, executive compensation, and transparency in financial reporting.

ESG policies are used to assess a company's broader societal and environmental responsibilities. They are increasingly important for investors and consumers who want to support businesses that align with their values and prioritize sustainability. It's important that these policies are never ignored or taken for granted if a brand is to stand.

CSR (Corporate Social Responsibility Policies)

It's a company's voluntary effort to contribute positively to society and the environment. CSR initiatives go beyond legal and regulatory requirements and often involve philanthropy, ethical business practices, and efforts to mitigate a company's negative impacts. Call them the charity bodies that see society as a place that consistently needs support in every way. Their initiative can include:

- Charitable donations to community organizations.
- Environmental sustainability efforts, such as reducing carbon emissions or conserving natural resources.
- Ethical sourcing and supply chain practices like good inventory management, having resourceful forecasting to project the demand and supply of products, or even risk management that can handle the mitigation of environmental disasters to sustainable development.
- Employee volunteer programs and efforts to promote workplace diversity and inclusion.

- Transparency in business operations and ethical marketing.

It can go on and on, but what's certain is that CSR is about a company's commitment to being a responsible corporate citizen by actively addressing social and environmental issues.

Ultimately, DEI incorporates some ESG and CSR policies and frameworks to ensure intersectionality and diverse inclusion are priorities within a company's policies. You want to instill a sense of belonging and responsibility in your workplace.

Looking at it statistically, McKinsey & Company affirms that diversity and equity matter today because Companies with diverse executive teams are 25–36% more likely to have above-average profitability. Also, an inclusive-minded workplace outperforms less inclusive ones because diverse leadership is 33% more likely to have industry-leading profitability (McKinsey & Company, 2020).

#5—Benefits of DEI

The Bulletin, on their part, states that equity ensures a fair shot at success, breaking down systemic barriers. The statistical data and confirmations above show that the BENEFITS of DEI in the workplace are limitless. To be more specific, DEI ensures:

- **Healthier Working Space:** Prioritizing DEI creates a healthier, more inclusive workplace culture. Fostering a sense of belonging, respect, and fairness among employees ultimately leading to higher morale, reduced stress, and improved mental well-being.
- **Top Talent Attraction and Retention:** Companies that value DEI are more appealing to a diverse pool of candidates seeking career advancement. Moreover, an inclusive workplace is more likely to retain employees who know their onions and are irreplaceable in terms of turnover costs and encouraging a stable and committed workforce.
- **Topnotch Decision-Making and Innovation:** Diverse perspectives and experiences are always the main menu, leading

to better decision-making and innovative solutions to challenges. When you have a workplace heavy with diverse thoughts due to cultural differences and experiences, it can give organizations a competitive edge in a rapidly changing business landscape.

- **High Profitability and Brand Reputation:** The DEI strategies often begets increased profitability, as diverse leadership and inclusive practices correlate with higher financial performance, an enhanced brand reputation, and a dedication to social issues.

- **Legal Compliance and Ethical Responsibility:** Undoubtedly, organizations dedicated to making DEI their motto for success always seek to comply with anti-discrimination laws and regulations. They channel their ethical responsibility to create a fair and just workplace that values all individuals, irrespective of their background identity or encircled personality.

Challenges for Workplaces Lacking DEI Initiatives

To understand this perspective clearly, you must access data that unveils the stark realities within workplaces lacking Diversity, Equity, and Inclusion (DEI) initiatives. These statistics shed light on the common challenges individuals encounter in such environments, and you may have a story that connects you to these data samples. As we delve deeper into DEI strategies, you'll find more data samples and perhaps bring about scenarios you have observed in your workplace.

- **Bias in Hiring:** Over the years, it has been shown in many ways that individuals with African American names can experience bias in hiring, potentially hindering interview opportunities and bringing workplace discrimination. This affects 25% of African Americans, Latinx, and Hispanics, impacting job satisfaction and well-being. Consider two equally qualified job applicants: Jamal Jackson and John Smith. Jamal, with a distinctly African-American name, might face subtle biases during initial screening, potentially resulting in John being selected for an interview despite their similar qualifications. This illustrates how implicit biases can impact interview opportunities. Or, imagine Maria, a Latina employee, who, despite her qualifications, is passed over for opportunities, and her contributions often go unrecognized. This discrimination affects her job satisfaction and overall well-being, highlighting the issue of workplace bias and its negative consequences.

- **Racial Workforce Disparity:** It's not new to discover that 77%, of the workforce in the United States remains Caucasian, highlighting the need for diversity efforts (De Jager, 2023). It's what Viola Davis, an acclaimed actress known for her roles in films and television, had been outspoken about when advocating for diversity and inclusion in the entertainment industry. She has openly discussed the disparities faced by actors of color, particularly African Americans, regarding limited opportunities, unequal pay, and underrepresentation in leading roles.
- **Disparity in Promotions:** Gender disparities persist in promotions, with fewer women reaching managerial positions, and when you know about women like Oprah Winfey in the media industry, it resonates with the journey of most women who fight to secure their positions in every organization to date.
- **Gender Pay Gap:** The gender pay gap persists, and the likes of tennis legend Serena Williams was a victim as she became vocal about the gender pay gap in professional tennis. Despite her incredible success and achievements, she has pointed out disparities in prize money between male and female tennis players, highlighting the need for pay equity in sports. Why should women receive lower salary increases despite seeking equal pay raises? They put in just as much as the males, and the sport isn't made easy just because it's a woman playing, so there should be no limitations.
- **Barriers for Disabled and LGBTQ+ Individuals:** People with disabilities face limited job opportunities, while LGBTQ+ and gender-diverse individuals encounter discrimination affecting their job satisfaction and health. Marlee Matlin, the acclaimed deaf actress, shared her experiences of being typecast in roles specifically for deaf characters rather than having equal chances to play a wide range of roles. Her advocacy today has called

attention to the need for greater inclusivity and open doors for disabled actors. It doesn't end there; LGBTQ+ individuals have had their fair share of workplace discrimination. In 2019, a U.S. Supreme Court case (Bostock v. Clayton County) highlighted workplace discrimination against LGBTQ+ employees. The case involved Gerald Bostock, who was fired from his job after his employer discovered he was gay. The Supreme Court's ruling in favor of Bostock affirmed that LGBTQ+ individuals are protected from workplace discrimination under Title VII of the Civil Rights Act of 1964. Many LGBTQ+ employees have shared experiences of discrimination, microaggressions, and exclusion in the workplace. These scenarios often involve employees being treated differently or unfairly due to their sexual orientation or gender identity. Advocacy and policy changes aim to create more connecting workplaces for LGBTQ+ individuals and the disabled community to ensure no one is left behind in building a more inclusivity-embracing workspace for all.

Also, in 2019, John Legend and other activists launched the "FREE AMERICA" campaign to raise awareness about mass incarceration and advocate for criminal justice reform. The campaign highlighted the stark disparities in sentencing and treating individuals in the criminal justice system. John Legend's involvement and advocacy efforts have contributed to significant changes in criminal justice policies in some U.S. states, bringing attention to the need for fairness and equity within the system.

$\backsim$

As we reflect on the benefits of diversity, equity, and inclusion, the undeniable power of data reinforces the urgency for change. If you find yourself among the statistics that reveal disparities, remember that data doesn't lie. It serves as a compass guiding us toward strategies for meaningful transformation. If you're ready to foster diversity, equity, and inclusion in your workplace, let's move forward to the next chapter. Strategy two will help you delve deeper into analyzing the need, a crucial step before you can pave the way for effective and lasting changes.

2

ANALYZING THE NEED FOR DEI IN THE WORKPLACE

Decisions are rarely black and white. By analyzing and collaborating
effectively, we can uncover better solutions.
—Jamie Dimon (BrainyQuote, 2001)

~

The Key to Identifying a Non-DEI-Oriented Workplace

Have you ever encountered the term "having a nuanced understanding of a challenge?" Well, it's not just about staring the problem in the face and thinking up a solution based on mind and sight assessment; it's crucially strategic for initiating change. This assessment involves in-depth examination, including surveys, focus groups, and interviews, to identify specific issues faced by underrepresented groups where DEI is concerned. This is called the Lighthouse Framework, a strategic blueprint for identifying and addressing DEI challenges and opportunities within an organization. The framework consists of several key components:

- **Data Collection and Analysis:** This first step involves surveys, interviews, focus groups, and other methods. This data is then meticulously analyzed to gain a deep understanding of the current state of DEI within the organization.

- **Comprehensive Assessment:** Organizations comprehensively assess their workplace environment, policies, and practices. This assessment includes examining employees' experiences from diverse demographic groups, identifying barriers to inclusion, and recognizing opportunities for improvement.

- **Pinpoint Specific Issues:** The framework emphasizes pinpointing specific DEI challenges underrepresented groups face. This includes recognizing areas where disparities exist and understanding the root causes of these disparities.

- **Create Targeted Strategies:** Armed with a nuanced understanding of DEI challenges, organizations can develop targeted strategies and initiatives to address the identified issues and create a more inclusive workplace.

- **Continuous Improvement:** The DEI Lighthouse Framework promotes a commitment to ongoing improvement. Organizations are encouraged to regularly review and assess their DEI efforts, making necessary adjustments and refinements to ensure progress.

- **Inclusive Leadership:** Leadership plays a crucial role in the framework, emphasizing inclusive leadership practices. Leaders are expected to champion DEI initiatives, set the tone for the organization, and lead by example.

- **Transparency and Accountability:** Organizations here must embrace communication as their DEI goals, progress openly, and hold themselves accountable for achieving meaningful results.

- **Employee Engagement:** Engaging employees from diverse backgrounds is a central component. By actively seeking input and feedback from employees, they get involved in decision-making, creating a sense of belonging.

- **Measurable Metrics:** The framework emphasizes the importance of using measurable metrics to track progress. One must define key performance indicators (KPIs) related to DEI and regularly assess their performance against these metrics.

- **Cultural Shift:** Ultimately, the DEI Lighthouse Framework aims to foster a cultural shift within the organization. It seeks to embed DEI principles into the organization's DNA, creating a workplace where diversity is celebrated, equity is prioritized, and inclusion is the norm.

In doing this, there will surely be a holistic approach to enhancing diversity, equity, and inclusion through policies, practices, and cultural aspects. That said, workplaces will set their priorities right in identifying the roadmap to success. For most, two things stand out:

1. **Gender Equity:** In gender equity, organizations recognize the importance of addressing gender disparities and inequalities in the workplace. The red flags are raised, especially in times of promotion and pay rates, which calls for the DEI initiative to set the pace for what is needed to achieve equilibrium among colleagues regardless of identity or biological formation.
2. **Competitive Standing:** With the DEI initiatives, competitive standing is imperative to help organizations foster diversity and inclusion for improved performance and competitiveness. Once a place is open to change, the opportunities for growth and productivity are endless.

To effectively prioritize successful roadmap initiatives, it is crucial to evaluate DEI not merely as a broadly accepted necessity but also as a distinct, individualized reality. This approach involves thoroughly examining the intricacies of non-DEI existence, identifying its roots, and actively minimizing its presence.

Evaluation and Assessment

Organizations can begin the mission of finding the loopholes using several personal methods of evaluation and assessment of non-DEI existence in the workplace:

- **Self-Assessment Surveys:** Employees can participate in self-assessment surveys that gauge their feelings of inclusion, opportunities for growth, and perceptions of bias or discrimination. These surveys often include questions about workplace culture, interactions with colleagues, and career advancement.

An example is Anabelle, a long-term employee with a construction company, who participated in a self-assessment survey asking about her sense of belonging. She shared, "The survey made me reflect on my experiences, and I realized I hadn't felt truly included. It led to conversations with HR, and they've since initiated changes to create a more inclusive environment."

- **Feedback and Reporting:** Implement a confidential feedback and reporting mechanism where employees can report bias, discrimination, or exclusion incidents. This allows individuals to share their experiences and helps organizations address issues in real time. Mark, an employee from Chicago who had just been recruited as a customer support for a bank and was in training, stated that:

When I had a concern about a microaggression while starting off and shadowing a senior manager, I used our reporting mechanism to share my ordeal of feeling uncomfortable with the show of harshness in getting the job done. I appreciated the confidentiality as it made me feel free to express my concerns without reservation. In fact, it led to a conversation with my manager, and the issue was addressed promptly, showing that the organization takes DEI seriously.

- **Focus Groups and Interviews:** During a focus group discussion, Maria shared her experience, saying she felt heard when she spoke about how being a person with a disability made her afraid of how the workspace would embrace her. She attested that there was no blame, but about making things better, as she was reminded, she is just as relevant as the next person who doesn't have a disability. For her, it meant she could be optimistic about DEI because the efforts made to create a sense of value and respect were established.

When organizations conduct focus group discussions or interviews with employees to delve deeper into their experiences and gather qualitative insights, these interactions allow employees to express their concerns and speak openly about what changes can make a difference.

- **Individual Goals:** Did you know that evaluating an individual's career progression, opportunities, and achievements within the organization can reveal potential biases? In doing so, questions such as: Are promotions, raises, and assignments distributed equitably will be brought up? It will draw attention to how this can be fixed for long-term goals.

Alex boldly stated these facts to his supervisor in a training session. He said he noticed a pattern in promotions favoring a particular group of persons, and this was odd for him, who had a long-term record with the organization. Why wasn't he due for a raise or promotion? So, he decided to track his achievements and raise the issue with his manager. So far, so good; he confirmed it worked out for the best as more equitable career opportunities were shifted his way since then. It's about being attentive to your rights as a workplace employee. Never see yourself as unworthy when you know the time and effort you put into the job.

- Mentorship: When you participate in mentorship and sponsorship programs, you will have a clear idea of assessing and accessing career development support. You will also understand that when you do not reap the benefits of mentorships, inclusive group programs, and all kinds of networking, the disparity plays out, and of course, DEI would mean no more than words with no action for you.

Step-by-Step Approach to Assess Work Environment

To make these methods above count, there needs to be a systematic step-by-step approach for leaders to assess their current work environment to ensure that DEI never dwindles or loses its presence but implements a strategy for change.

Step 1: Check the Website—This is usually the quickest way to discover the status of DEI in workplaces. Visit the company's official website and navigate to sections like "About Us," "Our Values," "Mission and Vision," or "Diversity and Inclusion." Look for any written mission statements or commitment to DEI and assess if the tone truly carries the goal of DEI beyond words. Companies often use their websites to communicate their dedication to DEI, and it can be through words, images, and the like so that everyone feels at home when they come into that online space. Take a look at Google. See how they made prominent features of their diversity initiatives for their workplace. It showcased their commitment to creating and sustaining inclusion and made more people realize that Google Group has amazing DEI ethics that go beyond time and personality.

Step 2: Online Data Search—Utilize search engines to find publicly available data and reports related to the company's DEI initiatives. This could include diversity reports, sustainability reports, or articles discussing the organization's diversity and inclusion efforts. Pay attention to any progress or challenges mentioned or, possibly, legal cases where the organization sustained protecting their employee in a situation surrounding discrimination or microaggression. These sorts of reports attract potential employees to desire to work in a space where their interests are utmost. Online platforms like LinkedIn are great spaces to explore the profiles of any company's leaders and employees and their professional backgrounds and affiliations, which mostly reveal insights into diversity efforts.

Step 3: Review Social Media—Scan for posts, articles, or comments related to DEI on social media profiles on platforms like LinkedIn, Twitter, or Facebook. Companies want growth and publicity for the right reasons, and that can best be achieved when they share updates, events, and initiatives related to diversity and inclusion on their social media channels. If there are real-time engagement posts between employees and others who have a passion for DEI, it can make a world of difference in any company's working environment evaluation.

Step 4: Calculate Diversity as it Stands—Gather data on the representation of different demographic groups within the company. This may include statistics on gender, race, ethnicity, age, and more. Look for diversity reports or data available in the company's annual reports or on its website, where you can combine all quantitative data with qualitative findings. Microsoft's diversity dashboard is a good example; it provides real-time data on workforce diversity, promoting transparency and accountability.

Step 5: Check Ratio of Diverse Leaders, Managers, and Team Leaders Existence—The composition of the company's leadership team, including executives, managers, and team leaders, is imperative in assessing whether individuals from diverse backgrounds are well-represented in leadership roles. Apple's CEO, Tim Cook, was, among many things, very passionate and vocal in his advocacy for DEI and its positive impact on the company's culture. For him, it was more like a channel to define how civilization aims to tilt in the direction of harmony if well embraced, as described by the Late Mahatma Gandhi, India's renowned leader.

Step 6: Employee Retention and Satisfaction—Analyze employee retention rates, particularly among diverse employees. How many have worked several years of service and have risen through the ranks? Review employee satisfaction surveys or feedback to identify whether certain demographic groups express lower satisfaction or face higher turnover rates. Are there more Asians speaking out on non-DEI than others? Are the disabled colleagues making cases for issues of inclusion and potential termination threats? These can raise many concerns about where the organization stands in the career growth of diverse employees. You can even conduct informational interviews with employees who represent different demographics. Their personal stories can provide invaluable insights into workplace dynamics.

Step 7: Mentorship or Training Programs—Investigate whether the organization offers mentorship programs or training initiatives focusing on DEI. These programs may include mentoring circles or leadership development opportunities for underrepresented groups. It is transformational and opens the door for all individuals seeking to be mentors and mentees to foster a culture of learning and growth. See how Facebook's Lean In Circles, which was inspired by Sheryl Sandberg's book, encourages mentorship and support among female employees, making them more aware of their gender role in the workplace.

Step 8: Do You Have DEI Training?—Check if the company provides DEI training programs for all employees. This measure helps raise awareness about diversity-related issues, reduce unconscious biases, and promote inclusive behaviors in the workplace. If it's missing, it's a problem. How will employees share meaningful conversations about these issues if they don't dialogue over it? Not every DEI conversation is fashioned to challenge the odds; instead, it becomes the gateway to harnessing positive change for an organization's present and future cultural structure.

Step 9: Check the Incident Reports—Issues relating to discrimination, harassment, or bias within the workplace must not only be reported but examined. Analyzing the frequency and nature of reported incidents and repeated negative trends in a transparent and anonymous fashion creates a room for openness and willingness to express opinions and inhibitions at all times.

Step 10: Do You Have ERG Software?—If the organization has Employee Resource Groups (ERGs) or affinity groups, assess the feedback and engagement levels within these groups. ERGs, which are the employees' voices, often provide valuable insights into their experiences, needs, and areas for improvement. J.H. Douglas (1959) stated, "Our ability to listen and take action on feedback is the secret to excellence." Airbnb is just one of the examples that showcase the vital role ERGs play in providing feedback and shaping the company's policies, including combating discrimination in their bookings. The success story of this brand speaks for itself, as it is now a globally welcoming approach to tourism in comfort.

Step 11: Observe Patterns in Discriminatory Onboarding or Missed Achievements—Investigate patterns of discrimination in various aspects, including the onboarding process, leadership appointments, and missed career advancement opportunities for diverse employees. Identifying these patterns helps pinpoint specific areas for intervention and necessary advocacy for unbiased processes and equal opportunities for all.

Step 12: Consider the Talent Attraction Strategies—Evaluate strategies such as recruitment efforts targeted at diverse communities, partnerships with diversity-focused organizations, or participation in job fairs and events aimed at diverse candidates. Are they compelling enough? Do they proactively show outreach efforts toward talent acquisition? Only time will tell how far and effective the DEI approach has been sustained with all the events put in place.

For you to understand the importance of these steps, imagine your company as a ship sailing through uncharted waters. You need a reliable compass to know if you're on course or if there are stormy seas ahead. These steps are like that compass, helping you gauge your company's current position and shed light on issues such as incident reports, employee grievances, a sense of discontent, and recurring missed opportunities for certain colleagues. With all that valuable information neatly organized in a spreadsheet. It becomes a treasure map with markers at key milestones, helping you measure your progress in fostering DEI.

Remember, DEI is not a one-time voyage; it's a continuous journey. So, you must regularly check your compass, adjusting your course as needed to navigate toward a more inclusive and equitable workplace.

ERG and ENG Software

Recall that in step 10, there was a mention of an ERG software to help checkmate all outcomes from engagements within employees and see the possible recurrency or non-recurrency on issues of DEI as well as the personalities involved. With this assessment mode, you'll find that there is much more to ERGs and its sister software ENGs (Employee Network Groups) in the journey to gathering data and concluding assessments efficiently. It not only assists in having a close to accurate measurement of the current status of the company's DEI, but it also labels out the needed changes that workers and the working environment should have to be DEI-friendly.

When you leverage ERGs and ENGs, you'll observe that it's a powerful way to gather essential data for your DEI assessment. Instead of the usual emails that might go unresponded or seen, these groups serve as bridges between your organization and its diverse workforce, offering a safe space for employees to share their DEI experiences. You can actually use these groups to conduct tailored surveys, focus groups, and interviews that capture a wide range of perspectives. Consider an ERG software platform where a Women in Tech group hosts a virtual panel discussion on gender diversity in the tech industry. The software allows members to register, participate in the discussion, and provide feedback afterward. This promotes engagement and collects valuable data on what women in the organization think about gender-related issues in their field.

The ERG software is the key to enhanced engagement and feedback collection, thereby streamlining ERG and ENG management and acting as a central hub for group activities. To make the most of ERG software, it's essential to cultivate an inclusive culture and encourage active employee participation in these groups. Remember, ERG software thrives when employees are motivated and feel supported in sharing their insights and experiences. If your company selects the Affirmity ERG platform with its robust analytics capabilities, the platform will allow the organization to track the impact of its ERGs over time. That's when you will notice a significant increase in engagement and a decrease in diversity-related complaints since implementing the software, which showcases tangible progress in its DEI efforts.

Now, don't get lost; the Affirmity ERG platform is one of several other ways data is being collected. Undoubtedly, the diversity leaders and HR teams are struggling to keep up with the evolution of DEI in the workplace. However, Affirmity's tools are the key to unlocking the full potential of workplace diversity through Employee Resource Groups (ERGs). These tools empower HR and diversity leaders to foster ERGs that drive leadership development, retain and nurture existing diverse talent, boost recruitment efforts, and streamline the onboarding process. Once you have Affirmity's solutions at hand, organizations can create an environment where employees are engaged, valued, and committed, ultimately leading to a more diverse and inclusive workplace that thrives.

Another great tool is the Qooper. Ever heard of it? Well, like Affirmity, it's an innovative tool that aims to enhance the effectiveness of ERG and ENG using some key elements of success:

- Qooper allows ERG leaders to manage their groups efficiently, facilitating communication, event planning, and collaboration among members.

- The platform enables the creation and management of mentorship programs essential for leadership development and knowledge sharing within ERGs.
- Qooper provides a centralized repository for ERGs to share resources, documents, and best practices, ensuring easy access for all members.
- It offers tools for collecting feedback and conducting surveys to gauge the effectiveness of ERG initiatives and gather insights from members.
- With Qooper, you get analytics and reporting features that help ERG leaders measure their impact, track progress, and make data-driven decisions.
- Best of all, the platform is designed to be mobile-friendly, allowing members to participate and engage with their ERGs from anywhere.

There is also Chezie, another champion of the ERG and ENG movement, and although these platforms support the journey to power up the DEI commitment in the workplace, they have their different strengths. Chezie stands out with a strong mentorship and resource-sharing focus, offering feedback tools and analytics. Affirmity specializes in data analytics and provides comprehensive diversity solutions and consulting services. Qooper, on the other hand, is a versatile platform known for scalability and integration with HR systems.

So, the choice depends on an organization's unique needs and priorities for fostering diversity and inclusion. Not to mention, as much as these tools revamp the power of technology in the pursuit of DEI assessment, it doesn't in any way negate the manual manner of data collection. It's still as effective as ever, and with the help of polls and surveys, complex data are retrieved and broken down, leaving no stone unturned in comprehending the challenges and needed changes surrounding the workplace and DEI.

Conducting Surveys

You can choose how you want to do it. What's more, is that statistics and data will always share with you the effectiveness and efficiency of all polls and survey strategies.

Types of Surveys

1. **Employee Engagement Surveys:** They come in various types, such as satisfaction surveys, vision surveys, leadership surveys, enablement surveys, recognition surveys, and more. Each type focuses on different aspects of employee engagement, and as specific as they come, it spells out data according to that particular tentacle of DEI and has a higher percentage of concern to the organization. Microsoft uses employee surveys to measure various factors, including job satisfaction and leadership effectiveness. They have made data-driven changes based on employee feedback, showcasing the importance of regular surveys.

2. **Sample Surveys:** You can use sample surveys from the provided source to create effective surveys for collecting data in your workplace. A human resources manager can find a sample satisfaction survey from the provided source. Then, they customize it for their organization to measure employee job satisfaction and identify improvement areas. These samples can cover various engagement themes regarding career development, leading to a long-term DEI assessment.

3. **Anonymity for Honest Feedback:** To ensure you receive honest and unbiased feedback, it's essential to maintain anonymity during surveys, polls, and quizzes. This helps employees feel comfortable sharing their thoughts and concerns. Research done by O.C. Tanner found that 79% of employees who quit their jobs cited a lack of appreciation as a key reason for leaving (Tanner, 2023). It means you, as much as the next employee, want to know you aren't seen as a working machine but as someone whose work counts for something important. Casual as it might sound, it's an essential part of welfare.

4. **Digital Surveys with Google Forms:** It's a convenient tool for conducting digital surveys. It's user-friendly and accessible, making it suitable for smaller teams and organizations.
5. **Culture Amp:** Here is an excellent choice for employee engagement surveys. It offers a comprehensive platform that covers the employee experience, from onboarding to exit, which is so encompassing and makes even the exit of any employee feel at home with no drama or tension.
6. **Connecteam for Hybrid or Remote Workers:** It supports surveys and helps manage teams, making it valuable for organizations with hybrid or remote work setups. It facilitates tasks like scheduling and communication, which is why, in the heat of the COVID-19 pandemic, Hybrid work became unavoidable. It was due to over 70% of established survey facts from employees stating the necessity for flexibility and adaptability (OECD, 2021).

Now you see why companies like Facebook's Meta Platform Inc., Sales-Force, and LinkedIn all stand out. They pay attention to employment engagement like a mother to her child. According to Mercer, 92% of companies use employee surveys as a tool to assess and improve employee engagement (Mercer, 2023). The Society for Human Resource Management (SHRM) even found that 77% of organizations offering employee wellness programs boost engagement and well-being (Miller, 2019). When the Work Institute suggested that 42 million employees would leave their jobs in 2021, it wasn't just a statement but a survey of how employee turnover remains a challenge for many organizations if DEI is handled with kid gloves (Work Institute, 2022). Now more than ever, there needs to be a hunger to face the challenges, fix them, and aim for a positive change.

To do this, it's your turn to create a custom spreadsheet. Start with the first column for the current situation, the second for supporting metrics, and the third for potential complications. The fourth column is where you outline your proposed resolutions. Leave the fifth column empty for now; you'll use it to measure success later. In upcoming chapters, we'll fill in columns 3 and 4 based on data insights and tailored solutions specific to your workplace.

Check the sample below for guidance.

THE SITUATIONAL ASSESSMENT CHART

1	2	3	4	5
Current Situation	Data Supporting the Current Situation	Possible Complications Resulting From the Current Situation	Potential Resolutions/Ideas to Improve the Current Situation	New Data After 3 Months of Testing the Resolution
• Employees don't feel that the hiring process is fair.	• 8/18/23 employees listed the same issue.	• Poor employee retention and a lack of diversity.	• Change the hiring process to include equitable processes based on people's skills, and post new job listings on diverse job boards.	• 12/6/23 Employees believe the hiring process is more fair. • Alternatively, the sample data could show: 12/8 employees now list a new problem showing the lack of in-house promotions. • (This 3-month metric 73 reveals a new problem altogether.)

EXAMPLE

Always remember that before embarking on the journey to transform your workplace culture and policies, it's essential to understand people's needs. To achieve this, you must gather input from your colleagues and assess the true state of your work environment. You must know that you cannot fix a broken system unless you take the pains to note what really went wrong and how it can be amended.

PITCHING A NEW WORKPLACE CULTURE THAT MATTERS

It's not what you look at that matters; it's what you see.
—H.D. Thoreau (Gracious Quotes, 2023)

∾

What Makes a DEI Idea Successful?

The answer is simple: Achieving success with your DEI initiatives and embarking on a transformative journey from start to finish. As H. Ford (1923) aptly said, "Coming together is a beginning; keeping together is progress; working together is a success." Therefore, for the success of your DEI ideas, you must prioritize them within your organizational strategy and recognize their role in shaping a better future.

McKinsey's "Diversity, Equity, and Inclusion Lighthouses 2023" report highlights that creating lasting change begins with delving into best practices and understanding how they can guide your efforts. You set a clear course and ensure your initiatives resonate with your organization's mission. As a ship relies on its compass, your DEI journey hinges on these best practices to steer you toward a workplace culture that celebrates diversity and fosters inclusivity, ultimately leading to success for all.

Five Rules of Engagement

In the planning, there needs to be outlined rules of engagement to enable a structured progression of where the ideas will take the organization. Here, five rules apply as best practices on the journey:

- **Rule 1: Thorough Understanding**—Show how well you understand the plan and its implications. It is not just about knowledge; it's your chance to demonstrate you've considered the broader context and potential challenges. This won't only make your co-workers and executives trust your initiative, but there will be a confidence that you are well-prepared and have all the skills to handle the proposed changes effectively.
- **Rule 2: Data-Driven Communication**—Executives value information that is concise, relevant, and supported by data. In life, facts are what move people to action. When presenting to higher-level colleagues, focusing on key metrics, real-time analytics, and evidence that directly relate to your proposal is crucial. Don't waste their time with unnecessary information that can slow down the decision-making process. Give them the real deal and never leave out all the pros and cons; that way, they know you're not just selling them some sob story of all the good stuff they know won't fly.
- **Rule 3: Initiative**—Taking initiative is a sign of proactiveness and leadership. Executives appreciate team members who follow instructions, identify improvement opportunities, and take action without waiting for explicit guidance. This demonstrates your commitment to the success of the project or initiative. When Ursula Burns started her career as a summer intern at Xerox, she eventually worked her way up to becoming the company's CEO in 2009. Ursula Burns' initiative and dedication were instrumental in her rise through the ranks of Xerox. Her leadership and innovative thinking helped steer the company through challenging times, including transitioning into a digital technology and services enterprise. It just shows

that initiative can take you far ahead of your co-workers once you are focus-driven.

- **Rule 4: Enthusiasm**—Not only is it infectious, but it can significantly impact how your ideas are received. One notable woman who showed enthusiasm for her initiative and won many over in the fashion industry is Anna Wintour. Since 1988, Anna Wintour has been the editor-in-chief of Vogue magazine and is widely regarded as one of the most influential figures in the fashion world. Her enthusiasm for fashion and keen editorial eye have significantly shaped the industry. When you're genuinely excited about a proposal or project, it energizes you and those around you. It can distinguish between a routine presentation and one that leaves a lasting impression. In fact, people are likely to take the project more seriously than you because there is an aura of passion flowing from how driven you are about the idea's success.

- **Rule 5: Being prepared for questions and potential challenges is a mark of thoroughness**—Nothing should take you by surprise, and executives who see this are more likely to trust your proposal if you've considered various scenarios and have well-thought-out responses to potential queries. It's the demonstration of your dedication to ensuring the success and viability of your plan.

These rules set the stage for having the perfect answers to key questions about your planned goal and the changes you look forward to. Questions like:

- What is the actual goal target of the idea?
- Who are the stakeholders that matter most in planning and executing this idea?
- By projection, what outcome will the idea likely deliver? (The Good, Bad, and Ugly).
- Do I have enough supportive and compelling data to support the plan?
- How can the nature of the data retrieved determine the next steps and measurable outcomes?

Once you align these questions in your planning strategy, then comes the best part. Using the Pyramid Principle!

The Pyramid Principle

Here, you can have an impeccable design laid down with all the data retrieved, the pros and cons in the course of planning, and the desired resolution after all ideas have been sifted and gathered. Let's take, for example, Apple Inc. and discuss one of its many ingenious ideas and how the Pyramid Principle assisted in expanding a situation and revealing the possibilities towards a fallback or a boom in production.

In the early 2000s, Apple Inc. faced a situation where their Macintosh computer sales stagnated, and the company was struggling to gain market share in the PC industry. You can see that in this sample, your first move is to start by explaining the current state or situation; that way, your audience will understand the context and be broad-minded about how it got to this point.

Secondly, highlight the issues or challenges your audience faces in the current situation so they know how invested they must be in the outcome, good or bad. Why do Apple's issues appear more complicated? It was because there was a declining market share, reduced profitability, and a lack of innovation in their product line, and competitors like Microsoft were dominating the market. Everything was evident and glaringly needed the "what next" big idea.

Thirdly, then comes the awaited dawn where a proposed resolution or change that addresses the complications is suggested, and you can just imagine how much that main idea has been long awaited. See how Apple's decision to introduce a series of innovative products changed the situation, starting with the iPod, followed by the iPhone and iPad. These products revolutionized their respective industries and allowed Apple to diversify its product line beyond computers. Good thinking!

By now, you see how the benefits brought about significant change. Apple's revenue and market share skyrocketed, and its value is second to none in the world today with its innovative products that changed how humans interact with technology. The main idea was a success guided by top-notch financial data, stock performance, and customer satisfaction metrics. To make an idea bought and renowned, emphasize the benefits of your proposed resolution by using accurate and compelling data to support your argument and encourage your colleagues to join by show-casing positive outcomes. No one will take your strategy lightly knowing how you have covered all your tracks efficiently.

There is a saying that for every ten men in battle, there is always a traitor, an insider who can sell the team out unless he is found out or won over. The same goes when you have an idea; that's when you should ensure there are no snags to your plans, like people who have all the influence and can use it to tumble your idea into a nightmare. So, to be prepared and not act unaware of potential complications, you should consider:

- **Getting everyone onboard:** Achieving buy-in from all stakeholders can be a significant challenge, both mentally and financially. It's crucial to address the potential resistance to change and allocate resources effectively to overcome these barriers. Ensuring that your corporate inclusion efforts align with organizational goals and values can help mitigate this challenge. You can even engage leadership in discussions about DEI's strategic importance. Use the advantage by sharing industry-specific success stories or case studies highlighting the advantages of diverse and inclusive workplaces. This act of conviction never goes wrong with the right data in hand.
- **Make DEI your culture:** Analyze how DEI principles will be integrated into various aspects of your company's operations, from recruitment and hiring to leadership development and decision-making processes. Just allow diversity and inclusion to be incorporated into training, discussions in affinity groups, and more, and see how people begin embracing the plan like a daily routine never to be missed.
- **Get rid of bias:** Aiming to address unconscious bias in hiring practices is essential because it undermines DEI efforts. Establish different hiring panels or committees to review candidates and make objective decisions. Implement blind recruitment techniques, such as removing identifying information from resumes during initial assessments. Regularly

review and update your hiring and promotion criteria to eliminate potential biases. With over 60% of respondents believing their workplaces exhibit bias, it's the perfect moment to recognize these biases and implement training and awareness programs that can help mitigate their impact.

- **Ageism:** Another common bias that can affect the opportunities and experiences of older and younger team members. What does age have to do with service delivery if the job can get done efficiently? When you promote mentorship and reverse mentorship programs, you bridge generational gaps within the workforce. Fostering age-related stereotypes and an age-inclusive environment is essential for DEI success.

- **Sexism:** Once a topic revolves around the male and female sexes, it remains a challenge in many workplaces. There is always a conflicting feeling of who deserves what and when which has affected the smooth working environment. It's time to establish clear guidelines and policies that prohibit gender-based discrimination and provide training to recognize and prevent it. Diversity in leadership roles should be encouraged as this can massively contribute to a more equitable workplace.

- **Halo effect:** Where one's positive traits influence perceptions of their other qualities, leading to bias in decision-making. No good judgment can come from a source when so many people are involved. You need feedback and comments to evaluate and reduce any biased conclusion so employees see the transparency of discussions and objective criteria rather than subjective impressions.

- **Measurement and accountability:** You need precision in providing key performance indicators (KPIs) and metrics to track the progress of your DEI initiatives. Every now and again, analyze data on hiring, promotions, compensation, employee satisfaction, and diversity representation at all levels of the organization. In fact, hold leaders and decision-makers accountable for meeting diversity and inclusion goals and celebrate successes along the way. It keeps everyone, executives and employees, on their toes where DEI is concerned.

Once you have all that covered, it's time to bring home the bacon! Enlighten the employees you've spent time trying to win over about the new culture you want to introduce that will set the company on a different level.

This is when you use the pitching Pyramid Principle.

Pitching

Pitching encompasses best practices and empowers individuals to effectively introduce new concepts, ideas, and policies in the workplace. Mastering this approach enhances pitching skills and boosts the chances of successful implementation. Understand that pitching is fundamental for professionals at all levels, as it allows them to present well-prepared plans and ideas, ultimately bypassing unconscious biases in decision-making processes. To be ahead in the game of pitching means:

1. Ensuring your pitch is clear and easy to understand by using simple language with less jargon or technical terms that your audience may not be familiar with.
2. Crafting a compelling narrative that engages your audience emotionally. Add stories to help people connect and remember your message better.
3. Showing confidence in your idea by speaking with conviction and belief in what you're presenting until it's contagious to your employees.
4. Thoroughly researching your topic and understanding your audience's needs and interests. You should anticipate questions and objections and prepare well-structured responses for whatever comes.
5. Sustaining the interest of your audience throughout the pitch. You can use visuals, AI prompts, anecdotes, and examples to illustrate your points; that way, people are engaged from start to finish.
6. You must be an active listener. Always pay attention to your audience's feedback and adjust your pitch accordingly, showing you value their input and want to get them involved in the process.

7. Being open to criticism and encountering resistance or questions. It doesn't mean the pitch isn't good; it just means you should adapt your pitch to address concerns effectively.

8. Respecting your audience's time by keeping your pitch within the allotted time frame.

9. Using visuals like slides or props to enhance your pitch and make complex information more accessible.

10. Making sure your pitch is relevant to your audience's needs and priorities. Say it tailored, and let your message resonate with them.

11. Following up with your audience after the pitch to address any outstanding questions or concerns. This shows your commitment to the idea.

12. Letting your body language send a compelling message. Maintain eye contact and use gestures purposefully while talking, as your audience will feel at home.

13. Above all, you get to practice your pitch multiple times to refine your delivery and increase your confidence. Rehearse like you would for a performance in front of a trusted colleague or mentor so they give you an honest review.

See how important pitching is? The more you practice, the better you can get at it. Who would have thought that the pyramid principle required this much skill to convince people? In fact, you'll need more than skills; you must have a broader understanding of what the Pyramid Principle truly represents and how it all began.

What Is the Pyramid Principle

In the dynamic era of the 1970s, a remarkable innovator, Barbara Minto, was on a mission to revolutionize the way we communicate complex ideas. For her, great ideas went underexplored because the originators weren't quite there in terms of delivery and conviction. At McKinsey & Company, Barbara was this diligently crafting woman who raised the idea of a technique that would become legendary—the Pyramid Principle.

What was her goal? Barbara aimed to empower consultants and professionals to articulate intricate concepts with clarity. Her visionary work was destined to change how we think about conveying ideas.

Fast-forward to 1987, Barbara Minto's legacy found its voice in the book *The Pyramid Principle: Logic in Writing and Thinking.* There she unveiled the blueprint for structuring information in a way that effortlessly guided even the most intricate ideas from paper to the reader's understanding and appreciation. This became the beginning of a profound shift in communication strategies.

Beyond management consulting, the Pyramid Principle became a versatile tool across diverse businesses, academia, government agencies, and nonprofit organizations. From crafting persuasive business proposals to distilling elaborate strategic plans, the best part is this approach has consistently delivered results. It's so embracing to the point where it's now a powerful cornerstone of effective communication and adequate comprehension of complex concepts.

What most people don't comprehend is that when you apply the Pyramid Principle, you're changing the standard information presentation format where you might start with background information or context and gradually lead up to your main point. The Pyramid Principle causes you to flip that order of expectation by commencing with the most critical message right from the start.

You can call it the "top-down" approach, where the key message is delivered so the audience immediately grasps the central idea without sifting through unnecessary details. Once you've laid out your main point, you then provide supporting information and context using a hierarchical structure. Why does the principle choose to go on this road? That way, your audience will understand the core message, making it easier for them to absorb the context and evidence you provide. They are left with memories of your idea because you shared it with clarity and effectiveness using three memorable steps:

- **Step 1: Impact**—You use compelling and unambiguous statements to set the stage for your entire message. When you initiate your discourse with your main recommendation or answer, you instantly engage your audience and present them with the core message. Think of it as a film director captivating viewers from the very beginning with a gripping scene. The objective is to ensure your primary message takes center stage and hooks your listeners' attention because when you avoid it, the audience gets lost amid an abundance of information.

- **Step 2: Thought-Out Strategy**—To give credence to your idea, substantiate your initial statement with several well-considered supporting arguments that will reinforce your central message and offer context or evidence. You should visualize these arguments as narrative elements in a movie, adding depth and maintaining audience engagement. It's essential that your supporting arguments are spot-on and logically organized. Make them what they should be; a summary of the ideas clustered beneath them that establishes credibility with your audience.
- **Step 3: Foster Trust**—In the ultimate phase, strive to reinforce the trust established by providing data and substantiation to endorse your proposed changes or ideas. Ensure the data enhances the credibility of your message and aids in persuading your audience regarding the validity of your recommendations. This can be like the resolution in a movie plot, where all narrative threads are tied up, leaving the audience convinced and content with how the story ends.

THE PYRAMID PRINCIPLE BLUEPRINT

01 THE ANSWER & RECOMMENDATION

The answer is simply a clear, concise, and effective core message that has four components: **Situation** , **Complication** , **Question** , **Answer**

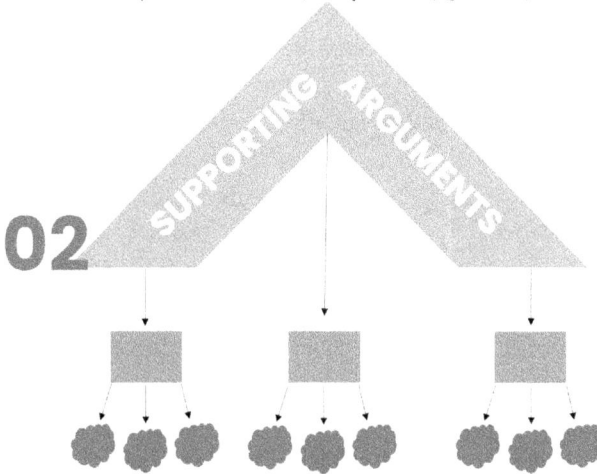

02 SUPPORTING ARGUMENTS

Arguments should then be sorted, grouped, and summarized in a logical way; each single thought should be backed by three supporting arguments.

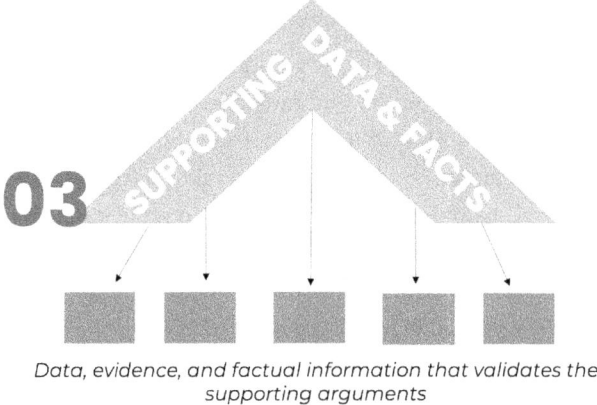

03 SUPPORTING DATA & FACTS

Data, evidence, and factual information that validates the supporting arguments

How to Choose a Vision

Once you adhere to these Pyramid steps, you can guarantee that your message resonates clearly and is not eclipsed by biased perspectives or viewpoints. Believe it or not, biased individuals will always rear their heads when you're getting somewhere with new ideas. You will find them even more interested once your idea spurs visionary thinking. This isn't unusual; all companies, organizations, and workers need a vision to achieve similar goals. So, how can you choose one to add to your plan?

1. **Mention Benefits:** Begin your vision by clearly outlining the benefits that your proposed changes will bring. Your executive summary should be concise, powerful, and barrier-free. It's what the famous Dove brand did in their 'Real Beauty' campaign. They emphasized the benefits of promoting realistic beauty standards in the executive summary. Stating how embracing diversity in beauty leads to increased consumer trust and brand loyalty. This initial step sets the tone for the entire vision, ensuring that it grabs attention and communicates the brand's intentions effectively.

2. **Have Shared Future Vision:** Promote inclusivity and encourage everyone within your organization to contribute to this vision. A shared vision not only aligns with DEI principles but also encourages collaboration and buy-in from various stakeholders.

3. **Align with Core Values:** Identify your company's core values, but also be open to evolving them if needed by seeking input from colleagues. You'll find and understand which values resonate with them and align with the envisioned future. This collaborative approach ensures your vision is firmly rooted in the organization's identity and purpose. Look what Athleta and The Body Shop stand for today; they combine their core values with environmental sustainability, inclusivity, and ethical behavior so customers and employees can enjoy a sense of confidence, respect, and social responsibility all in the world that's passionate about ageless beauty. The message here is what will make women convinced about the brands.

4. **Simplify Your Values:** In a world of information overload, try staying simple. Keep your values human, straightforward, realistic, and easily recallable. Clarity is essential to ensure that your vision is not only understood but also embraced by all employees, regardless of their role or level within the organization. In 2011, When Patagonia, a clothing company, ran a full-page advertisement in The New York Times with a bold headline that read, "Don't Buy This Jacket" on a Black Friday, they had a mission. They were featuring one of their best-selling products, a down jacket. The aim was to explain the environmental impact of the jacket's production, from the resources used to its carbon footprint, so that consumers would consider the environmental consequences of their purchases. The core value here was to show the world that they were a company that stood for integrity by prioritizing the planet over profit. Smart way to convince an audience, wouldn't you say?

5. **Seek New Values:** Building on what already exists is a powerful way to maintain continuity while evolving. Additionally, actively seeking new values that reflect the changing landscape of your organization and the world so you don't seem obsolete in the eyes of your audience is a nice way to stay in the game and make a difference. Don't just collect all inputs because they are available; let them come from a diverse group of team members to ensure that your vision remains fresh, relevant, and up-to-date.

6. **Filter and Refine:** Stitch Fix, co-founded by Katrina Lake, underwent a process of filtering and refining its values to align with its mission of personal styling. They refined values like "Client-Centric" to emphasize their dedication to providing personalized fashion experiences. It's all about prioritizing values that best represent your organization's goals and aspirations and filtering out values that may be less relevant or conflicting. A refined vision with a focused set of values allows for a clear and impactful message that resonates deeply with your team.

Now, armed with your well-thought-out plans and innovative ideas, you're perfectly poised to inspire your audience to embark on crafting a powerful business plan. This plan can take the form of a dynamic spreadsheet or an engaging slideshow, delving into your present circumstances, the hurdles you face, and the ingenious solutions you've conceived. While certain sections may be a work in progress, infusing them with initial data-driven insights is a fantastic way to get started. Consider this as the spark that ignites the flame of motivation, the first step towards creating a comprehensive framework. You can further refine and develop this foundation in the chapters that lie ahead. So, go ahead, and take a look! Your journey to success begins here.

Ensure your strategy remains accessible as forthcoming tactics guide you to fill every facet of your presentation board or slideshow. Now, in the next chapter, uncover the principles of initiation and learn how to rally all aboard the DEI journey to spark up transformative shifts.

4

HOW TO NURTURE A CURIOUS INCEPTION MINDSET TO WELCOME CHANGE

All of us do not have equal talent, but all of us should have an equal
opportunity to develop our talents.
—John F. Kennedy (Kennedy J.F, 1964)

∽

The DEI LightHouse Strategy

Before the world tilted toward the hunger of ensuring an environment that's inclusive and conscious of all, irrespective of human factors, everything was almost sedentary. People appreciate only those they know and don't feel the need to be open to encountering new people, places, or activities. For them, the more was never the merrier; instead, that was a case of chaotic living that caused things to go topsy-turvy. This was the mindset, and it felt good and acceptable, but was it enough?

Of course not. With the dawning of migration and crosscultural interrelations, the DEI became the next best choice to help more work environments experience innovative ideas. At this point, it's widely recognized that implementing training programs and workshops is crucial in fostering a DEI mindset and ensuring organizations stay firmly committed to upholding a culture of diversity and inclusion. In fact, a staggering 92% of business leaders concur that a strategic workforce education initiative should serve as the catalyst for achieving their diversity and inclusion objective (InStride, 2021). This is good, but many more things are involved that bring the DEI LightHouse Strategy initiative to play.

The DEI LightHouse Strategy doesn't just believe in making robust plans and pitching them with style and precision; they are all about accountability and investment.

One of the DEI LightHouse Strategies, "Define Vision, Purpose, and Values," compels employers to set a compelling DEI vision aligned with their broader mission. It entails defining core values centered on fairness, respect, and transparency and actively engaging leadership to garner support. Employee involvement in shaping the vision and values is paramount. Transparent communication, backed by education, ensures that everyone understands the significance of DEI. Measurable goals and accountability mechanisms must be established, alongside a commitment to reviewing and adapting policies. External engagement broadens the scope of impact. A continuous improvement mindset underscores this strategy, as organizations continually aim to foster inclusivity and equity.

For instance, in the case of Lighthouse Corporation, this strategy was implemented by creating a robust DEI vision statement that emphasized the company's commitment to diversity and inclusion. This vision was reinforced by a set of core values, which were integrated into the corporate culture. Leadership buy-in was achieved through targeted workshops, and employees played a pivotal role in refining the vision. Regular training sessions ensured that all staff members were well-informed, and metrics were implemented to assess progress and hold leadership accountable. Lighthouse also actively engaged with external organizations and stakeholders to advance its DEI goals, creating a more inclusive workplace environment over time.

To effectively utilize this strategy, as a leader or a manager, start by defining specific, measurable, and time-bound goals for DEI within your organization. These goals should align with your broader mission and values, ensuring everyone understands the significance of these objectives. Next, make strategic investments in DEI initiatives that support your goals. This may include training programs, mentorship opportunities, or initiatives to promote diversity in hiring and leadership positions. It's essential to allocate resources and budget to these efforts; it's your way of showing commitment to driving change.

Believe it or not, accountability is a crucial component of this strategy. Hold yourself and your leadership team responsible for meeting the established DEI goals. Regularly review progress, collect data, and communicate results transparently to all stakeholders. Engage with external organizations and stakeholders to gain additional insights and promote broader change within your industry. Create a comprehensive DEI plan to ensure everyone in your organization understands, accepts, and embraces these changes. This plan should include strategies for educating employees at all levels, fostering an inclusive culture, and addressing bias and discrimination when they occur. By providing ongoing education and training, you empower your workforce to participate in the transformation process actively.

Additionally, encourage employees to share their visions, goals, and statements related to DEI. This collaborative approach can lead to a more inclusive and diverse workplace, as it incorporates a variety of perspectives and experiences. Furthermore, highlight the benefits of these changes, such as improved employee morale, creativity, and productivity, in your proposal to gain widespread support.

How to Control Biases

This is not to say that you can easily evade certain biases and reservations during your planning because you can't. For most managers and leaders, biases are ingrained in how they strategize, and connect, and becoming more aware and prepared for this takes a lot of steps.

1. **Awareness of Biases:** Always recognizing that the presence of unconscious biases is the foundational step in addressing them, which involves acknowledging that everyone, regardless of their background or intentions, may hold biases. This self-awareness

encourages individuals to examine their beliefs, attitudes, and behaviors critically. It's essential to understand that biases can manifest in various forms, such as racial, gender, age, or cognitive biases.

2. **Unconscious Bias Training:** It's a program that is important in bridging the gap between awareness and action. They provide individuals with the knowledge and tools to identify and manage their biases. Effective training modules delve into the science behind bias, emphasizing that it is a natural part of human cognition. Such programs empower individuals to challenge their biases and make fairer decisions by fostering empathy and understanding.

3. **Unpacking Unconscious Biases:** When it comes to unconscious biases, there is a wide range of stereotypes, prejudices, and discriminatory behaviors. It's vital to delve deeper into these biases to comprehend their effects on individuals and organizations. By examining specific scenarios and real-world examples, you can grasp how biases influence everyday interactions, affecting everything from hiring decisions to employee morale. This deeper understanding serves as a motivator for change.

4. **Organizational Improvement:** Addressing unconscious bias is not solely an individual endeavor but a collective responsibility. Organizations must foster a culture of inclusion and diversity where everyone feels valued and heard. This involves leadership commitment, policies promoting equity, and inclusive recruitment, retention, and advancement practices. Employees at all levels should actively contribute to building an environment free from bias and discrimination.

5. **Efficacy of Training Programs:** Organizations should regularly assess the impact of their unconscious bias training initiatives. This involves tracking changes in attitudes and behaviors and monitoring key metrics related to diversity, equity, and inclusion. Feedback mechanisms, surveys, and follow-up assessments can help refine and improve training programs.

Recall that in sharing details of training and its effectiveness, each form of bias training serves the crucial purpose of addressing specific prejudices and stereotypes, fostering an inclusive work environment, and promoting fairness and equity among all employees. With various bias training programs, organizations can create a more comprehensive approach to tackling unconscious biases and promoting diversity and inclusion.

Trainings Focussed on Bias Control

- **Gender bias training** addresses prejudices and stereotypes related to gender, promoting equality and fair treatment of individuals regardless of gender identity. Being a woman or a man should have no base in determining the execution of any duties as long as it gets done efficiently.
- **Racial bias training** focuses on confronting and mitigating biases related to race and ethnicity. It emphasizes the importance of treating people equitably, irrespective of their racial background. Your ethnicity is a pride you should carry everywhere, whether it shows in how you dress or the speaking phonetics you possess.
- **LGBTQ bias training** aims to create a more inclusive workplace for individuals of diverse sexual orientations and gender identities. You get educated about the challenges faced by LGBTQ+ individuals, which fosters empathy and ensures that the work environment is welcoming and respectful.
- **Age bias training** addresses stereotypes and biases related to age, ensuring that older and younger employees are treated fairly and respectfully. After all, it is said that age is nothing but a number and that there should be no limit to how much a person can deliver in duties. Room is and should always be made for all.
- **Disability bias training** raises awareness about prejudices faced by individuals with disabilities and promotes a more accessible and inclusive work environment.
- **Religious bias training** helps employees recognize and confront biases based on religious beliefs. Here, you learn to

appreciate the importance of accommodating diverse religious practices and not favoring one religious group over another.

- **Lookism bias training** targets biases related to physical appearance, challenging stereotypes that may affect hiring, promotions, or workplace interactions. It encourages a more inclusive perspective by highlighting that individuals should be assessed based on their qualifications and skills rather than their appearance.
- **Lesser-known bias training** covers many biases that may not be as widely recognized as others. These biases can include biases related to socioeconomic status, personality type (e.g., extrovert vs. introvert), and communication style. If you're interested in how upper class a person is before giving room to their ideas or how worthy an organization is to have your ingenious idea, there can be a problem. Also, if someone prefers to stay more reclusive, that shouldn't be an issue of concern; instead, addressing these biases will foster a more inclusive and accepting workplace.

Diversity and Inclusion Trainings

Every training that must be worthwhile and exciting can occur in many ways. The easiest way is to have individuals do a one-on-one interactive online session, allowing swift communication of ideas from anywhere. But that's not all:

- **Unconscious Bias Online Training:** This method has gained popularity due to its scalability and accessibility. In today's digital age, it's a practical way to reach a geographically dispersed workforce. All you need to do is make it interactive, engaging, and tailored to various learning styles, making them essential tools for raising awareness about unconscious biases. However, organizations should complement online training with real-life discussions and applications to ensure the lessons translate into tangible behavior change.
- **Diversity Training Programs:** Encouraging employees to participate in diversity training programs demonstrates a commitment to inclusivity. It's a proactive step that sets the tone

for the organization's culture. When employees see leadership endorsing these programs, they are more likely to engage willingly. You should offer programs to accommodate different learning preferences and address specific diversity and inclusion challenges within the organization so no topic area is displaced.

- **Awareness Training:** If you are the foundation for any meaningful diversity and inclusion initiative, you would understand that awareness training is akin to turning on the lights in a dark room. Without awareness, biases remain hidden, so leaders and managers should view this training as a starting point rather than a final destination. Following up with more targeted training and practical applications of diversity principles is crucial to drive lasting change.

- **Basic Diversity Training:** There is nothing more promising in training than having all participants share a common language of diversity. The vocabulary and understanding of diversity and inclusion concepts align the workforce with the organization's diversity goals. It won't only keep this training engaging and relevant, but it will avoid a one-size-fits-all approach.

- **Skill-Based Diversity Training:** While awareness is vital, skill-based training takes it further by equipping employees with practical skills. Effective communication, conflict resolution, and teamwork in diverse settings are critical skills for the modern workplace. Skill-based training empowers employees to navigate complex situations and contribute positively to diverse teams.

- **Diversity Audit Training:** Diversity audits provide valuable insights into an organization's strengths and weaknesses in the diversity and inclusion arena. You can think of it as an analytic of DEI where, with the data retrieved, training key personnel becomes authenticated and ensures the audit is conducted thoroughly and impartially. It also underscores the organization's commitment to transparency and continuous improvement as attention is given to all loopholes that need covering and smoothening.

- **Intermediate Diversity Training:** Diversity is a multifaceted topic that delves into deeper discussions, exploring intersectionality, privilege, and allyship. Such training encourages participants to think critically about diversity issues and fosters a culture of ongoing learning and growth. With these parameters, you can feel free and open to discuss any area of DEI, especially those that seem ignored and overlooked for fear of sensitivity.
- **Mobile Learning:** Know the power and swiftness at which mobile technology is taking over in providing ease of communication and a practical solution for organizations with remote or globally distributed teams. It aligns with the changing dynamics of work, where flexibility and remote work are becoming increasingly prevalent. Mobile training ensures all employees can access essential diversity training materials regardless of location.

You can see excellent diversity training opportunities, and inclusion isn't left out. However, training demands time and money, and with a reasonable budget, **inclusion training** is another beneficial option with great potential for an action plan for change.

Inclusive training takes on a more educational approach designed to foster a sense of belonging and respect for all individuals, regardless of their background, abilities, or perspectives. **Why does it matter?** Because it creates a workplace environment where employees feel valued and empowered to contribute their best. Inclusive training not only ticks the diversity box; it actively promotes diversity, equity, and inclusion (DEI) as essential organizational values. It boosts workplace morale by creating a culture of respect and collaboration, improving job satisfaction and overall well-being.

What Are the Benefits?

McKinsey & Co. (2023) found that companies with more diverse executive teams are 25–36% more likely to have above-average profitability. This data underscores the business case for inclusive training as much more than morals, but also reaping the tangible benefits of a diverse and inclusive workforce in productivity and retention. Diverse teams bring a more comprehensive range of perspectives and ideas, which can lead to more innovative solutions and better decision-making.

Another benefit is perspective-taking. It's a valuable training module that encourages employees to step into the shoes of their colleagues from diverse backgrounds. It's a powerful empathy-building exercise that fosters understanding and reduces biases. When your mind is too joggled to consider different viewpoints and experiences of other employees besides yourself, empathy and open-mindedness come into play, contributing to a more inclusive workplace. Suggesting such modules for free or low-cost training can be a cost-effective way to enhance diversity and inclusion. For instance, two co-workers, Michelle and Sally, disagree during a team meeting because Sally believes Michelle constantly interrupts her repeatedly during her presentation. Using a perspective-taking exercise, each employee is asked to switch roles and see the situation from the other's point of view.

Guess what happens?

In Michelle's role, Sally realizes the interruption was out of excitement to share her ideas. On the other hand, Michelle understands how frustrating it can be to have someone interrupt during a presentation and recognizes the need to be more mindful of it in the future. Both employees gain empathy for each other's perspectives, leading to improved communication and a more harmonious working relationship.

"I am, but I'm not" is another effective and free training exercise that encourages participants to reflect on their identities and the unique aspects of their personalities. You are prompted to recognize that people are multifaceted, with many dimensions to their identities. This exercise can be eye-opening, helping employees appreciate the complexity of diversity beyond visible characteristics. It fosters a sense of unity by acknowledging our shared humanity and individuality.

Morgan: *"I am an extrovert, but I'm not always the life of the party."*

Shirley: *"I am introverted, but I'm not anti-social; I enjoy deep one-on-one conversations."*

Carlo: *"I am a parent, but I'm not always available outside of work hours."*

Priya: "*I am young, but I'm not inexperienced; I bring fresh ideas to the team.*"

Everyone identifies with a trait and isn't ashamed to make it known so there is an understanding among themselves.

Equity Training

This brings us to the final destination of the journey: equity. As straightforward as it might sound, equity is another initiative that would do well with the help of training that establishes its meaning and how it is a means to an end where DEI is of note. Regarding employment equity online training, you are guaranteed one of the most valuable resources primarily designed for HR professionals and those in leadership positions. If you want to address issues relating to workplace employment equity by making it a comprehensive but straightforward subject, this training is all you need. It includes in-depth modules on understanding employment equity legislation, creating equitable workplace policies, and implementing strategies to achieve a diverse and inclusive workforce. Not to mention the ease at which HR professionals and leaders can access crucial information that is up-to-date with the latest regulations and best practices. It also provides a platform for interactive learning, enabling participants to engage in discussions, ask questions, and share insights with colleagues.

If there is one thing that makes online training worthwhile, it's the convenience to busy employees who need the flexibility to complete the course and also the real-life case studies and practical examples that illustrate the impact of employment equity on organizations. With these scenarios, HR professionals and leaders grasp the significance of DEI in the workplace. When workers know there is no pressure to finish a course because of the first interest in comprehension and application, it enhances their knowledge and skills in employment equity.

This training is an essential resource for all staff members within an organization because it is designed to provide a foundational understanding of employment equity principles and practices. Here, you will find topics such as the legal framework surrounding employment equity, the importance of diversity in the workplace, and strategies for promoting equity and inclusion.

Another key benefit of the training is its accessibility to all employees, regardless of their role or level within the organization. You get to appreciate the organization's commitment to creating an equitable workplace and its role in supporting these efforts, thereby leaving room for questions and concerns relating to DEI to be adequately responded to in the most professional fashion. Organizations can create a shared understanding of the value of diversity and inclusion by equipping staff with basic employment equity knowledge. This, in turn, contributes to a more harmonious and productive workplace. Basic training can also serve as a foundation for more specialized equity training for HR professionals and leadership.

Checklist of Key Employment Equity Facts

Designing a brief checklist of key employment equity facts helps educate colleagues and garner their support for equity initiatives. When you have details like the purpose of employment equity, its legal framework, and its role in promoting fairness and justice in the workplace, employees will be clear as to how passionate the organization is about an equitable workforce.

Note that the purpose of employment equity is threefold:

1. To redress past discrimination
2. To promote equal opportunities for all
3. To eliminate employment barriers that perpetuate inequality

By sharing this fundamental understanding, organizations can emphasize their commitment to social justice and inclusivity. With a checklist, employees can now demystify employment equity, where the topical engagement is no longer restricted but open to dialogues and reviews. It can be a conversation starter that encourages employees to ask questions, seek clarification, and actively participate in equity-related initiatives within the organization.

Remember that establishing a strong groundwork for transformation and initiation will never be easy but stimulates a more inclusive and harmonious workplace across all dimensions. While it might entail some expenses, it stands as an indispensable component of your proposal or concrete reforms. Now, you can go a step ahead in creating a unique checklist and, while at it, look into how vital it is to use these pragmatic approaches for seamlessly integrating DEI principles into your day-to-day workplace operations. Chapter five has so much more to tell you.

YOUR FEEDBACK IS VALUED!!

You're halfway through "Impactful Inclusive Leadership," and I'd love to hear your thoughts. Your feedback not only helps me but also fellow leaders seeking valuable insights.

It's simple to leave a review on Amazon: Visit the book's Amazon 'Write a customer review' page by clicking the link or scanning the code below.

By sharing your experience, you're contributing to a community of leaders helping each other thrive. Your words of wisdom can inspire and guide them, making their journey smoother and more fulfilling.

Your insights matter – thank you for being part of my journey!

5

THE ACT OF MARRYING CULTURAL DIFFERENCES AND IDEAS

Diversity is the art of thinking independently together.
—Malcolm Forbes (Teambuilding, 2022)

∾

The Lighthouse Impact

Have you ever considered the remarkable advantages of diversity in the workplace once you begin to actualize your plans? It's a powerful catalyst for success. As diverse companies are 70% more likely to seize new market opportunities (Hewitt et al., 2013), you will also find that diverse teams are 87% more inclined to make decisions that not only benefit the company but also enrich the lives of everyone involved (Sucich K., 2022). To make headway to seeing these benefits come to life, you must by now identify the journey so far in instilling the DEI strategy.

In the Lighthouse model introduced in an earlier chapter, what outcomes were derived from applying that approach? Have you been able to envision the right practical tools and strategies that will make DEI much more than a culture? With answers to these questions, you will feel ready to enter the fourth stage of the DEI Lighthouse framework.

It's a framework that highlights the remarkable success in the realm of DEI achieved in 2023. The Lighthouse organizations have set the standard by not only recognizing DEI as a priority but also by actively designing innovative solutions to address DEI challenges within their workplaces. A standout example of their impactful initiatives is the implementation of a comprehensive leadership development program in India. This was one of the many testament to their commitment to fostering diversity and inclusion in the workplace, particularly in a region where such efforts are crucial. Beyond geographical boundaries, Lighthouse has shown its desire for global engagement, thereby underscoring the universality of DEI's importance. So, as you progress in developing your plan, recognize especially the insights gained from these leading organizations, as they can serve as a solid foundation for your own DEI proposal.

Best Strategies to Ensure DEI

Imagine you hold a powerful position of making life-changing decisions for your company in hiring, firing, and promoting; what would be the best strategies to ensure DEI plays its part in the outcomes of your resolutions?

1. **Recruitment Process Overhaul:** Conventional recruitment approaches may unintentionally exhibit bias towards particular groups. In such moments, leaders should contemplate a comprehensive reform of these processes to ensure equity and inclusiveness. Embracing novel strategies and methodologies can broaden the talent spectrum, thus enhancing diversity in the pool of potential candidates. No need for the old ways of being straight jacket when you can give room for broader perspectives by being open and less stereotyped.

2. **Welcome Ideas:** Fostering diversity requires leaders to inspire employees to value different viewpoints and backgrounds. Implementing training initiatives, such as exercises that encourage considering other perspectives, can aid employees in

recognizing the constraints of their ideas and becoming more receptive to the ideas of others. In fact, you might consider combining ideas to create a holistic perspective that will meet the company's needs extensively.

3. **Retention Measures for Diverse Talent:** Potent recruitment and advancement strategies should be supplemented with robust retention measures. If you don't feel like you're growing, then the work can never seem worth your time and years. Progression goes beyond high pay but a rising career, and leaders should guarantee the celebration and dissemination of success stories from individuals of diverse backgrounds to motivate others. When you encounter top executives from all backgrounds who rose through the ranks in wealth and career, it spurs you for job success.

4. **Acknowledge Cultural differences:** There cannot be a more joyous time to appreciate culture and rejoice in disparities within the workplace than now. Not only have cultural differences nurtured a feeling of belonging and mutual esteem among employees, but it has also coopted a sense of festivities in various ways. Organizations now introduce the observance of cultural occasions and disseminate accomplishments and triumphs from diverse employees. They even go the length of establishing a long trail of the success journey of these employees to show how their differences never stopped their successes. An inspiration to all and a backbone to the future of DEI strategies.

5. **Diversify Teams:** Diversity should extend beyond just entry-level personnel and encompass teams engaged in various projects and endeavors. The selection of employees from diverse age groups, racial backgrounds, and genders for project teams serves as a safeguard against the domination of discussions by a single, uniform perspective. When you go to watch the Super Bowl, there are no age limits to who enjoys the game; it's a combination of all, and that's what DEI aims to achieve long term.

6. **Who is your Diversity Expert?** Leaders should contemplate the recruitment of a Chief Inclusion Officer or an adept specialist

tasked with ongoing evaluation of the organization's diversity endeavors. With them on board, updates on the highs and lows of DEI are always brought forward for assessment and next steps. You bring professionals who are proficient in conducting an exhaustive analysis of diversity within the organization, and you are sure to get invaluable, data-centric insight to guide decision-making. Can you picture having someone like Dr. Johnnetta B. Cole, former president of Spelman College and Bennett College and renowned diversity expert on the organizational board of directors? Her work in academia and beyond has contributed significantly to promoting diversity and inclusion, so think how her input will leave an indelible mark on the company's DEI transformation system. It's an approach that can't be overlooked by any leader who wants to see their DEI practice tools make meaning.

7. **Check Leadership Diversity:** Leaders should assess the diversity within their leadership teams. Is there adequate representation from various demographic groups? These questions help evaluate the system, identify gaps in diversity, and inform the need for further recruitment efforts in alignment with equity-focused strategies. It's a big step toward creating an inclusive culture. When you feel like you're working with a team of executives who are more male than female or more 40+ than their late 20s, it can be the best time to bring in a diversity expert to level the ground and set the stage for a profiting DEI strategy.

8. **Empower Multilingual Workforce:** Once you embrace a multilingual workforce, rest assured that your organization will have employees eager to speak multiple languages and share discussions on cultural disparities to foster better relationships and an inclusive environment. A place where language barriers are reduced, and individuals from diverse linguistic backgrounds feel valued, heard, and appreciated because they bring something unique and possibly unfamiliar to the floor. If you're smart about the benefits of DEI, you can use this approach to create culturally sensitive marketing campaigns where employees connect with customers from diverse

linguistic backgrounds. As a result, they will expand the company's market reach and increase customer loyalty. It's called thinking out of the box.

9. **Enforce Anti-Discriminatory Policies:** The implementation and strict enforcement of anti-discriminatory policies are essential in creating an inclusive environment. Policies that will set the tone for respecting individual differences and promoting equality. They create a sense of fairness and establish a foundation for an inclusive culture. No one will experience the look of snivelry or riddle knowing that there are laws governing against such.

10. **Engage Focus Groups:** The use of focus groups and gatherings of like-minded individuals can be a valuable strategy for gaining insights and facilitating open, honest discussions on diversity and inclusion topics. Focus groups provide a platform for employees to share their experiences, perspectives, and suggestions for improvement, enhancing understanding and promoting inclusion. It's like having college students discussing with their faculty heads issues of bullying caused by discrimination and having the victims share their fears and the way forward. There can't be a more constructive conversation than this, as it will give the group a chance to see DEI with a keener eye.

Focus Groups

The best part about the focus group is that it's open to all, young and old, employees and employers. Everyone has the unique opportunity to embrace DEI in the workplace in many ways. It can be:

- **Celebrate Cultural Diversity:** Start by embracing traditions and encouraging employees to share their culture, festivals, and practices. Celebrate these diverse occasions within the workplace to foster inclusivity and understanding. There can be special ways to mark occasions through cultural food feasts and dances, allowing some employees to mark their international days in their own ways, possibly by wearing their native wears and more. You can also offer cultural awareness and sensitivity training to educate employees about different cultures and traditions, promoting respect, curiosity, and a stronger mutual and working relationship. Also, leaders might contemplate providing employees with the option to choose a specific number of holidays, even if the company doesn't officially recognize them. This allows them to take time off to celebrate their cultural observances, such as Yom Kippur, Diwali, and others, while still receiving personal paid leave.
- **Promote Inclusive Communication:** If you have the discipline of active listening, it can make people appreciate your sense of empathy and eagerness to help others and give room for all. This is what inclusion is all about in the workplace. In meetings and discussions, ensure everyone's voice is heard before decisions are made. There is the confidence it gives employees knowing they're free to express their likes and dislikes, and it won't reflect on their position or employer's opinion of them. Alternatively, for those who are shy or uncomfortable, establish anonymous feedback mechanisms so they can express their opinions without fear of retribution, encouraging open dialogue.
- **Stimulate Innovative Thinking:** When a team is allowed to think more diversely by including individuals with various perspectives, experiences, and backgrounds, you will find that the problem-solving approach will be less one-track-minded

and more encompassing. The more avenues there are for workshops on creativity and innovation, the greater the chances of innovative thinking and unique insights coming to the table.

- **Personalizing Connections:** Employees should be encouraged to have connective conversations with their employers and colleagues on a personal level. A sense of belonging and camaraderie through mentoring circles is always a welcome way to strengthen growth-oriented conversations that will let employees know there is a place to get valuable support and meaningful connections.

- **Cross-Cultural Collaborations:** With global exchange programs or overseas assignments where employees use communication platforms like Teams, Slack, and Webex to share business ideas and discuss the latest global changes, there can be a diverse work environment culture even from a mile away. Such experiences broaden perspectives and enhance global understanding of issues as these employees speak from their encounters with the economic situation within their confines all under an organization. If you have seen journalists share conference meetings about global issues and the approach toward broadcast, that is a reflection of DEI at work in the workplace.

- Inclusive Hiring Practices: Begin by unleashing the power of Diverse Talent from the get-go of recruitment. Don't just check boxes to show you have met hiring requirements, recognizing the importance and value of having diverse hands on board. Candidates' different life experiences can spark innovation, creativity, and unique problem-solving. So, when you revamp your hiring practices to welcome diversity, you know you're opening the door to a world of possibilities.

- **Respectful Communication:** There is a saying that respect is reciprocal, and it is so true. Once there is equal and respectful dialogue every now and again, it's the cornerstone of any inclusive workplace. It's not just about what you say but how you say it. Being mindful of how your words and actions affect others, regardless of their background, shows you are sensitive to people's feelings and demeanor. When you and the colleague next to you decide to contribute equally and respectfully to conversations, the workplace becomes a more harmonious and productive environment.

- **Leverage Employee Resource Groups:** By now, you should be familiar with the benefits of Unity and Growth within ERGs and how they offer a unique space for connection and learning. These groups are instrumental in broadening engagements and expression to eye-opening experiences, helping everyone appreciate colleagues' challenges, triumphs, and aspirations from various backgrounds. It's a chance to stand together and work toward shared goals.

- **Learning and Expanding Diversity Horizons:** Personal growth through education is a journey. When you dedicate time to learning about different cultures, traditions, and perspectives, you enrich your life and ability to support and appreciate diversity. It's a commitment to lifelong learning that benefits both individuals and the workplace. You will learn to meet people halfway whenever they are slow to comprehend due to language or act in a certain way due to cultural background. Nothing will come as a surprise or discomfort. Instead, you become more accommodating in a diverse workplace, knowing there is something unique about everyone.

- **Be the Change You Wish to See:** Once you treat others as you want to be treated, this golden rule becomes the fundamental principle for which you promote DEI as an activist and an employee. Beyond being a workplace practice, it should be a way of life where we set the tone for an inclusive and respectful environment. It's a personal commitment to be the change we wish to see in the world, one interaction at a time.

Activities to Promote DEI in the Workplace

You will find a range of activities that not only promote diverse thinking and acceptance in the workplace but also infuse a sense of fun and engagement into the process. Nothing too serious, just some exercises designed to create a personal connection among colleagues by introducing a more inclusive and understanding work environment. Once you explore these activities, you'll discover how each one can contribute to a workplace that values diversity and celebrates differences while ensuring that everyone's voice is heard and appreciated.

Here is how you can get started:

Activity 1: The Shape of Others

Here, develop empathy by understanding the factors that have shaped your colleagues' perspectives over the years to this point. Everyone shares a personal object or memento that represents a significant event or aspect of their background. This highlights the unique qualities that each person brings to the team.

Instructions

- Create small groups of colleagues, possibly five or ten each.
- Get each participant to share the key life experiences and influences that have shaped their beliefs and viewpoints. Could be cultural background, upbringing, personal experiences, or role models.
- Encourage active listening, and questions and answers sessions to understand each person's unique journey better.
- Afterward, reconvene as a larger group and discuss the eye-opening moments and insights gained from this activity.

Activity 2: The Rose and the Thorn Exchange

Let employees share successes and struggles, a combination of the positive and negative aspects of their professional or personal lives. It will build trust and understanding and deepen empathy and solidarity.

Instructions

- Begin by sitting in a circle and taking turns sharing both a "rose" (a personal or professional success) and a "thorn" (a challenge or adversity) you've faced.
- Celebrate achievements spoken of and create empathy and understanding for the obstacles others may have encountered.

- Above all, focus on active listening and providing support to colleagues sharing their stories. There could be teary moments, and it's a sign that progress is being made and people are beginning to get intentional about honest reveals.

Activity 3: Confronting Stereotypes

Challenge and deconstruct stereotypes by opening a discourse on biases. There is no shame in discussing what mindset you have about a certain person's ideology and having it demystified in open dialogues. Ever heard of "Inclusion Starts With I"? Accenture, a professional services company, developed this program for employees so they could take a self-assessment to explore their own biases and learn how to promote a more inclusive workplace. This activity has been instrumental in sustaining DEI and debunking prejudices that can be found in the workplace.

Instructions

- Prepare a list of common stereotypes or biases related to different groups or backgrounds. What do you think about a certain mode of dressing or eating of a particular culture and lay it on the table for discussion?
- With that stereotype stated, in pairs or small groups, participants take turns drawing each stereotype from a hat and discussing their personal experiences or insights related to that stereotype. Where have they witnessed it or been confronted concerning it?
- Someone from the group who belongs to the school of thought surrounding that stereotype can give clarity about it. Then, to encourage open dialogue about the impact of stereotypes and how they can be harmful, the stereotype is presented with a better understanding from an authentic source.
- It's all with the goal of debunking myths and empowering participants to challenge stereotypes when they encounter them rather than using them for office gossip and poor judgment.

Activity 4: The Shoe Swap

When you put yourself in someone else's shoes, you learn empathy in the most personal way, and that is the whole idea behind this exercise. Google performed this exercise once, where they had colleagues switch roles for a period of time just so everyone could get a feel of what working in another department was like. Everyone got a taste of their coworkers' workspace, the joys, and pains, and there was more appreciation among them. The mode of making it worthwhile can be by:

Instructions

- First, ask participants to pair up with a colleague from a different background or perspective, and it should be someone they are unfamiliar with and whose departmental responsibilities are alien to them. It creates room for curiosity and excitement.
- Then, the show switching begins with their partner for a set period. Each person attempts to experience the world from their partner's perspective and encounters with clients, leaders, and coworkers.
- Afterward, the period elapses, and partners discuss their experiences, what they learned, and how it felt to walk in someone else's shoes, especially if they believed their partner's responsibilities were a walk in the park. At this point, there will be an opinion change and an appreciation of what everyone does in the workplace, no matter how little.

Activity 5: Bias Awareness

The impact of bias in the workplace will continually be treated with kid gloves unless more awareness programs are introduced concerning it and how to streamline it best. More exposure to bias and discrimination can be a great start, and it doesn't always need to feel serious or uptight. It can be in the form of games and activities involving bias and diversity. By playing out these scenarios, employees gain a deeper understanding of how to promote inclusivity in the workplace.

Instructions

- Share thought-provoking articles, videos, or stories about diversity and inclusion with your colleagues.
- Let employees reflect on the content and its implications so they know how much damage can be caused by bias and how impactful DEI can be to dispel these negatives.
- Host a group discussion where everyone shares their thoughts, insights, and any actions they plan to take after gaining new perspectives. What they would like to do differently moving forward would be a great way to start.

If you really want to feel at home with diversity at play, see it as a gateway to boundless innovations and unbridled creativity. A way of unlocking a world of untapped potential and unique viewpoints where you not only accept but celebrate the differences, recognizing that each person brings their own set of experiences and insights to the table. It's these diverse thoughts and talents that have the power to elevate your organization to new heights. But, it takes more than mere acceptance; you must also actively work on creating an equitable environment. Equity isn't just a buzzword; it's the foundation for a fair and just workplace. When everyone is given equal opportunities and support, this, in turn, fuels collaboration, and overall job satisfaction. Your plan's success hinges on these interconnected principles of DEI working together harmoniously. So, embark on this journey of transformation, where diverse thinking and equitable practices become the cornerstones of your organization's success.

6

INVITE SKILLS, INNOVATION, AND ACHIEVEMENT

Too many of us still believe our differences define us.
—John Lewis (Teambuilding, 2022)

∾

The Opportunistic Equity Method

I t's obvious to see the fruitfulness of DEI so far and the lagging effect for organizations who have taken it trivially over the years. Hope is not lost, and adding to these findings, there has been an opportunistic equity strategy where equal chances are offered to employees seeking to rise in their careers and gain earned promotions. It's why equity isn't just another strategy to encourage commitment and reward for hard work; it's a means to reveal how there should be a level playing ground for all employees.

In 2019, the National Center for Education Statistics showed a significant disparity in access to training programs among racial and ethnic groups. African Americans and Hispanics were revealed to be more likely to enroll in such programs, which may stem from the challenges they face due to lower graduation rates and limited opportunities. The statistics underscore education's pivotal role in shaping future earning potential, as a Bachelor's degree can translate to an additional $400,000 in lifetime earnings. This stark economic reality serves as a compelling motivator for individuals from minority groups to advocate for equitable access to education and career advancement opportunities. It clearly indicates that underrepresented communities increasingly recognize the importance of standing up for their rights and demanding more inclusive and equitable workplaces and educational environments (Instride, 2021).

So, what really constitutes the essence of equity in the workplace? Is it just about having everyone get fair-share in everything as long as they have earned it? It could be, or there is so much more to it that requires a deeper outlook before proper implementation, considering you have a plan that is passing through stages of the DEI Lighthouse Framework. There has to be adequate context to the idea as you proceed, and it starts with offering clarity to what employment equity signifies.

The Fourth DEI Lighthouse Framework emphasizes the importance of actively designing solutions that will stand the test of time. Organizations need to move beyond superficial diversity efforts and work on structural changes, and this involves ensuring that all employees, regardless of their background, have equal opportunities to thrive within the organization. As a leader, rethink recruitment, promotions, and workplace culture. Ask questions about what's going wrong with the system and seek opinions to help mitigate whatever is hampering the smooth sail of DEI, and while you're at it, be sure you truly understand all about employment equity.

When it comes to employment equity, you must look at it beyond being discrimination but, as a tool to address systemic imbalances. Cases where some groups have historically faced more barriers than others in terms of access to career growth, possibly because of their color, personality, orientation, and more. You might have been forced to make tough choices because you didn't get the kind of opportunities others received. Such disparities are why these initiatives aim to level the playing field and provide everyone with a fair shot at success.

But first, as you strive to engage any plan, recognize that it's vital to distinguish between employment equity and discrimination. Employment equity is the antithesis of discrimination because while it promotes fairness and equal opportunities, discrimination perpetuates inequities and awakens an awareness of color, religion, status, and more. Once you can differentiate both adequately, you will give sound advocacy for more equitable plans that involve a proactive approach to fostering inclusion. A plan that goes beyond paperwork but reveals an honest approach with genuine commitment and implementation to take actionable steps from the organization's leadership to the employees concerned.

You need to see it to believe it. That's what implementation involves, beginning with creating a culture where everyone feels valued and has an equal chance to contribute their best. Collective ongoing effort within the organization becomes part and parcel of the mission and vision until it runs deep in the company's DNA. Achieving the implementation process which can be done by Human Resources or senior executives takes convincing employees of the benefits of having and building an equitable system for the now and the future.

Benefits of Equity

- **Safe Environment:** The enormous safety employees attain knowing their promotion and their background or identity does not determine career advancement is the first step to making a successful entry for implementing employment equity. You put your best foot forward to work because you feel valued and accepted without judgment.
- **Promoting Innovation and Creativity:** When people from different cultures and orientations come together to work and share ideas, there is a quality of work that comes out of that combination that is exceptional because it's a source beyond a regular path. Like a meal with different ingredients and spices, this is a mix that spurs outstanding innovations and inclusivity.
- **Enabling Opportunity for Youths:** Young people, as well as minorities, with the help of employment equity, begin to see the opportunities that exist for everyone, regardless of their background. Suppose they believed their passion for success was a pipe dream because of the issue of discrimination. In that

case, it gets dispelled as the representation of employment equity is critical in inspiring and empowering underrepresented groups to pursue their aspirations and be rest assured of having equal opportunities.

- **Increases Trust and Collaboration:** If there is one thing a diverse workforce attracts with the right framework for equity, it is trust among employees. Once they see that their organization values and respects differences, the trust enhances collaboration because employees, as diverse teams as they have become, now have a deeper understanding of each other, leading to improved teamwork and problem-solving.

- **Better Retention Plan:** DEI principles create a sense of belonging for employees from underrepresented communities. It is vital to attract, retain, and promote diverse talent in the system. Employees who see your commitment to their satisfaction and consistent loyalty through adequate equity will give them all to ensure the organization moves to greater heights. That way, growth and progress are all around.

- **Uniquely Tailored Plan:** Every organization's employment equity plan is tailored to specific needs and circumstances. There is no one-size-fits-all solution, and companies must design strategies that align with their goals, culture, and existing diversity landscape as it spurs creativity. Based on the brand, an approach could work better for one and not the other. Google and Gucci can never have similar employment equity plans. Although these brands aim to serve the public, they represent two industries and focus on different missions and visions.

- **Tracking, Monitoring, and Revision:** Employment equity requires ongoing monitoring and revision to make it count. Data-driven assessments help organizations identify areas that need improvement, allowing them to adjust their strategies for more effective equity initiatives. No need to fret if the figures don't look great because they fluctuate depending on time, trends, and feedback as the implementation progresses.

As time elapses, the benefits of equity in employment show itself as a non-negotiable necessity that all leaders embrace and aim for to make employees hunger to be part of any workspace. All HR and executives must take extra steps in fashioning out ways to make a success out of convincing employees that their unique skills, talents, and achievements aren't only appreciated but are valued and respected.

The goal is to be open to every possibility by:

1. **Creating Room:** Create an inclusive environment that accommodates various health conditions and disabilities, whether the blind, autistic, or aged. Knowing blind people might require braille to enable their reading or hard-of-hearing individuals some form of hearing aid, make all necessary adjustments to the workspace. You can have assistive technologies and offer flexible work arrangements to ensure all employees perform at their best. Nothing should make employees feel depressed to executive their jobs and feel as involved as everyone else.

2. **Wage Equity:** Pay equity is a fundamental aspect of DEI, and when there is a regular review and adjustment to wages, employees are compensated fairly based on their skills, experience, and job responsibilities. No favoritism but an address to any wage gaps that may exist among different demographic groups.

3. **Wage Transparency:** Promote wage transparency in your organization. Ensure that employees understand the criteria used for determining their compensation. Transparent pay structures align with the principle of equal pay for equal work and play a crucial role in addressing historical pay disparities based on gender, race, or age. By making salary information accessible, organizations build trust among their workforce, boosting morale and employee confidence in the fairness of the compensation system. Also, with it, you can motivate employees to enhance their performance and skills, knowing how their pay is determined. Additionally, it ensures compliance with legal requirements related to pay gaps and contributes to attracting a diverse and inclusive talent pool. Ultimately, wage transparency is a powerful tool for promoting fairness, reducing bias, and fostering a workplace environment where every

individual's contributions are recognized and compensated justly.

4. **Equity Awareness Structure:** You can create a workplace culture that values equity and shows it by educating employees about the importance of equity and inclusion. Open dialogues about equity-related issues, workshops, and providing resources to help employees understand their rights and responsibilities will raise a continual assessment of the effectiveness of all things equity, from awareness to initiatives. So, along with these programs, you regularly monitor and evaluate workplace equity through surveys, feedback mechanisms, and key performance indicators. The data becomes useful for making data-driven decisions about the right awareness initiative and so much more to identify areas for improvement.

5. **Equity Goals:** Transparency in setting and sharing equity goals demonstrates a commitment to a fair and inclusive workplace. You can have clear and shared goals, thereby becoming a rallying point for all employees so everyone has a sense of shared responsibility. It encourages everyone to contribute to these objectives, and with regular assessment and adaptation, the organization will learn and grow in its equity journey.

6. **Team Empowerment:** Diverse teams are not just about optics; they're dynamic engines for creativity and innovation. My perspective emphasizes that when you prioritize diverse leadership and encourage varied voices at all levels, you invite a range of perspectives that can lead to novel solutions. This diversity isn't just a checkbox but a catalyst for staying competitive in a rapidly evolving global landscape.

7. **Reforming Hiring Practices:** Rethinking hiring practices to reflect equitable policies isn't just about compliance but fundamental fairness. It's a shift that allows you to showcase your organization's commitment to merit-based hiring. By focusing on skills and qualifications, you ensure that candidates are selected based on their ability to excel in their roles, creating a more capable and diverse workforce.

8. **Involving Online Presence:** Your website is often the first interaction potential employees have with your organization. As

a leader, use it to highlight your diversity and inclusion initiatives. It communicates that your workplace is not just a collection of employees striving for company success but a vibrant community where diversity is celebrated. This makes your organization attractive to candidates who value equity.

9. **Inclusive Onboarding:** Onboarding goes beyond the logistical processes; it's the first exposure a new employee has to your workplace culture. So when you want to entice a new hire by convincing them through an inclusive onboarding process, it sends a clear message that your organization values every individual's unique skills and talents and is eager to create an environment where all employees can thrive, irrespective of their background.

Activities to Promote Equity in the Workplace

To promote equity and encourage acceptance, understanding, and implementation of diversity and inclusion in the workplace, engaging activities can be organized. As a leader and an executive, you can spring up the best ideas to spur DEI in the workplace and surprise your employees.

Activity 1: Virtual Travels Details

Virtual travels can be enhanced by dedicating specific sessions to regions or countries with unique workplace cultures. Include guided discussions after each session to reflect on how these cultural insights can be applied to build an inclusive work environment. All you have to do is encourage team members to share personal experiences related to the featured culture, reinforcing the importance of understanding and appreciating diversity.

Activity 2: Spot the Brand to Support Details

This activity can go beyond brand recognition. Organize follow-up sessions where team members share their experiences with products from diverse brands. Discuss how supporting these brands positively impacts the economy and the employment of underrepresented groups.

Go above and beyond by inviting entrepreneurs from these brands to share their journeys, providing a deeper understanding of the challenges they face, and making employees understand that: "Hey it's not as bad as people make it out to be."

Activity 3: Real-Life Storytelling Details

To make real-life storytelling more impactful, encourage participants to highlight moments of growth and transformation regarding their perceptions of diversity and inclusion. These stories can serve as catalysts for organizational change, inspiring others to rethink their perspectives and biases, whether right or wrong, while considering having a trained facilitator to ensure these conversations remain respectful, constructive, and valuable to all parties.

Activity 4: Differences Aside Details

Provide resources such as articles, books, or documentaries in advance that focus on various aspects of DEI. Encourage participants to engage with these materials and come prepared to discuss their key takeaways. Create a welcoming environment where participants can ask questions and seek clarification about issues they may not fully understand or turn it into a game where somehow fun is created so the topic doesn't seem uptight or create a kind of nervous tension.

Activity 5: Office Potluck Details

To add depth to the office potluck, encourage participants to bring food and share stories or traditions related to the dishes they bring. Imagine the fun of having a variety of foods brought to the table; it spices up the networking occasion. This personal touch helps team members connect on a deeper level and appreciate the cultural significance of the food. Consider incorporating a rotation system so each team member can host a potluck and share their heritage. Such an organization will be the envy of many growing companies once they observe and notice the exchange of respect, harmony, and connection employees have with each other and their employers. The environment will ooze with DEI as an achievement and a way of life.

Clearly, it shows that your differences don't define you. Instead, they might be your Pandora's box. So, embrace them, welcome the changes at work, or incorporate your plan as a leader. At the same time the focus remains, as always, on establishing ways of bringing inclusion to the workplace.

7

BOLD INCLUSION—THE BEGINNING OF VALUE, RESPECT, AND PRICELESS TEAMWORK

Diversity is a mix, and inclusion is making the mix work.
—Andres Tapia (Teambuilding, 2022)

∽

Climbing the Fourth Step

B y now, you already know that diversity and inclusion are what make the workplace a place to thrive. Glassdoor (2021) reveals that among job candidates, roughly two-thirds, or roughly 67%, express a strong preference for organizations that boast a diverse workforce. This preference highlights the growing importance of workplace diversity in the eyes of potential employees.

Furthermore, a striking 74% of millennial employees firmly believe that their respective organizations demonstrate greater levels of innovation when they cultivate a culture of inclusion. This sentiment underscores the critical link between diversity and innovation, emphasizing that companies embracing a wide range of perspectives tend to excel in innovative thinking. Intriguingly, almost half of millennials, specifically 47%, actively factor in a company's commitment to diversity and inclusion when evaluating potential employers. This statistic illustrates that a significant portion of the workforce, particularly the millennial generation, is making a conscious effort to align their career choices with organizations that share their values and prioritize diversity and inclusion (Deloitte, 2023).

There is no other way to say it: DEI is the future of successful workplaces, and now that we are at the fourth step of the Lighthouse Framework, the final stage to make a difference. It is time to uncover the contexts that reveal practical daily changes that can be achieved using DEI starting with defining inclusion from a more personable perspective.

Inclusion extends beyond just creating a sense of belonging at work. It involves nurturing an environment where diversity isn't just tolerated but celebrated. When it comes to inclusive organizations, it's about actively investing in policies and practices that ensure people from all backgrounds feel respected, valued, and empowered to contribute their unique talents. Such environments foster innovation, as people are more likely to share diverse perspectives, resulting in creative problem-solving metrics because no one's ideas are shut down. Now, there are several ways in which an inclusive organization can sustain its vision permanently:

- **Ground Up:** Building inclusion from the ground up is the way to go, where individuals at all levels of an organization play important roles in driving change beyond the responsibility of senior management. Frontline employees, middle managers, and executives, all with their unique perspectives and power, make a workplace more inclusive through collaboration; a multi-level approach is often more effective than top-down strategies.
- **Integration of Inclusive Practices:** In all daily routines, inclusive practices should become second nature beyond policy documents and training sessions. This means inclusivity becomes a part of the cultural DNA of the organization, ingrained in the day-to-day activities, thereby making it more likely to be sustained.

- **Voice for All:** Giving every individual a voice doesn't just mean providing a platform for speaking out; it's about actively listening, valuing, and acting on those voices. Inclusive organizations not only encourage feedback but also demonstrate that they take it seriously, leading to greater engagement and trust among employees.

- **Uniqueness and Belonging:** Acknowledging uniqueness and fostering belonging requires a proactive approach to valuing differences, such as background, experiences, and perspectives. They make sure every employee feels that their distinct qualities contribute to the organization's success, fostering a deep sense of belonging.

- **Consistent Recognition:** Recognizing and celebrating the uniqueness of each employee is not a one-time event. Inclusive organizations continually affirm the value of diversity. This recognition isn't just about big gestures; it can happen through daily interactions, feedback, and acknowledgment of contributions, no matter how small.

- **Learning and Development:** In an inclusive environment, learning and development are tailored to individual needs and aspirations. It's not just about generic training; it's about providing opportunities for growth that are relevant and meaningful to each employee, ensuring their potential is fully realized.

- **Collaboration:** This is about teamwork, diversity of thought, and harnessing the power of varied perspectives to drive innovation and solve complex challenges. Collaborative efforts are highly valued and encouraged, driving productivity and creativity.

- **Resource Accessibility:** Ensuring employees have access to necessary resources means addressing potential barriers, whether physical, technological, or cultural. An inclusive workplace actively seeks to remove these barriers to create an environment where all can thrive.

- **Intrinsic Motivation:** Cultivate a culture where employees feel intrinsically motivated to contribute tirelessly to the growth of an organization. They are aligned with the organization's mission and values, which, in turn, fosters a strong sense of belonging and engagement.

- **Transparency and Support:** Transparency extends to sharing information about the organization's DEI initiatives and progress. Support means not only offering resources but also introducing a culture where employees feel comfortable seeking assistance and mentorship, leading to personal and professional growth.

No doubt, with all these in place, Inclusion benefits organizations by improving employee morale, driving creativity and innovation, and increasing productivity. For workers, it offers the opportunity to work in an environment where they can thrive and achieve their potential, contributing to a more fulfilling and successful career.

Steps to Imbibe Inclusion in the Workplace

Above all, knowing the potential inclusion brings to the table makes it paramount for individuals to seek ways to imbibe the rule of inclusion as a character in the workplace. It starts by taking these steps:

- **Embrace Your Authenticity in the Workplace:** Being authentic in the workplace not only fosters a more inclusive environment but also enhances your well-being. When you are genuine, you're more likely to connect with your colleagues on a personal level, which can lead to better teamwork and collaboration. Make yourself felt and understood through your ideas, and your team members will see you as a colleague who represents authenticity.
- **Practice Thoughtful Communication:** Thoughtful communication is a cornerstone of effective workplace interactions. It not only helps prevent misunderstandings but also promotes a culture of respect and consideration. Taking a moment to reflect on your words can save you from unintentional offense and help you convey your thoughts more clearly. When you send a message in a group chat, be mindful of your tone and diction as well as the emojis used so you don't

create doubt as to your character due to statements made
casually.

- **Connect Through Personal Experiences:** Sharing your own
experiences can be a powerful tool for building empathy and
understanding among your colleagues. It helps humanize the
workplace, making it easier for others to relate to you and your
perspectives, which in turn encourages a more inclusive
atmosphere.

- **Respect by Using Correct Pronouns:** Using correct pronouns is
a sign of respect for your colleagues' identities. It not only
ensures that they feel acknowledged and valued but also sets an
example for others, creating an inclusive space for everyone.

- **Champion Diversity and Differences:** Celebrating diversity in
the workplace isn't just the right thing to do; it's also a source of
strength. Differences in perspectives, backgrounds, and
experiences can lead to more innovative solutions and richer
collaboration. Supporting these differences contributes to a
more vibrant and inclusive work environment.

- **Stay Informed About Inclusive Language:** Language and
terminology evolve, and keeping up with these changes is a sign
of being respectful and inclusive. Your willingness to educate
yourself and adapt your language demonstrates your
commitment to fostering a diverse and welcoming workspace.

- **Enhance Clarity with Universal Phrases:** Using universal
phrases in communication helps ensure that everyone is on the
same page. It minimizes misunderstandings and ensures that
your message is accessible to all, regardless of their background
or knowledge.

- **Respect Nonbinary Identities with Gender-Neutral
Language:** Genderless language is a simple yet impactful way to
be inclusive of nonbinary individuals. It sends a powerful
message that you acknowledge and respect diverse gender
identities, contributing to a more inclusive workplace.

- **Foster Understanding Through Thoughtful Questions:**
Showing thoughtfulness and a willingness to learn by seeking
clarification when faced with unfamiliar concepts or terms
fosters an environment where asking questions is encouraged.

This can lead to richer discussions and a deeper understanding of each other's perspectives.

- **Educate Yourself About Colleagues' Experiences:** Commit to educating yourself about others' experiences and challenges, recognizing the value of your example in fostering inclusion. Life is much more than just about us; it's about the people around us and how their experiences can shape our reality. So, never make anything in life about just you, especially when you are part of an inclusive workforce.

- **Show Respect Through Active Listening:** Active listening is fundamental to respectful and inclusive communication. When you don't interrupt, you signal that you value your colleagues' input and respect their expertise. This can lead to more meaningful and constructive interactions.

- **Recognize and Appreciate Contributions:** Acknowledging and appreciating individual contributions is a form of recognition that can boost morale and motivation. Redirecting questions to the right experts shows respect for their expertise and ensures that individuals are recognized for their specific contributions.

- **Provide Constructive Feedback Without Personal Attacks:** Feedback that focuses on situations rather than personal attacks encourages a culture of respect, open communication, and continuous improvement. It fosters an environment where everyone feels safe to share ideas and make mistakes without fear of personal criticism.

- **Actively Interrupt Microaggressions:** Interrupting microaggressions is not only an act of allyship but also a way to actively contribute to a safe, inclusive environment by sending messages that such behaviors are not tolerated. It encourages others to follow suit and support colleagues who may be experiencing microaggressions. You can use examples to buttress practicing microaggression interruptions and help build the skills needed to address these issues effectively. It's a proactive step toward creating a more inclusive and respectful workplace.

Once the employees have successfully accomplished their part in practice, it doesn't end there. HR, leaders, and executives must fulfill their end of the bargain by finding easy and accommodating ways to invite inclusion into the workplace.

1. **Prioritize Inclusive Policies:** Begin by ensuring that your organization has comprehensive, up-to-date, inclusive policies in place. These policies should cover various aspects of diversity, equity, and inclusion, including hiring practices, employee development, and cultural awareness training. Building a culture of inclusion often requires buy-in and active support from leadership and HR teams.

2. **Lead by Revealing Pronouns:** Demonstrate your commitment to inclusivity by disclosing your pronouns. Encourage all team members to follow suit, creating an environment where everyone can express their gender identity comfortably. Providing this visibility is particularly vital for transgender and nonbinary individuals, offering a welcoming and respectful atmosphere.

3. **Incorporate Cultural Celebrations and Observances:** Show genuine appreciation for the diverse backgrounds and traditions of your employees and colleagues by incorporating a range of cultural celebrations and observances into the company calendar. This sends a clear message that the organization values and respects the varied cultural heritages of its workforce.

4. **Establish Safe and Inclusive Spaces:** Proactively create safe and inclusive spaces within the workplace, including facilities for nursing mothers, prayer rooms, or quiet spaces for meditation. These efforts ensure that employees from all backgrounds feel respected and accommodated.

5. **Foster Inclusivity Through Team-Building Events:** Planning and participating in inclusive team-building events is an excellent way to encourage connections among employees from diverse backgrounds. As a leader, consider the types of activities and events that will be inclusive and supportive, ensuring everyone feels a sense of belonging.

6. **Recognize and Reward Equitably:** Guarantee that recognition and rewards are distributed fairly. Implement a system that acknowledges and values the contributions of all employees, regardless of their background, tenure, or level of achievement. This practice motivates and engages all team members, fostering a sense of belonging.

7. **Accessibility for All Employees:** As HR, an executive, and a leader, it's imperative to ensure that the workplace is accessible to all employees. This includes accommodating remote workers, individuals with disabilities, and those with different accessibility needs. Embracing accessibility fosters an inclusive and supportive environment where all can thrive.

8. **Adopt Inclusive Language Year-Round:** Demonstrate an unwavering commitment to respect and inclusivity by consistently using inclusive language throughout the year. Avoiding offensive language or terminology fosters a culture of understanding and acceptance.

9. **Join Inclusion Allies Programs:** Participate in inclusion allies programs to deepen your understanding of diversity and inclusion issues. These programs provide valuable insights and equip you to support employees from underrepresented backgrounds actively. By actively engaging in these programs, you become a champion of inclusivity.

10. **Display Multilingual Signage and Materials:** Reinforce the message of welcome and inclusivity by installing multilingual signage and providing materials in various languages. These materials also serve as gentle reminders to employees that they are part of a diverse, global community, regardless of the language spoken in the office.

All these approaches don't work in isolation; there has to be a regularity of events where there is prompting the question of how can you assemble a team that not only values inclusivity but also forms strong bonds, enhancing their ability to collaborate innovatively and creatively. Doing this often will inform everyone that anyone is welcome to propose activities to introduce what can be called a tighter-knit and more innovative team. You can test with activities.

Activity 1: The Chat Away

The focus is on open and candid discussions within the workplace. Drawing inspiration from the talk show format of Steve Harvey and Ellen DeGeneres, this initiative aims to create a platform where employees feel encouraged to share their experiences and perspectives openly. The goal is to establish a space for honest inclusivity, allowing diverse voices to be heard and valued. Much like the talk show hosts, the objective is to generate meaningful dialogues around various social issues, so the work environment becomes that place where lessons are learned, and innovative ideas are embraced.

Instructions

- Encourage employees to openly share their experiences and perspectives.
- Create a platform where diverse voices are welcomed and valued.
- Take inspiration from talk shows like Steve Harvey and Ellen DeGeneres, where candid conversations are celebrated.
- Feature guests from diverse backgrounds, promoting inclusivity and understanding.
- Embrace the emotions that may arise during discussions, with the understanding that lessons learned contribute to personal and collective growth.
- Ensure that the chat-away moments lead to a workplace culture where inclusivity holds significance.

Activity 2: Picture Albums

Create team picture albums to celebrate the diversity within the organization. These albums will visually capture the unique backgrounds, cultural experiences, and encounters of team members through vibrant colors, collages, and canvas.

Instructions

- Gather photos that represent the diverse backgrounds, cultural travels, and experiences of team members.

- Design visually appealing collages that showcase the richness of cultural diversity within the team.
- Experiment with different artistic mediums, such as canvas, to add a touch of creativity to the picture albums.
- Take inspiration from the "Share a Coke" campaign by Coca-Cola, emphasizing personalization and representation of various cultural backgrounds.
- Use the picture albums as a means to promote inclusivity and connection within the team.
- Aim for the lasting impact achieved by campaigns like "Share a Coke" by making the picture albums a symbol of cohesion and celebration of diversity.

Activity 3: A Thousand Words

Embrace the timeless tradition of storytelling infused with modern creativity. This activity encourages employees to share their stories through visual elements, combining the richness of personal experiences with creative images.

Instructions

- Invite employees to share personal stories emphasizing unique perspectives and experiences.
- Emphasize using creative images, graphics, or visual elements to enhance the storytelling experience.
- Compile the visual stories into a showcase or gallery, either virtually or physically, celebrating individual uniqueness.
- Encourage continuous participation, creating a dynamic and evolving tapestry of employee experiences.

Activity 4: Privilege and Allyship

This activity explores privilege and allyship. It educates employees on the concept of privilege and encourages them to be allies for their colleagues. If an employee has faced some form of abuse in her past, of course, she wouldn't know what it's like to feel supported and loved by a partner because she never had it. However, it doesn't mean she needs to feel alien to a discussion that surrounds either side of the coin as regards love and abuse. For such an individual, they must be carried along to understand the privileges of support and also appreciate that they aren't alone but have allies they can trust to stand by them. It builds understanding and support among employees so that there is a space for open dialogue. Here, no one feels alienated from discussions on various life experiences.

Instructions

- Conduct a session explaining the concept of privilege, using examples to help employees grasp its nuances.
- Prompt employees to reflect on their own experiences and acknowledge areas where privilege plays a role.
- Facilitate discussions on the importance of allyship, emphasizing the role each employee can play in supporting their colleagues.
- Relate the concept to real-world examples, such as the advocacy initiatives of companies like Ben & Jerry's, illustrating the power of allyship in driving positive change.

Activity 5: The Name Game

This activity centers on fostering a workplace culture that respects individuals' names and pronouns. It emphasizes the significance of using correct terms to create an inclusive environment.

Instructions

- Begin with a brief educational session on the importance of using correct names and pronouns, drawing attention to the evolving landscape of gender identification.
- Reference notable figures like Laverne Cox, who advocates for transgender rights and emphasizes the impact of using correct pronouns.
- Encourage an open dialogue where employees can share their preferred pronouns, fostering an understanding of diverse gender identities within the team.

- Ensure workplace materials and platforms incorporate spaces for individuals to specify their preferred pronouns, promoting visibility and respect.
- Implement periodic reminders and updates on the importance of using correct names and pronouns to reinforce a culture of inclusivity.

Note: Sensitivity and respect are paramount during this activity to create a safe space for open discussion.

Activity 6: Inclusive Design Workshops

Organizing workshops where employees collaborate to design products, services, or workplace elements with inclusivity in mind is another activity that might seem casual but can be most rewarding of all. This promotes a more equitable and innovative environment. For instance, in a technology company, the HR department wanted to make their workplace more accessible for employees with disabilities. They organized an inclusive design workshop, bringing together employees from various departments and an inclusive design expert. The workshop focused on identifying challenges, brainstorming solutions, and creating prototypes for inclusive design changes. These changes, such as accessible ramps and sensory-friendly workspaces, were then implemented! Think of the amount of inclusivity that will be created for the disabled group and how valued they will feel knowing their participation is desired and appreciated.

How about this setting:

Instructions

- Clearly define the objective of making the workplace more accessible for employees with disabilities.
- Assemble a diverse group, including employees from various departments and an inclusive design expert.
- Break the workshop into phases—identify challenges, brainstorm solutions, and create prototypes for inclusive design changes.

- Ensure the inclusive design expert guides participants, providing insights into best practices.
- Select and implement feasible solutions, such as accessible ramps and sensory-friendly workspaces.
- Communicate changes to the workforce, emphasizing collective effort, and celebrate the success of the workshop.

So, with these activities incorporated into the workplace, organizations can be sure to head on to foster inclusivity and innovation. These are activities that provide opportunities for employees to learn from each other's diverse experiences, creating a culture that values differences and encourages creativity. With the insights and strategies provided in the previous sections, you'll be well-equipped to assemble a comprehensive and confident plan. The final two strategies delve into the critical aspects of modeling best practices, leading by example, and effectively addressing any potential challenges that may surface during your DEI integration. Notably, the solutions you develop for these challenges will further enhance the overall effectiveness of your DEI plan, as discussed in Chapter Three. Now, let's shift our focus to your role in this transformative journey.

8

THE PRIZE OF MULTICULTURAL WORKPLACES

Earn your leadership every day.
—*Michael Jordan (Sankofa, 2023)*

❧

You

In the scheme o f DEI, there is one thing that completes the meal: you. If you didn't know, understand that the prize for making a multicultural workplace is all about how you commit yourself to this needed change in the workplace. In case you missed it, you hold the four aces; you represent the 92% of leaders and executives who believe training and workshops presented by passionate DEI drivers are the prize of gaining a multicultural workplace (Instride, 2020).

You are guided to delve deep into your DEI mindset and become the driving force behind the change you want to see. You are not only a participant but a mentor, inspiring and leading by example to ignite DEI progress. You might be curious why you have become the protagonist in this 8th strategy. It's because you're the one with the idea; therefore, the realms of change demand more from you.

- **A Deep Commitment and Accountability:** Within the DEI Lighthouse Model, a profound commitment is essential. This means being responsible for the changes, investing in them, and actively modeling the desired transformations within the organization.
- **Being the Epicenter of Change:** As a leader, you are the focal point for all transformative efforts. To initiate and sustain progress, embrace diversity, consistently monitor key metrics, seek feedback, and acknowledge and reward those who contribute to the change journey.
- **Kickstarting with Role Model Leadership:** To inspire others to follow your lead in championing diversity and inclusion, actively engage in the process, and display the qualities of a role model leader. Effective role models can overcome obstacles and serve as beacons of positive change.
- **Involvement and Role Modeling:** To drive the transformation you envision, it's crucial to be as involved as you expect others to be. By taking the lead and actively participating, you become a role model for the changes you aspire to instill within the organization. This involves demonstrating the qualities that others should emulate.

Note that effective role model leaders exhibit qualities that make them worthy of emulation. These qualities include resilience, determination, adaptability, empathy, and the ability to inspire and guide others.

Ways to Exhibit Role Model Persona

So what are the ways you can exhibit the role model persona so others follow accordingly and you, in turn, see the right DEI results?

1. **The Hard Work Foundation:** No one likes to be overworked or work so hard it takes away their fun time or makes them lose their sense of concern for other things in life. But, when you really work hard with a goal, it forms the cornerstone of effective role modeling. You stay dedicated to tasks and maintain a mentality where excuses aren't tolerated or entertained because you know once you begin to think of all the

reasons why it can't or won't work, a lot of people will be disappointed, considering how much confidence they have in you. Probably more than you did in yourself. Consider the determination and diligence displayed by Oprah Winfrey, who overcame significant obstacles to achieve success in media. She was committed because she understood that this wasn't just about her, or women in the media or women in the workplace, but women of color who needed to feel safe anywhere in the world, and that's why Oprah serves as an inspiration for all today.

2. **The Trust Mechanism:** This is an element of being a role model that helps more people buy into your idea and participate in your cause. You should prove to your team that you can be trusted by consistently exhibiting fairness in judgments, honesty in dealings, and reliability in moments of struggle. If there is office gossip going on because of a manager who messed up or an executive whose integrity is in question, don't be the one to spread the already bad news and discourage it within your team. As a leader, building trust among employees gives them the assurance that their issues are in the hands of someone who takes confidentiality seriously.

3. **Accountability Mode:** If you're afraid to be blamed when things go wrong, especially when you represent the center of a project, then ask yourself if you really want to be a role model. In this position, you must learn to take responsibility for your actions so you inspire others to do the same. In cases of mistakes or missteps, admit them and communicate your plan for correction because roles come with failures and successes, and you need to have a taste of both, so you appreciate what it means to develop. Leadership accountability assists organizations in preparing for seasons when a business experiences downsides and economic loopholes occur, at such times all hands must come together to ensure transparency for survival. This was one of the measures that made people appreciate Elon Musk's accountability mode during challenging times at SpaceX, where he showcased the importance of taking responsibility and addressing issues directly.

4. **Respect Response:** The respect response is paramount in all interactions role models have and will have going forward between themselves, employees, and stakeholders. Showing respect to individuals, whether they are customers, employees, or vendors, proves you understand the importance of value and that every individual has self-worth in your eyes. It's especially vital when addressing behavioral issues, which often pop up in workplaces when intentions and statements are misinterpreted or misconstrued. When Indra Nooyi, the former CEO of PepsiCo, exemplified respect by promoting a culture of inclusivity and respect for diverse perspectives within her company, she did it with the intent to uphold DEI as a business imperative. Indra sustained that if you want to get the most suited hands at work in any business, it starts with the entire population. If you comb through a larger number, there is no telling the amount of talent and skill you will find hungry to give their all (Peterson, 2020).

5. **Optimistic Positivity:** Maintaining a positive outlook during times of change is essential.There is such a thing as toxic positivity, where you stand confident and reassured in your mind that no matter the challenges that come, everything is going to be alright, and you maintain keeping the workplace that way because, for you, optimistic positivity is the anchor for DEI.

6. **Demonstrating Integrity:** As a role model, you must adhere to the same rules you expect your team to follow. Never exempt yourself from being subject to the rules just because you are a leader and executive. If employees don't see you uphold the existence of DEI as a necessity, what should they do? Howard Schultz, the former CEO of Starbucks, has shown remarkable integrity throughout his career by consistently following company policies and setting an example of integrity. He projected a culture of trust and ethics within Starbucks. He looked at how renowned the business is and how it maintains its status despite the challenges of COVID-19 and many other economic meltdowns.

7. **Persistence Metrics:** Role models display steady persistence in the face of obstacles. Whether you're at the entry level or a seasoned professional, becoming a role model in your workplace starts with showcasing qualities that others can look up to. Microsoft's CEO, Satya Nadella, made a difference when he championed DEI in the tech industry by implementing programs for equal opportunities and employee support, a commitment that set high standards for the industry.

As you become more visible in your role as a leader, mentor, or someone actively embodying the principles you want to instill in others, the time comes to shift from personal change to inspiring those around you. Whether you're striving to make (DEI) stand out or other transformative values, leading by example is paramount. It involves showcasing your drive for DEI through your actions and communication. Sharing your own DEI journey, complete with its trials and triumphs, can inspire others, create an atmosphere where every voice is heard and respected, and welcome open dialogues and active listening. When experience can be told in stories recounting real-life tales of individuals who've overcome DEI challenges, serves as an impactful source of motivation. Recognizing and celebrating even small DEI victories reinforces your dedication. As a mentor or leader, you play a proactive role in nurturing personal growth, providing educational opportunities, and setting ambitious yet achievable goals. With your ability to inspire, you can lead your organization toward a future of positive transformation and innovation in several ways unimaginable:

- Set high goals aligning with your chapter three plan, and aim for them, no matter what, to prove your ambition for success and how goals are an essential part of your plan. These goals should be in tune with your strategic DEI plan, and once there is a continuous striving to achieve these goals, you lead by example and inspire your colleagues to be equally dedicated to the cause.
- Use empathy to show how much you care about other cultures and minorities in your journey as a DEI advocate. When you can trigger the right kind of emotion in people using shared

personal stories of cultural experiences or moments of inclusivity, it can go a long way in demonstrating genuine care for other cultures and minorities. As a leader, you dig deep into what makes a person thick and ensure they know how valued they are; by extension, others will accord the employee the same level of care, respect, and value, and possibly more.

- Show interest and appreciation for things they achieve at home or work by celebrating them in any way possible. A significant aspect of inspiring others is recognizing and appreciating their achievements, both in their personal lives and at work. As you actively root for them and acknowledge their successes, you create a culture of support and inclusivity where every individual's contributions are put out there, not as a show-off but as a show of support.
- Practice good communication, inclusive language, active listening, and knowing the pronouns colleagues prefer. By consistently using inclusive language, actively listening to your colleagues, and respecting their preferred pronouns, you set a clear example of respectful and inclusive communication. This practice empowers your team to do the same.
- Empowering your colleagues by suggesting and creating shared opportunities is a hallmark of inspirational leadership. It shows that you are committed to their growth and development. I've witnessed firsthand how these opportunities can bring diverse talents to the forefront.
- Share the personal and professional benefits of DEI, and speak plainly about the insights with your colleagues. When the positive impact it has had on your own journey is stated, many will want to engage with DEI initiatives and embrace its rewards actively.
- Using storytelling to inspire others to speak up and share their own experiences and challenges related to diversity and inclusion, along with your personal growth, can encourage them to open up and celebrate their own differences. I've found that storytelling creates an emotional connection that motivates others to share and embrace their unique narratives.

- Demonstrating a genuine interest in learning about your colleagues is a cornerstone of encouraging inclusivity. By investing time in understanding their backgrounds, experiences, and interests, you show that you value their uniqueness. This, in turn, creates a sense of belonging and trust within the team.
- In meetings or casual conversations, asking the right questions is an effective way to inspire others. Thought-provoking questions encourage meaningful dialogue, critical thinking, and the sharing of diverse perspectives. I've observed how this practice promotes a culture of open and inclusive communication.
- Building intentional relationships with colleagues from diverse backgrounds is a personal commitment every role model must hold dire. It's a conscious effort to connect with individuals, regardless of their cultural origins. This approach not only strengthens professional bonds but also sets a powerful example of building an inclusive workplace.

All the personal growth mechanism shared takes us to the realm of effective communication, as this is an action often conveying more than words alone. Nevertheless, mastering the art of combining body language, speech, and tone can significantly impact your ability to influence and connect with your colleagues. Let's delve into strategies for enhancing your communication in a professional setting.

Strategies to Enhance Communication

Active Listening Skills

In this setting, you should be able to:

- Maintaining **eye contact** demonstrates your engagement and respect for the speaker, thereby building trust and rapport. You're sending the message that you value what they have to say and that they have your full attention.
- People often communicate as much through their body language, facial expressions, and tone as they do with words. By

paying **attention to these cues**, you can gain a deeper understanding of the speaker's emotions and perspectives. For instance, a coworker may say they're fine, but their slouched posture and averted gaze might suggest otherwise.

- Interrupting can be perceived as disrespectful and may hinder open dialogue. **Allowing the speaker to finish** their thoughts shows that you respect their perspective and are willing to listen before forming your response.
- When you listen without judgment, you create a safe space for honest and open communication. **Avoiding hasty judgments** allows the speaker to express themselves freely without fear of criticism.
- Instead of immediately providing your own opinions or solutions, focus on **understanding the speaker's viewpoint.** Your goal is not to fix the issue but to grasp their perspective fully.
- **Asking questions** not only demonstrates your interest but also helps clarify and deepen your understanding. It's a way to show that you're actively engaged in the conversation.

Effective Communication

With active listening comes a more detailed idea of how communication is made impactful from role models to employees:

- **Authenticity** is essential in building trust. Being yourself in your communication is more genuine and the best in a transparent environment where colleagues can relate to you more readily, seeing how much of a realist you are.
- In a professional setting, **clear and transparent communication** is vital. Transparency in your messages ensures that others can comprehend your intentions and expectations without confusion. Nothing is misread or misunderstood because you made it so.
- **Simplifying your communication** is crucial, especially in the workplace. Avoid jargon or overly complex language that might confuse others. Being direct ensures that your message is clear and easily understood. Sometimes, in a bid to sound

professional, we add too much to straightforward ideas, and in the end, nothing is established. You have to be intentional about being understood.

- **Storytelling** is a powerful communication tool. Sharing relevant stories or anecdotes can make your points more relatable, memorable, and engaging. It helps convey complex ideas in a way that's easy to grasp and can bring about valid emotional responses.
- **Non-verbal elements** can reinforce your message. Gestures, body language, and tone can emphasize your sincerity and intent, contributing to a more comprehensive understanding of your communication. The way you laugh when employees make an error will determine if the laugh is out of anger, mockery, or a way to lighten the mood so they don't feel like an error is a death sentence.
- **Receiving feedback** gracefully and acting upon it demonstrates your willingness to improve and adapt. It's a sign of a growth-oriented, learning mindset and also that you are willing to take the fall for any error so that you can make things right.
- The most compelling form of communication is your **actions**. Following through on your commitments, demonstrating consistency, and acting on your words build trust and credibility in your workplace relationships.

Actionable Steps

Having considered all these, what about actionable steps that can lay the foundation for change? Do you have any in mind, or perhaps you have tried to think out a few possible moves that will encourage collaboration in the most productive fashion? It could be in:

- **Understanding Your Coworkers:** It's you going beyond surface-level interactions by diving deep into understanding the backgrounds, experiences, and unique perspectives of your colleagues. Invest time in developing genuine connections on a personal level, even knowing a little bit about their life outside the office and how it might be influencing their attitude to their work or opinion on certain issues. By taking this initiative, you'll find yourself better equipped to truly appreciate the rich tapestry of diversity within your team and organization.

- **Uncovering Learning Goals:** Your role as a mentor or leader goes beyond giving guidance; it's about actively engaging with your mentees or team members. Spur them into conversations and sessions where they can speak freely, as it will give you the chance to take the time to explore what they aspire to learn and the skills they're eager to share. This approach is transformative, leading interactions into a two-way knowledge exchange where everyone contributes to personal and professional growth. In fact, the mentor and the mentee might find they both admire something unique about each other's approach, personality, or culture and want to know more or less about their different ways of doing things.

- **Promoting Leadership and Inspiration:** Encouraging your colleagues to step into leadership roles and inspire others is one of the many ways to promote DEI as a growth tool. It creates an environment where team members can lead and acknowledge the incredible value of each other's unique perspectives. This is the gateway to allowing innovations and fresh ideas to thrive and also nurturing a sense of empowerment among your peers. This brings to mind Sheryl Sandberg at Facebook, who champions women's leadership in tech. She inspired countless others to step up, get into training, explore their capacity to learn tech, as technical as it might seem, and then lead. Today, women make up 28% of the workforce in computer and mathematical occupations, and within the field of engineering and architecture occupations, women hold 15.9% of the available jobs (Women in Tech, 2023). Yes, the figures can be better, and it will be with more DEI initiatives to build upon, especially in the area of inclusion.

- **Building Strong Rapport:** One of the most rewarding foundations of a successful DEI strategy rests on meaningful relationships. Ensure you have these flowing interactions with your colleagues and team members where you can establish a level of trust and mutual respect through genuine connections. This is how an inclusive environment is nurtured, where everyone feels valued and heard. While Tim Cook, the CEO of Apple, is a simple man who values his privacy more than anything, he understands the importance of DEI and has cultivated strong relationships with both employees and customers, reinforcing the importance of genuine connections.

- **Prioritizing Minority Development:** In your capacity, make it a priority to advance the professional growth of underrepresented minorities within your organization. Remember, you are a role model, so ensure they receive equal opportunities and the necessary support for their development. A stellar example is Mellody Hobson, who has been a driving force behind diversity and inclusion efforts at Ariel Investments, working to elevate the representation of minorities in the financial sector.

- **Advocating Senior Leadership Buy-In:** Advocating for DEI initiatives and gaining buy-in from senior leadership is a critical part of every role model. You should convey the potential benefits and profound impact of these changes and show how great DEI can be for any workplace, especially yours when embraced at all levels of the organization. So many companies, knowing how helpful and insightful DEI has been since it was introduced, have had no choice but to create an agenda to stabilize its existence as it is a force that has come to workplaces to unveil a new culture of working in sync with each other.

- **Proactive Issue Identification:** Stay vigilant and proactively search for hidden challenges within your workplace, whether subtle or under-the-radar. Identifying these concealed issues allows you to address them early, preventing potential obstacles and cultivating a more inclusive and equitable environment. Much like how Google consistently seeks out invisible biases in its algorithms to ensure fairness and equality in its services. So, because they are up to speed in time, it cannot affect their productivity as they are able to nip it in the bud sooner rather than later.

- **Activate Activity Arcades:** With practical activities that will help connect role models with their coworkers, the journey toward DEI becomes easier. To engage in these activities is to forge individual relationships, build meaningful connections, and lay a proper foundation for collaborative efforts in advancing DEI and getting more familiar at the same time.

Activity Attempts

- **Three Statement Impact:** Most call this a "two-true and a-lie" game where coworkers form groups and exchange facts and fallacies about each other. Within the group, the game plan is to guess what is true and what is a lie in these statements. In doing so, it encourages team members to share personal anecdotes and colleagues to gain insight into each other's backgrounds and experiences for a deeper understanding of individual differences.

- **Find-A-Way:** This engaging exercise is all about survival and using each person's uniqueness to make headway for everyone. Here, team members discuss the items they would choose to have if stranded on a desert island. This conversation often reveals personal preferences and priorities, opening the door to understanding diverse viewpoints. If you know the game show "Survival," you will see that it's never easy to mingle or adjust to people who feel like strangers, but when DEI comes into play, there is no such thing as a stranger because it's all about inclusion and acceptance.

- **Nailed It:** Immerse yourself in a lively and inclusive Cultural Bingo game designed to deepen connections and celebrate diversity. Each participant receives a Bingo card filled with prompts related to cultural backgrounds, hobbies, and personal experiences. Here's the twist: your task is to do some friendly "snooping" to learn more about your fellow participants and fill in the Bingo squares accordingly. Engage in conversations, ask questions, and observe shared spaces to discover unique qualities. Once a row or column is complete, share your newfound knowledge with the group. This game goes beyond the ordinary, transforming diversity appreciation into a fun and meaningful experience that fosters a stronger sense of community. Let the cultural connections unfold, and enjoy the shared journey of discovery!

- **Quick Question:** Quick icebreaker questions, such as sharing the number of cups of coffee consumed in a day or favorite vacation destinations, is another way to lighten that overly busy and corporate atmosphere in the workplace with lighthearted conversations. It also gives room for personal preferences to be acknowledged and understood rather than misread like why a coworker always wears dark shades in the office. It could be because they have an eye issue or they are shy. Or, why does another coworker never use makeup? It could be for religious or personal reasons. All these are questions that can be answered when people get up close and personal.
- **Top Five:** This activity invites participants to share their top five favorites, whether it's movies, books, or travel destinations. So easy and fun and creates room for longer chats as people will be open to speaking more as to why they like this instead of that. It's a great way to explore common interests and spark conversations that transcend work-related topics.

Once you can activate any of these activities by introducing and playing along, count yourself ready and worthy as a role model. You're already embodying the essence of a leader by actively engaging in DEI, regardless of your official title. Your efforts are instrumental in instigating change where it's needed. Now, you recognize that initiating change also means committing to modeling it and mentoring those around you. So, you're at the last piece of the puzzle going into the final chapter, which involves identifying pragmatic approaches to address challenges as the organization navigates this evolving landscape.

OVERCOMING DEI HUMPS
THE FINAL LAP

*No culture can live if it attempts to be exclusive. —Mahatma Gandhi
(Teambuilding, 2022)*

❧

DEI and What Lies Ahead

As we navigate the intricate path of Diversity, Equity, and Inclusion (DEI) in the workplace, the challenges are endless. Workplace discrimination is an unfortunate reality that is deeply ingrained. To completely eliminate bias in today's world is a continuous effort because people still feel that sense of racial concerns as well as personal segregation. While DEI training is a cornerstone that helps ease these growing concerns, some of the most prevalent complications that hinder DEI initiatives must be faced and addressed.

In 2023, transgender workplace discrimination has come to the forefront, shining a light on the urgency of the issue with a 90% statistical figure showing it as the most prominent of all discriminatory behaviors (Fenton, 2023). It's a cause for concern, even though comprehensive data remains limited. For instance, looking into the story of Laverne Cox, a notable transgender actress. Cox, known for her groundbreaking role in the hit series "Orange Is the New Black," faced discrimination and adversity on her journey to stardom. Despite the challenges she encountered, she emerged as a prominent advocate for transgender rights and an influential figure in the fight against discrimination. Her story emphasizes the need to tackle workplace discrimination head-on and find proactive solutions for the successful embrace of our DEI initiatives.

Dismantling workplace discrimination and promoting DEI is a multifaceted endeavor, one that demands recognition of the fact that significant transformation takes time and a ton of effort from role models and coworkers. It's imperative to understand that the DEI Lighthouse model emphasizes continually monitoring and adjusting your DEI plan. This phase of the journey is a linchpin in your pursuit of seeking a more inclusive workplace, requiring you to consistently assess your progress, anticipate potential obstacles, and ensure that your colleagues' needs align with the core values of your plan. Using the assessment framework elaborated upon in Chapter Two, you can systematically track progress every three months, showcasing your dedication to cultivating an environment where inclusivity thrives.

Also, in instances of entrenched workplace discrimination, where despite rigorous efforts, problems persist, it becomes essential to contemplate seeking legal counsel. Employment equity lawyers who specialize in addressing discrimination cases can be invaluable partners to your organization. They bring their expertise to the table, offering guidance on legal avenues and the necessary steps to rectify injustices. The pursuit of justice is a fundamental right, and these professionals can assist in ensuring that any discrimination is met with the appropriate response.

To mitigate the impact of workplace discrimination, understand common forms of discrimination and acquire the tools to respond effectively. Addressing these concerns proactively, before they escalate to the point of necessitating disciplinary actions, is paramount. Getting acquainted with prevalent types of workplace discrimination, such as gender or racial bias, empowers you to take preventative measures and remediate issues when they arise. Recognize that the strategies expounded upon in your Chapter 3 plan prove indispensable in navigating these challenges. Not only do they equip you to tackle existing problems, but they also serve as a barrier to maintaining the effectiveness and integrity of your DEI initiatives so they remain robust and sustainable.

Complications

To give clarity to the actuality of DEI and discrimination, let's dive further into the likely issues in the workplace that spark the tension of discrimination:

Complication 1—Transgender Discrimination

Addressing transgender discrimination in the workplace is not just a matter of compliance but a vital mission, especially in a world where an alarming 90% of transgender employees have reported encountering harassment and inappropriate treatment within the past year (Fenton, 2023). To effectively combat transphobia (negative thought, action, or inaction towards transgender people) or to eradicate trans-prejudice, you need to deploy some practical strategies. One of the pillars of this effort is to ensure discretion and support for transgender colleagues experiencing discrimination. Giving them that safe haven so they can voice their concerns and ensure they are heard and revered is a key step.

In addition to promoting discretion and support, enact policy changes that bolster disciplinary actions in the face of discrimination. These changes send a crystal-clear message throughout the organization that discrimination, including transphobia, is unequivocally unwelcome and intolerable behavior. This, in turn, nurtures a workplace culture brimming with inclusivity.

Stepping into a leadership role, you mustn't underestimate the significance of providing practical and technical support to transgender employees. Recognizing their unique needs and offering a helping hand when necessary is a cornerstone of creating a supportive and appreciable atmosphere. Transphobia and unconscious bias training shouldn't be a one-time event but a continuous one. It will be a constant reminder of the organization's dedication to inclusivity and equip employees with the tools to challenge discriminatory attitudes and behaviors persistently.

Furthermore, to lower emotional disorders coming from transpeople's encounters with toxic workplaces, an extended warm welcome to them and non-binary colleagues is paramount. Start by dropping any expectations tied to pronoun usage and ensuring that everyone is well-versed in and respectful of their preferred pronouns. This harmonizes with an environment where individuals are free to express their gender identities without the looming specter of judgment or discrimination.

In the quest to eliminate the social stigma attached to gender diversity, consider the power of a sensitization initiative or a specialized workgroup. As a role model, try to run sensitization campaigns to educate your workforce about the unique challenges and experiences of transgender individuals, nurturing understanding and empathy.

Moreover, it's not just about words; actions speak loudly. Embed a robust anti-discriminatory policy within your organization, complete with unambiguous consequences for those who transgress. This sends a strong signal that discrimination in any form, including transphobia, is met with swift and proportionate repercussions.

Recognizing the significance of medical procedures for transgender employees is a cornerstone of support. It necessitates understanding and accommodating potential leaves required for medical appointments or procedures. Respect for employee privacy and choices in this domain is a must.

Respecting name changes is another vital strand of this tapestry. When a transgender employee decides to change their name, it's not just about making the switch but updating internal records, email addresses, and any professional order memberships. This administrative commitment symbolizes your respect for their identity.

Conducting anti-harassment meetings can be a turning point as well. By outlining explicit expectations for every employee, these meetings lay the foundation for an environment free from discrimination and harassment, where everyone is treated with dignity and respect. Let's not overlook the small gestures. Offering employees the option to indicate their preferred pronouns in emails and other communication channels is a subtle yet potent way to bolster support for transgender colleagues. This initiative contributes to a culture where sharing pronouns becomes a norm, fostering inclusivity.

Lastly, ensuring the availability of gender-neutral safety spaces or restrooms is not just about facility management; it's about ensuring safety and comfort. Transgender individuals frequently face violence and harassment in public restrooms that don't align with their gender identity. By providing gender-neutral facilities, you're not just facilitating inclusion; you're safeguarding the well-being and peace of mind of your transgender employees. This paves the way for them to navigate the workplace confidently and without the specter of discomfort.

Complication 2—Racial Discrimination

Tackling the pervasive problem of racial discrimination in the workplace is an ongoing quest for equality and justice. Shockingly, studies reveal that racial discrimination affects a significant portion of the workforce, with statistics ranging from 24% to 58% (Fenton, 2023). This goes beyond acknowledging the issue; it necessitates proactive involvement and transformative actions.

One potent strategy to combat racial discrimination is the formation and active participation in Employee Resource Groups (ERGs). As mentioned in an earlier chapter, these groups offer a platform for open dialogues and an exploration of diverse cultures, backgrounds, and experiences. It's a crucible for unity, where employees come together to share their distinctive perspectives and grow a workplace that embraces diversity with open arms.

In addition to ERGs, organizations must adopt a strict zero-tolerance approach to racism. Like transgender discrimination, this entails instilling comprehensive anti-racism policies, procedures, and clear-cut consequences for discriminatory behavior. This is not a mere bureaucratic task; it signifies embracing a set of core values that permeate every facet of the organizational culture. It's high time to shed light on and weed out any policies, behaviors, partnerships, or client relationships that run contrary to the commitment to eradicate racial discrimination.

A workplace free from discrimination necessitates a concerted effort to raise awareness. It's a collective responsibility to educate everyone about the richness of diverse cultures, the significance of different voices, and the persistence of injustices. The more informed and empathetic employees become, the more formidable the collective crusade against discrimination will be to make DEI thrive.

Respect and professionalism should be the bedrock of every workplace interaction. In leadership, awaken everyone's respect for cultural diversity, both in behavior and communication, and cultivate an environment where every individual feels valued and acknowledged. Furthermore, pledging to steer clear of racial slurs, offensive humor, or pranks is of paramount importance. When in doubt, it's best to leave such content outside the workplace. What may be a joke to you might be hurtful to someone else and cause an emotional breakdown. Watch your ways when it comes to statements, gestures, and dispositions.

Employees must proactively support anti-racism endeavors by promptly reporting any discriminatory conduct they encounter. Never keep silent but empower individuals to take a stand against injustice and reinforce the principles of equality and justice. Each report can be a significant step toward shaping a more equitable work environment.

In cases of racial discrimination complaints, it's imperative for organizations to treat them with gravity and handle them equitably. Every complaint should be subject to the correct procedures and resolved fairly and transparently. This ensures that justice prevails and sends a powerful message that discrimination is unwelcome.

The significance of maintaining an open-minded approach when addressing racial discrimination issues cannot be overstated. It is crucial to approach each situation with empathy, striving to grasp different viewpoints and lived experiences. This nurtures a culture of inclusivity and guarantees that every individual's voice is acknowledged and respected.

In instances where racial harassment adversely affects an individual's well-being and mental health, unwavering support is non-negotiable. The person experiencing discrimination should never feel isolated; their mental and emotional well-being must be a priority to avoid cases of depression and purported suicidal tendencies. The organization should stand alongside them in the battle against racial discrimination and all forms of aggressive behaviors.

Complication 3—Generational Discrimination

Now, a complex challenge affects a significant 45% of employees who demand proactive solutions that move beyond surface-level awareness (Fenton, 2023). An issue so threatening that as far back as 1967, the United States put forward an Age Discrimination in Employment Act to help successfully combat ageism. The idea is, why look at age if the ability, both mentally and physically, is still there to work and deliver? Also, why make people over 40 years of age feel like their life is over? Organizations must implement comprehensive strategies that bridge generational divides and foster an inclusive work environment.

An essential shift in addressing ageism revolves around recognizing and rewarding employee performance rather than tenure. By moving away from tenure-based rewards, organizations can cultivate an environment where employees are acknowledged and appreciated based on their accomplishments and contributions, ensuring that merit takes precedence over age-related biases. If Martin, a 55-60-year-old man, can still work well and hard at a factory as one of the attendants, then why should his position be sent over to someone young just because the organization believes Martin is unfit to keep working? It's a prejudiced way to judge efficiency and productivity in the workplace.

Hiring and promotion practices must be recalibrated to focus on skills, competencies, and potential, irrespective of age. Embracing a holistic evaluation of employees, free from age-based bias, creates a culture of meritocracy, where individuals from all generations have equal opportunities for growth and advancement. Tough decisions, such as layoffs, should never be driven by age-based considerations. It's crucial to avoid unfairly targeting older employees solely due to their age during challenging periods. Fair and unbiased evaluation, prioritizing skills and performance, ensures a just approach across generations.

Organizations can achieve a significant transformation by revising policies and wholeheartedly embracing a multi-generational workforce. This approach encourages teams with diverse age groups to collaborate and share their unique experiences and knowledge, recognizing the inherent value each generation brings to the organization's success.

Inclusive teams, projects, and team-building exercises provide a solid strategy to combat ageism. By promoting diversity within these contexts, organizations create a workplace where employees of all ages feel comfortable, valued, and empowered to collaborate effectively. Through these measures, organizations can cultivate a workplace that's free from generational discrimination, where every employee is appreciated for their unique contributions, regardless of their age. Remember Colonel Harland Sanders? It was in his early 60s he started Kentucky Fried Chicken (KFC). He began franchising his restaurant concept and the KFC brand in the early 1950s, and the first KFC franchise opened in 1952 when Sanders was around 62 years old. He went on to become a well-known and successful entrepreneur, helping to build KFC into one of the world's most famous fast-food chains. Now, everywhere in the world, KFC is the chicken delight for everyone. His skills had nothing to do with age but everything to do with efficiency, commitment, and ingenuity.

Complication 4—Gender Discrimination

Gender discrimination remains a persistent issue affecting a substantial 42% of employees (Fenton, 2023). Also, the findings, featured in the Academy of Management Journal and stemming from research conducted at the USC Marshall School of Business, highlight that workplace environments where gender discrimination exists can diminish the overall sense of belonging for both male and female employees (Gonzales, 2022). This complex problem includes disparities such as the gender pay gap and unequal promotion rates. To address this pressing concern, different strategies must be employed.

Transparency is the cornerstone of tackling gender discrimination. Companies must be forthright about matters like wages, job positions, promotions, and the reasoning behind promoting one employee over another. Openness can help eliminate gender biases by ensuring that employees are privy to the same information so they don't assume the worst.

Empowering women is essential to breaking through the glass ceiling by actively supporting them with the skills and potential to excel in senior positions. Another proactive approach that can help dismantle the barriers women often face and further implement gender-neutral recruitment processes through blind evaluation methods is a practical step to ensure candidates are assessed solely based on qualifications and skills rather than their gender. It promotes fairness and equality in hiring practices.

Also, conducting an equal pay review by identifying wage inequalities and standardizing salaries based on skills and qualifications rather than historical pay packages is a vital step toward wage equity.

Clear company policies and explicit consequences for harassment, discrimination, and inappropriate comments send a strong message that such behaviors will not be tolerated in the workplace. This promotes a culture of respect and inclusivity.

Recognize that gender discrimination extends to parental leave policies. Providing shared parental leave options can alleviate the discrimination men often face with paternity leave. Inclusivity in these policies encourages a more equal work environment.

Both men and women should have representation to ensure balanced and comprehensive policies in place. Inspiring and actively encouraging women to succeed without needing to justify their aspirations is a critical component of combating gender discrimination. This support and guidance can be a driving force for women to reach their full potential tirelessly and without any low self-esteem.

Promoting a culture of meritocracy, where skills and performance are prioritized over gender, helps recognize and reward deserving individuals. With this, everyone is given an opportunity to succeed. The fight against gender discrimination also demands that organizations offer equal opportunities for brainstorming, professional growth, and participation, creating a level playing field for everyone.

Lastly, it's essential to combat sexism and harassment with a robust anti-sexism and sexual harassment policy. This zero-tolerance stance against gender-based harassment, stereotypes, and discriminatory behavior reinforces a culture of respect and inclusivity.

Incorporating these strategies can help organizations address gender discrimination comprehensively so the workplace becomes a place where every employee feels at home and a part of something meaningful, irrespective of their gender.

Complication 5—Sexual Orientation Discrimination

Sexual orientation discrimination, which affects approximately 33% of employees, has grown over the years to become a bane in most working environments (Fenton, 2023). This statistic is not just a number; it represents the experiences of real people facing discrimination based on their sexual orientation. By acknowledging this fact, we take the first step in creating a workplace that values DEI.

Addressing orientation discrimination involves more than just awareness; it requires action. While introducing pronouns is a valuable step, it is equally important to implement concrete policies, conduct comprehensive training, and establish clear consequences for discriminatory behavior. These actions send a strong message that discrimination is not tolerated in the workplace and should not be kept silent. Beyond policies and training, offering resources and leave options for adoption or same-sex marriages is a tangible way to show support for LGBTQ+ employees. This not only recognizes their unique needs but also demonstrates the organization's commitment to equality.

Health insurance for same-sex partners is another move that can be made intentionally so employees, regardless of their relationship status, receive the same benefits. It reflects the organization's dedication to providing equal opportunities and privileges.

Supporting and welcoming transitioning employees to educate others can foster a deeper understanding of the challenges they face. This helps create an environment where everyone feels safe to be their authentic selves, and it promotes a culture of empathy and inclusivity.

Using appropriate terminology, particularly in job descriptions, is a simple yet effective way to support more gender-neutral language that not only respects all individuals but also sends a powerful message that the organization values diversity.

By incorporating these strategies, organizations can not only address sexual orientation discrimination but also lay the foundation for a workplace where every employee feels committed to work progress because their opinions and personalities are respected and regarded. This is the way to uphold legal and ethical standards and makes good business sense, as diverse and inclusive workplaces tend to be more innovative and successful.

So, empower yourself! Create a checklist using the one shown in Chapter 2 *(below)* that encompasses ideas for addressing the most prevalent workplace discrimination. Take the initiative to integrate the third column into your DEI pitch or plan, allowing for a comprehensive approach. Consider potential solutions for each discrimination type, mirroring the table example provided. Keep in mind that the final column is a dynamic aspect to be revisited every three months as you evaluate and measure the progress of your implemented changes. Draw inspiration from the sample to guide you through this transformative and impactful activity.

THE SITUATIONAL ASSESSMENT CHART

	1	2	3	4	5
	Current Situation	Data Supporting the Current Situation	Possible Complications Resulting From the Current Situation	Potential Resolutions/Ideas to Improve the Current Situation	New Data After 3 Months of Testing the Resolution
1	• Employees don't feel that the hiring process is fair.	• 9/18/23 employees listed the same issue.	• Poor employee retention and a lack of diversity.	• Change the hiring process to include equitable processes based on people's skills, and post new job listings on diverse job boards.	• 12/6/23 Employees believe the hiring process is more fair. • Alternatively, the sample data could show: 12/6 employees now list a new problem showing the lack of in-house promotions. • (This 3-month metric73 reveals a new problem altogether)

EXAMPLE

So, knowing what you know now, can you say discrimination can be erased? Of course not, but understanding that its impact can be diminished is imperative. As the architect of your DEI plan, envision wielding a strategic tool to navigate workplace intricacies with finesse. You should always picture presenting not just an idea but a comprehensive blueprint meticulously designed to address and alleviate the subtle echoes of discrimination. This chapter encapsulates the essence of transformation, a poignant call to leadership, and a reminder that the power to reshape the workplace lies within your grasp. Begin with an idea, proceed with a plan, and get everyone on board regardless of character, personality, or orientation but focused on productivity. You will see that there is more strength in diversity than numbers.

YOUR FEEDBACK IS MEANS A LOT!

Hey there fellow leaders and readers,

I hope you've been enjoying this incredible resource. But here's the thing - your experience can be even more fulfilling, and it all starts with a simple question: How can you help others on their leadership journey?

Leaving a review for this book isn't just about sharing your thoughts; it's an opportunity to deliver value to fellow leaders, managers, and professionals who are seeking guidance and inspiration. Your words can make a difference in someone else's experience.

1. Click the link or scan the QR code below to leave an honest review on Amazon.

2. Share your thoughts, insights, and how this bundle has impacted your leadership journey.

By leaving a review, you're not just helping us; you're paying it forward to other leaders who are on their path to success. Your words of wisdom can inspire and guide them, making their journey smoother and more fulfilling.

So, let's come together as a community of leaders, share our experiences, and help each other thrive. Leave your review today and be a part of this incredible journey!

With warm regards,

Marguerite

CONCLUSION

This comprehensive journey through the intricacies of implementing Diversity, Equity, and Inclusion (DEI) in the workplace has equipped you with the essential knowledge and strategies. From understanding the core concepts to analyzing the need for specific interventions, you've delved into the intricacies of transforming workplace culture. Armed with data-driven insights, you've witnessed the power of introducing DEI concepts to organizational culture and policies, realizing that change can emanate from any level within the hierarchy.

As we move forward, the focus sharpens on fostering a curious mindset and breaking through biases via strategic training initiatives. Your role as a change agent is highlighted, emphasizing that innovation and transformation start with you. The exploration of practical ideas and exercises brings diversity into the workplace, stressing the importance of baby steps and collective efforts. No leader or executive should ever work with the assumption that they can do it alone. They need a team and a multifaceted one where you find all kinds of characters and personalities participating, and like a meal cooking, the end product becomes sumptuous.

Equity becomes a guiding principle delicately woven into the fabric of your organizational practices. This chapter underscores that DEI isn't just an acronym; it's a commitment to creating an environment where everyone has equal opportunities and feels valued. The final strategy encapsulates the culmination of your efforts, offering practical advice and exercises to enrich your workplace with inclusivity.

As you navigate the path to change, these chapters will place a mirror before you. It reinforces the truth that to advocate for transformation, you must embody it. The concluding message is clear: you are the epicenter of change. By incorporating the insights gleaned from these pages, you're not merely reading about DEI; you're actively shaping a workplace where diversity thrives, equity prevails, and inclusion becomes the norm.

In this final act, the spotlight is on you. Addressing the pervasive issue of workplace discrimination, this chapter acknowledges the difficulties in eradicating biases but provides a nuanced perspective. It recognizes training as a crucial tool and shifts the focus to addressing common complications in DEI workplace changes. Armed with the collective wisdom accumulated throughout this journey, you are poised to make a profound impact. The narrative concludes not just as a chapter but as a call to action, a powerful testament to your ability to drive change and champion inclusivity in a world that needs it. The journey has just begun; now, go and make a difference.

Embarking on the journey toward success was no overnight feat for me; it was a dedicated 20-year pursuit specifically tailored to benefit those facing discrimination in the workplace. My focus is now centered on crafting strategies that empower companies to leverage Diversity, Equity, and Inclusion (DEI) for the betterment of all, employing data-driven insights as the compass for change.

As we conclude this chapter, I invite you to become an integral part of the conversation. Your experiences, insights, and innovative approaches to measuring or implementing DEI strategies are invaluable. Let's break free from conventional boundaries and explore new perspectives collectively, harnessing the brilliance of previously overlooked creatives.

Your stories matter, and I'd love to hear them. Share your journey, your challenges, and your triumphs with me. Your voice adds a unique dimension to the ongoing narrative of creating inclusive workplaces. Don't hesitate to leave a review on Amazon, contributing to a communal pool of knowledge that can guide others on their DEI journey.

For those navigating the challenges of a demanding industry or company, I recommend exploring the book *Fearless Female Leadership*. It's a valuable resource tailored for women facing unique hurdles, providing insights and inspiration to navigate the professional landscape with resilience and courage.

As you continue your hard work and creative pursuits, I extend my heartfelt wishes for success and fulfillment. Your commitment to fostering change within your sphere of influence is commendable, and I believe that collectively, we can shape workplaces that embrace diversity, champion equity, and thrive on the principles of inclusion. Here's to your journey and the transformative impact you're poised to make. Cheers to the best and everything you truly deserve.

REFERENCES

～

SOURCE REFERENCES:

Affirmity. (2022, October 21). Employee Resource Group platform. https://www.affirmity.com/software/employee-resource-group-platform/

Analysis quotes. (n.d.). BrainyQuote. https://www.brainyquote.com/topics/analysis-quotes

Aspirale. (2023, May 4). *What is unconscious bias training for employees and why it's essential | Clear Law Institute.* Clear Law Institute. https://clearlawinstitute.com/blog/2021/06/07/why-unconscious-bias-training-for-employees-is-essential/

Barney, N., & Rosencrance, L. (2023). *diversity, equity and inclusion* (DEI). HR Software. https://www.techtarget.com/searchhrsoftware/definition/diversity-equity-and-inclusion-DEI

Benefits of Diversity in the workplace: What youth and Parents should know. (n.d.). https://www.bgca.org/news-stories/2022/December/benefits-of-diversity-in-the-workplace-what-youth-and-parents-should-know?gad=1&gclid=CjwKCAjwv8qkBhAnEiwAkY-ahoEBqCjblmm5PWro8K3d1456Fhg_6R3-I8UQUZpolakeNHrdBYmswhoCNbgQAvD_BwE

Best practices and tips for employees. (n.d.). US EEOC. https://www.eeoc.gov/initiatives/e-race/best-practices-and-tips-employees

British Heart Foundation. (n.d.). *10 Tips for Active Listening.* https://www.bhf.org.uk/

Bunch, H. (2022). *8 Tips: How to increase your knowledge on Diversity and Inclusivity — School store vending machine.* School Store Vending Machine. https://www.spiritboxnation.com/news/2020/6/10/8-tips-how-to-increase-your-knowledge-on-diversity-and-inclusivity

Council, F. C. (2020, March 24). *Mentoring For The First Time? 14 Tips To Start Off On The Right Foot.* Forbes. https://www.forbes.com/sites/forbescoachescouncil/2020/03/24/mentoring-for-the-first-time-14-tips-to-start-off-on-the-right-foot/?sh=799a977821a1

Diversity, equity, and inclusion plan template and tool | Office of Diversity, Equity and Inclusion. (2023, April 3). City of Philadelphia. https://www.phila.gov/documents/diversity-equity-and-inclusion-plan-template-and-tool/

Dunn, L. (n.d.). *What is Diversity, Equity & Inclusion (DEI)?* https://www.inclusionhub.com/articles/what-is-dei

Ellingrud, K., Ellsworth, D., Madner, S., Musallam, R., Sandhu, I., & Yee, L. (2023, January 13). *Diversity, Equity and Inclusion Lighthouses 2023.* McKinsey & Company. https://www.mckinsey.com/featured-insights/diversity-and-inclusion/diversity-equity-and-inclusion-lighthouses-2023

Employment Equity Training - The Mindspa Institute. (2023, July 10). The Mindspa Institute. https://themindspa.co.za/employment-equity-training/

Equity in the Workplace: What It Is and 9 Ways to Lead By Example. (n.d.). https://www.betterup.com/blog/equity-in-the-workplace

Esparza, A. (2023). 12 Diversity, Equity, & Inclusion Activities To Kickstart Your 2023 DEI Initiatives. SnackNation. https://snacknation.com/blog/diversity-inclusion-activities/

EVERFI. (2023, August 24). *How to avoid age discrimination in the workplace.* https://everfi.com/blog/workplace-training/how-to-avoid-age-discrimination-in-the-workplace/

Fenton, M. K. (2023, June 8). Employment Discrimination Statistics In 2023. *Wenzel Fenton Cabassa, P.A.* https://www.wenzelfenton.com/blog/2022/07/18/employment-discrimination-statistics-employees-need-to-know/

Firstup. (2021). *15 ways to improve diversity and inclusion in the workplace.* Firstup. https://firstup.io/blog/15-ways-to-improve-diversity-and-inclusion-in-the-workplace/

Gino, F. (2021, August 30). *Unconscious bias training that works.* Harvard Business Review. https://hbr.org/2021/09/unconscious-bias-training-that-works

Green, R. S. (n.d.). *5 Ways to support Transgender and Gender Non-Conforming People in the workplace.* Great Place to Work®. https://www.greatplacetowork.com/resources/blog/5-ways-to-support-transgender-and-gender-non-conforming-people-in-the-workplace#:~:text=2.%20Display%20pronouns,can%20create%20tension

Hall, S. H. (2023, April 21). *9 Ways to measure the success of your DEI Strategy in 2023 - Senior executive.* Senior Executive. https://seniorexecutive.com/9-ways-to-measure-the-success-of-your-dei-strategy/

He, G. (2022, November 30). *70 Powerful Diversity And Inclusion Quotes For The Workplace.* teambuilding.com. https://teambuilding.com/blog/diversity-and-inclusion-quotes

Heinz, K. (2023). *What does Diversity, Equity and Inclusion (DEI) mean in the workplace?* Built In. https://builtin.com/diversity-inclusion/what-does-dei-mean-in-the-workplace

Hodgson, N. (2022, November 10). *Tackling transphobia in the workplace.* Raconteur. https://www.raconteur.net/talent-culture/transgender-discrimination-workplace

How to Define Company Values (And Why It Matters) | By Gustavo Razzetti. (n.d.). https://www.fearlessculture.design/blog-posts/how-to-define-company-values-and-why-it-matters

How to prevent sexual orientation Discrimination. (n.d.). Croner-i. https://app.croneri.co.uk/topics/discrimination-and-equality-sexual-orientation-discrimination/how-prevent-sexual-orientation

Indeed Editorial Team. (2023, April 6). *13 Ways to Inspire and Motivate People in the workplace.* Indeed.com. https://www.indeed.com/career-advice/career-development/ways-to-inspire-people

James. (2022, March 8). What is Employment Equity? | Teamsters 987. Teamsters Alberta | Edmonton and Calgary. https://teamsters987.com/what-is-employment-equity-and-is-it-discrimination/

John F. Kennedy Quote. (n.d.). A-Z Quotes. https://www.azquotes.com/quote/547771?ref=equal-opportunity

Kohler, C. (2021). *What is unconscious bias training and does it work?* TopResume. https://www.topresume.com/career-advice/workplace-unconscious-bias-training

Kurter, H. L. (2020, July 22). *4 Ways To Create A More Diverse Workplace That Inspires Innovation.* Forbes. https://www.forbes.com/sites/heidilynnekurter/2020/07/22/4-ways-to-create-a-more-diverse-workplace-that-inspires-innovation/?sh=32c7793634af

Kurter, H. L. (2020, June 9). 4 Ways You Can Tackle Racial Discrimination In Your Workplace. *Forbes.* https://www.forbes.com/sites/heidilynnekurter/2020/06/09/4-ways-you-can-tackle-racial-discrimination-in-your-workplace/?sh=6be27fd60409

LAURIER, J. (2017, October 5). *Preventing and ending discrimination and harassment of transgender employee.* The Globe and Mail. Retrieved November 11, 2023, from

https://www.theglobeandmail.com/report-on-business/careers/leadership-lab/prevent-
ing-and-ending-discrimination-and-harassment-of-transgender-employees/arti-
cle36456796/#:~:text=It%20is%20also,of%20these%20leaves

Leadership Role Models | Qualities & Examples - Video & lesson transcript | Study.com. (n.d.).
study.com. https://study.com/learn/lesson/role-model-leadership-style-examples.html

Leikvoll, V. (2023). Scale Up to 70% by Beating These 22 Unconscious Biases. Leaders.com.
https://leaders.com/articles/business/unconscious-biases/

Leyshon, J. (2023, February 7). *10 ways to eliminate gender bias in the workplace.* Sage Advice
United Kingdom. https://www.sage.com/en-gb/blog/eliminate-gender-diversity-
workforce/

Making and handling complaints - Race discrimination - Acas. (2023, August 21). Acas.
https://www.acas.org.uk/race-discrimination/making-and-handling-race-discrimina-
tion-complaints

Malyk, M. (2022). *What is Inclusion Training? Importance, Types, and Methods.* www.easylla-
ma.com. https://www.easyllama.com/blog/what-is-inclusion-training/

Murray, R. (2023, March 8). The difference between DEI, CSR, and ESG - She+ geeks out.
She+ Geeks Out. https://www.shegeeksout.com/blog/the-difference-between-dei-
csr-and-esg/

Nguyen, D. (n.d.). Software Platform For Employee Resource Groups | Chezie.
https://www.chezie.co/

Officevibe. (2023, July 17). *5 diversity and inclusion activities for the workplace.* Officevibe.
https://officevibe.com/blog/diversity-and-inclusion-activities

OHCHR. (n.d.). *The struggle of trans and gender-diverse persons.* https://www.o-
hchr.org/en/special-procedures/ie-sexual-orientation-and-gender-identity/struggle-
trans-and-gender-diverse-persons

Online Employment Equity – Copperline training. (n.d.). https://copperline.co.za/corpo-
rate-training-courses/online-employment-equity/

Online, R. T. (2021, December 7). *Six traits of an effective role model for all managers.* Ready
Training Online. https://readytrainingonline.com/articles/effective-role-model-traits/

Partners, F. (2023). *5 Tips: How to create a more Diverse Workplace.* Frederickson Partners.
https://www.fredericksonpartners.com/news/blog/5-tips-how-to-create-a-more-
diverse-workplace/

Pathak, A. (2023, April 27). *9 Powerful Steps To Eradicate Gender Inequality In The Workplace.*
Nurture an Engaged and Satisfied Workforce | Vantage Circle HR Blog. https://blog.-
vantagecircle.com/gender-inequality-in-the-workplace/

Pathak, A. (2023). 26 Diversity and Inclusion Questions For Employee Surveys. Nurture an
Engaged and Satisfied Workforce | Vantage Circle HR Blog. https://blog.vantagecircle.-
com/diversity-and-inclusion-questions/

Pathak, A. (2023). 6 Types Of Diversity Training For An Inclusive Workplace. Nurture an
Engaged and Satisfied Workforce | Vantage Circle HR Blog. https://blog.vantagecircle.-
com/types-of-diversity-training/

Pathak, A. (2023). *7 Effective Ways To Promote Workplace Equity! Nurture an Engaged and
Satisfied Workforce* | Vantage Circle HR Blog. https://blog.vantagecircle.com/workplace-
equity/

Patterson, D. (2023, May 3). *3.5 Employment standards and employment equity.* Pressbooks.
https://ecampusontario.pressbooks.pub/humanresourcesmgmt/chapter/3-5-employ-
ment-equity/

Peterson, M. (2023, January 11). 11 essential traits of an inclusive workplace. Limeade.

https://www.limeade.com/resources/blog/inclusive-workplace/

Powerful diversity workplace statistics to know for 2023 | InStride. (n.d.). https://www.instride.com/insights/workplace-diversity-and-inclusion-statistics/

Qooper | ERG Software. (n.d.). https://www.qooper.io/erg-software

Reiners, B. (2023). *50 Diversity in the workplace Statistics to know*. Built In. https://builtin.com/diversity-inclusion/diversity-in-the-workplace-statistics

Sankofa, C. (2023, October 5). *Lead by Example Quotes To Talk About It And Be About It*. Everyday Power. https://everydaypower.com/lead-by-example-quotes/

Say, J. (2021, February 2). *Top 50 Inspirational Vision Quotes (SUCCESS)*. Gracious Quotes. https://graciousquotes.com/vision/

Shi, D. (2022). *How to get better at using inclusive language in the workplace*. Fast Company. https://www.fastcompany.com/90753901/how-to-get-better-at-using-inclusive-language-in-the-workplace

Singh, D. (n.d.). *Your DEI-Centered Business Plan*. https://www.deannasingh.com/blog/dei-business-plan

Staff, I. (2023, July 12). *6 top tips for preventing ageism in the workplace - Insperity*. Insperity. https://www.insperity.com/blog/preventing-age-discrimination/

Staff, L. E. (2023, August 22). *15 Tips for Effective Communication in Leadership*. CCL. https://www.ccl.org/articles/leading-effectively-articles/communication-1-idea-3-facts-5-tips/

Stainforth, D., & Null. (2023). A PRACTICAL GUIDE TO EMPLOYMENT EQUITY. Measuredability. https://measuredability.com/employment-equity/

Team, E. (2022, August 16). *Ageism in the Workplace and 7 Ways to Fight it | Embroker*. Embroker. https://www.embroker.com/blog/ageism-in-the-workplace-and-how-to-fight-it/

TestGorilla. (2023). *An HR professional's guide to DEI initiatives*. TestGorilla. https://rebrand.ly/a8sci5v

The Pyramid Principle - How to Effectively Pitch projects | Planio. (n.d.). Planio. https://plan.io/blog/pyramid-principle-pitching/

The Williams Institute at UCLA School of Law. (2023, February 14). *LGBT people's experiences of workplace Discrimination and Harassment - Williams Institute*. Williams Institute. https://williamsinstitute.law.ucla.edu/publications/lgbt-workplace-discrimination/

Tmason. (2022, April 11). 27 *Fun getting to know you activities for work teams*. Outback Team Building & Training. https://www.outbackteambuilding.com/blog/getting-to-know-you-activities/

West, W. (2023). *10 Actions You Can Take Today to Be More Inclusive At Work*. The Diversity Movement. https://thediversitymovement.com/10-actions-you-can-take-today-to-be-more-inclusive-at-work/

What is diversity, equity, and inclusion? (2022). McKinsey & Company. https://www.mckinsey.com/featured-insights/mckinsey-explainers/what-is-diversity-equity-and-inclusion

Wong, L. (2023, March 30). Employee Engagement Surveys: Everything you need to know | Poll Everywhere blog. *Poll Everywhere*. https://blog.polleverywhere.com/employee-engagement-survey

Wong, L. (2023, March 30). Employee Engagement Surveys: Everything you need to know | Poll Everywhere blog. *Poll Everywhere*. https://blog.polleverywhere.com/employee-engagement-survey

WorkTango. (2023, August 9). *15 tips for building a more inclusive workplace* | WorkTango. https://www.worktango.com/resources/articles/how-to-build-an-inclusive-workplace

Yankovsky, D. (2023). *8 Tips To Boost Workplace Diversity In 2023*. Connecteam. https://con-necteam.com/further-workplace-diversity-tips/

5 Ways to Assess a Company for DEI Before you Apply. (n.d.). https://resources.scru-malliance.org/Article/5-ways-assess-company-dei-apply

7 ways to be an inclusive co-worker – Inclusive Employers. (n.d.). https://www.inclusiveem-ployers.co.uk/blog/7-ways-to-be-an-inclusive-co-worker/

8 Great Job Boards for Diverse Professionals – AAUW: Empowering Women Since 1881. (2020, September 2). AAUW: Empowering Women Since 1881. https://www.aauw.org/re-sources/career/boost-your-career/8-great-job-boards-for-diverse-professionals/

10 ways to inspire others and change their life | Tony Robbins. (2021, December 31). tonyrobbin-s.com. https://www.tonyrobbins.com/business/how-to-inspire-others/

11 Ways to Increase Workplace Diversity - ASME. (n.d.). https://www.asme.org/topics-resources/content/11-ways-to-increase-workplace-diversity

11 Ways to Increase Workplace Diversity - ASME. (n.d.). https://www.asme.org/topics-resources/content/11-ways-to-increase-workplace-diversity

25 effective diversity team building activities in 2022/2023. (n.d.). https://www.gomada.-co/blog/diversity-team-building-activities

IMAGES REFERENCES:

** All images created by author**

AUTHOR BIO

Born in a quaint New England town, Marguerite has carved a remarkable path in the professional realm, boasting over two decades of unparalleled leadership. Now 44 and residing in New Jersey with her supportive husband and two beautiful children, her journey has seen her evolve from the humble beginnings of her hometown, through the corporate corridors of Chicago, and into the dynamic streets of New York. Throughout this journey, Marguerite has held several esteemed leadership roles in both large and small organizations, consistently breaking through glass ceilings and challenging the status quo.

Witnessing firsthand the untapped potential of countless talented women who were often overlooked in the corporate world, Marguerite's keen observations and personal experiences ignited a deep passion within her. This led to the creation of her debut work, "Fearless Female Leadership," a meticulously researched and engagingly written book that celebrates the unique prowess of women in leadership. In this book, she masterfully intertwines thought-provoking insights with compelling narratives, spotlighting the unique strengths and struggles of women in positions of power.

With her latest book, "Impactful Inclusive Leadership," Marguerite broadens her scope beyond championing women's potential. She dives into the essential tenets of Diversity, Equity, and Inclusion (DEI), crafting a compelling call to action. This work urges leaders of all stripes to cultivate truly inclusive environments where diversity is celebrated, and equity is a foundational principle.

Marguerite Allolding stands not only as a advocate for change but as a beacon of hope and an embodiment of the transformative power of leadership that is both fearless and inclusive. Her unwavering commitment to empowering women and advocating for DEI inspires everyone to strive for a world that thrives on the pillars of equity and inclusion and recognizes the strength in diversity.

∽

Founder and CEO of SHE LEADS STRATEGIES
https://www.SHELEADSSTRATEGIES.com

Also by Marguerite Allolding

9 ESSENTIAL STRATEGIES TO OVERCOME
GENDER BIASES, BUILD **CONFIDENCE**
AND EMPOWER **YOUR CAREER**

FEARLESS
FEMALE
LEADERSHIP

MARGUERITE ALLOLDING

Click link or scan QR code below to find Fearless Female Leadership: 9 Essential Strategies to overcome Gender Biases, Build Confidence and Empower Your career.

★★★★★

9 POWERFUL STRATEGIES THAT ENCOURAGE DIVERSITY,
FOSTER EQUITY, AND CULTIVATE
INCLUSIVITY TO TRANSFORM YOUR WORKPLACE

IMPACTFUL
INCLUSIVE
LEADERSHIP

MARGUERITE ALLOLDING

Click link or scan QR code below to find IMPACTFUL INCLUSIVE LEADERSHIP: 9 Powerful Strategies That Encourage Diversity, Foster Equity, and Cultivate Inclusivity to Transform Your Workplace.

www.ingramcontent.com/pod-product-compliance
Lightning Source LLC
Chambersburg PA
CBHW062049270326
41931CB00013B/3004